Will Parfitt is a registered psychotherapist who is well known as an inspiring and innovative group course leader. He has been a student of the Kabbalah for more than thirty years, and has taught Kabbalah for twenty years. Will is the director of PS Avalon, which offers several distance education courses, including the Kabbalah and the Tree of Life. He has published many articles in his field, and is the author of several books.

Will has extensive experience of working with psychospiritual development, and travels internationally to run courses on a variety of subjects, including both the Kabbalah and Psychosynthesis, in which he completed training in 1981. He lives in Glastonbury where he offers coaching, mentoring and professional supervision.

D1638442

By the same author:

The Elements of the Qabalah
The Elements of Psychosynthesis
Walking Through Walls

THE COMPLETE GUIDE TO THE KABBALAH

HOW TO APPLY THE ANCIENT MYSTERIES OF THE KABBALAH TO YOUR EVERYDAY LIFE

WILL PARFITT

RIDER

LONDON · SYDNEY · AUCKLAND · JOHANNESBURG

1 3 5 7 9 10 8 6 4 2
Copyright © Will Parfitt 1988, 2001

The right of Will Parfitt to be identified as the Author of this work has been asserted by him
in accordance with the Copyright, Designs and Patents Act, 1988

First published as *The Living Qabalah* by Element Books in 1988
(revised as *The New Living Qabalah* 1995)

This extensively revised and updated edition (including new material
throughout and additional chapters on practical applications of the
Kabbalah) is published in 2001 by Rider, an imprint of Ebury Press,
Random House, 20 Vauxhall Bridge Road, London SW1V 2SA

www.randomhouse.co.uk

Random House Australia (Pty) Limited
20 Alfred Street, Milsons Point, Sydney
New South Wales 2061, Australia

Random House New Zealand Limited
18 Poland Road, Glenfield
Auckland 10, New Zealand

Random House South Africa (Pty) Limited
Endulini, 5A Jubilee Road,
Parktown 2193, South Africa

The Random House Group Limited Reg. No. 954009

Papers used by Rider are natural, recyclable products made from wood grown in
sustainable forests

Diagrams from originals by Will Parfitt

Printed and bound by Mackays of Chatham plc, Chatham, Kent

A CIP catalogue record for this book is available from the British Library

ISBN 0 7126 1418 4

CONTENTS

PREFACE

The Tree of Life features as a potent symbol in the myths of many different cultures. The relationship between humans and trees stretches back to the earliest history of humankind. Trees have been our protectors, our homes, our foodstuff, they have sustained us, they give us pleasure and occasionally pain. Trees are important to us in our modern world for many reasons, not least because of the oxygen they give and the carbon dioxide they remove from the air we breathe. Trees have always been and still are of prime importance to all life forms.

Trees figure in our myths, legends and cultures sometimes individually, sometimes in groups as copses, and sometimes as whole woods or forests. Trees often represent basic values such as life itself, growth, health, fertility, wisdom and strength. On the darker side, their shadowy nature sometimes leads them in myth to entrap and even destroy humans. There are also idiosyncratic trees that have particular power such as large ancient oak or yew trees with whom we may have an individual as well as a collective relationship. Trees carry weight in the human psyche; they are powerful and sometimes fearful, particularly when we treat them badly. It is of prime importance in our modern world that we acknowledge and treat trees for what they are, living sentient beings of another order.

In many traditions, a special 'world tree' stands in some central place in the universe and is associated with the origin of all life. The Tree of Life in the Judaeo-Christian Bible is such a tree and is perhaps one of the earliest appearances of our modern Kabbalistic Tree of Life. As in many tree myths, this Tree connects everyday life with both spirit and the visible world (what is 'above') and shadow and the underworld (the roots, what is 'below' or hidden). As with a real tree, the trunk is then a potent symbol of what links together the different worlds. Such is also true of, for instance, Yggdrassil, the world tree of North European mythology which is divided into realms of gods, giants, humans and the dead. This is also the case with the Kabbalistic Tree of Life with its division into four worlds representing different aspects of the make-up of not only human life but all life forms.

In the Hebrew myth, the first humans, despite a warning against doing so, eat of the fruit of the Tree. Whilst apparently a negative act – they are thrown out of the garden of Eden – it also leads them, in the words of their Creator, to 'become like us', that is, sentient beings with their own free will. In some Christian traditions, Jesus is described as the Tree of Life and in the Book of Revelations it says this Tree of Life will grow again at the time of the New Jerusalem. Central to Rosicrucian mythology is the belief that when the cross of human suffering is planted in the ground it takes root like a tree and starts to blossom with beautiful flowers.

The Kabbalistic tradition offers the same world view, that through coming to earth, with its attendant difficulties and suffering, we are offered the opportunity for redemption. Unlike some traditions, however, Kabbalists believe this redemption may be achieved through the pleasures of earth as much as through the difficulties. Indeed, Kabbalistic mythology suggests that actually coming to earth is the goal in itself and the most difficult thing to attain. To truly 'be here now' is of course the aim of most Eastern spiritual systems, too.

When we look at a basic tree, we see it has many branches and leaves originating from a single trunk, strongly suggesting the development of diversity from unity. This is the origin and template for the evolutionary tree of which we are all part, and for individual family trees. The way a tree comes out from the ground as a single shoot and grows with great diversity and complexity is a potent symbol for the creative growth process both on a personal and collective level. If our life task is to really be here now, to fully 'come to earth', it is interesting to note that the word 'matter' (the very stuff of life) is etymologically linked with the trunk of a tree. The word matter is also linked with the Latin word 'mother'. The Kabbalistic Tree of Life is sometimes drawn as a female symbol (♀) symbolically showing the link between the Tree and the source of energy from whence we all emerge.

This completely revised and updated version of an earlier book of mine (*The New Living Qabalah*) is intended to offer an easy and yet powerful way to connect with the Kabbalistic Tree of Life and to learn how to use its mysteries and revelations in your everyday life. We will study the leaves, branches, roots, all the parts of the Tree of Life, always grounding our work back to the core, the trunk of the tree, represented for us humans by our bodies, our psyches, the world we live in, and the continually evolving relationship between what we experience inside us and what is happening outside us. May your work with the Tree of Life bring you fully to earth, at peace with yourself and with the myriad of other life forms in our ever evolving universe.

PART I

FOUNDATIONS

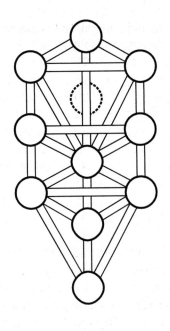

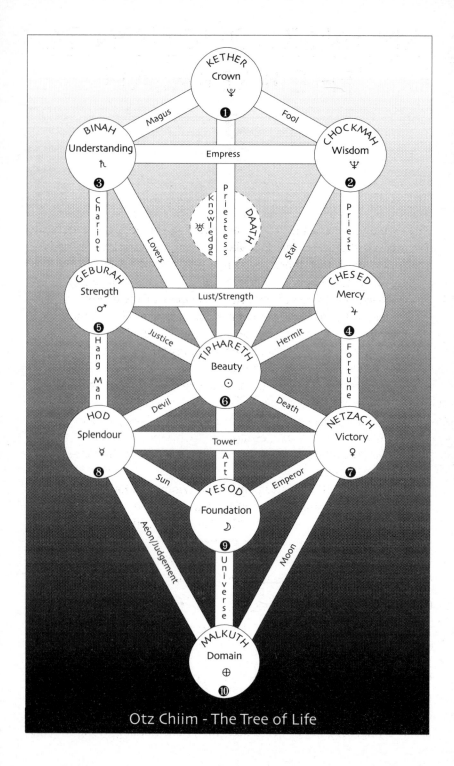

Otz Chiim - The Tree of Life

CHAPTER 1

AN INTRODUCTION TO THE KABBALAH

Why would anyone want to study and practise something as apparently obscure and strange as the Kabbalah? What possible relevance could it have to today? In fact, there are so many uses for the Kabbalah we can never tire of its company, whatever we are doing. One way we can choose to use it is to make connections between *all* the different aspects of our lives – all the different events, experiences, ideas, images and relationships we encounter. These connections, called correspondences in the Kabbalah, help us to make sense of life and to live it to the full.

We all like to have mystery in our lives, things to unravel and explore, things that bring flashes of 'aha' when we discover their secrets. Using the Kabbalah offers plenty of such opportunities. Through the correspondences, we can come to understand symbols, myths and dreams, not only of our own psyche but also of other people. We come to know ourselves, and can know and respect others for their similarities to us and their differences.

At the heart of the Western Mystery Tradition, the Kabbalah is a way of personal development and self-realization based on a map of consciousness called the Tree of Life. The Tree of Life can be used to express self-realization through a vision of love and harmony. This vision is exciting to live with, to express and experience in our lives. It can bring a sense of purpose and meaning to those aspects of our lives where previously we felt disconnected or lost.

The Kabbalah is particularly relevant to our modern world because it emphasizes that our ordinary, daily lives are an expression of our spirituality. Including both the light and shadow aspects of the psyche, the Kabbalah offers us a detailed, coherent world view, both of the nature of human existence and the relationship between ourselves, other beings, and our world.

The Kabbalah is very clearly not a path of transcendence. It is not about saying: 'Hey, I don't like it here, there is something wrong with this planet, I'm going to do everything I can to shoot off somewhere else; let me tune in and go to the higher spheres.' What the Kabbalah says is: 'If you want to do that, fine, but then bring that energy back to earth to ground it. Find some way to make your connections manifest on the planet, otherwise there is no point in being here.'

The Kabbalah is definitely *a path with a heart*. Central to the Kabbalah is a diagram or map called the Tree of Life. The purpose of this map is to help us sort out different aspects of our psyches, and more clearly be able to work with heart energy rather than just with intellectual knowledge. We have minds, feelings and bodies so we can be incarnated here on the planet earth to do our work, whatever that might be. What the Kabbalah says is if we just tease thoughts, feelings and sensations apart a little bit and start looking at what each of them means in relationship to our whole being, then it is easier to start finding out what the energy is behind them – and identify what's really moving us. For instance, I might want to be hugged. I believe that is all I want. Stepping behind that, I can ask myself: 'What do I *really* need?' Then moving back a step further, I can ask: 'What's trying to come through, what's trying to emerge in this?'

The Kabbalah, as a path with a heart, says that basically it is always love that is trying to emerge. That's not to deny the importance of power, or all the other qualities and aspects of our lives, but when we move to our hearts and really ask ourselves what it is we are here for, in one way or another we find it is something to do with the expression of love. When we stay connected to love we realize the inherent harmony throughout the whole of creation. This harmony, which includes all differences, including those that without it lead to abuse and war, is the most profound expression of love.

We might expect such vision, insight and understanding would be the result of something complicated, a system inevitably difficult to pick up and utilize. In truth, what Kabbalah represents is easy to learn, and continues to develop and change as we develop and change in our lives. The Kabbalah is of value to everyone travelling the path of personal and spiritual development, whichever their preferred way.

Using the Kabbalah, we learn how to experience and express all the different energies in our bodies. We can come to a greater understanding of the relationship within ourselves between physical, emotional, mental and spiritual energies, making whole our fragmentation. We learn to act from the heart and become more able to heal ourselves, other people and our relationship with the environment. We can grow and learn to connect with our own unique purpose for incarnation.

What is the Kabbalah?

Its doctrines have spiritual contemplation, pure inspiration, or 'intellectual intuition' as their point of departure and not the autocratic activity of reason.

Leo Schaya

ה   ל   ב   ק

H   L   B   Q

The Kabbalah is the foundation stone of the Western Esoteric Tradition as, for example, the Yoga Sutras, the Upanishads, the Bhagavad Gita and other cryptic and holy works are the foundations of the Eastern Tradition. The Kabbalah is a great body of theoretical and practical philosophy and psychology interwoven into the religious texts of the Jews, and in a vast complex of alchemical, astrological, occult, Rosicrucian and Masonic symbolism, including the Tarot. It has been called *The Mysticism of the West*. When it comes to the documentation of these practical esoteric teachings, the West compares badly with the East because of the oral origin and tradition of the teachings, their persecution through the Middle Ages, and the general disinterest of the modern world.

There are different theories about the origins of the Kabbalah, but no one really knows. Some writers say that there were two or three inspired people just after the time of Jesus Christ who received the basic design, concept and idea of the Tree of Life from God. Perhaps it was invented by Jewish mystics in the early Middle Ages. Another theory says that an angel came and secretly shared the Kabbalah with Adam and Eve when they were being kicked out of the garden of Eden. This angel thought it was something we humans wouldn't be able to live without. Another version puts the origins of Kabbalah with the Egyptians, 'borrowed' by the Jews when they came out of exile with Moses and Aaron. Personally I like this idea – that the Kabbalah comes from the ancient Egyptians. Ultimately you can choose the myth which serves you best in giving the Kabbalah meaning and value in your life

There are many different ways to describe the Kabbalah. In one sense we each carry our own individual Kabbalah within us, so there are as many Kabbalahs as there are individual people. Yet, just as we all have some experiences in common, so aspects of each individual

Kabbalah are common – perhaps some are universal. There are particular historical 'group Kabbalahs', such as the Jewish and Greek ones, but the 'universality' of these is often based upon common belief rather than experience.

True awareness springs from direct experience. The truly universal and *living* Kabbalah is based upon individual and shared experience. The Tree of Life is a living 'entity' through which we may communicate our individual experiences to others, and through which we may share in the experience of others. The uses of the Kabbalah from the innermost, spiritual levels to the most earthly matters are elucidated in a practical way in this book.

As you read these words, be aware that you have made a commitment *to yourself* to learn about the Kabbalah and the Tree of Life. It is *your* choice. You are embarking upon a study of wisdom and understanding whose richness is unbounded. The benefits of the practical Kabbalah will unfold as you delve deeper into the Mysteries. Everything you gain from studying the Kabbalah is directly proportional to the amount of energy you are willing to put into it. The key to success is a familiarity with the system which is only gained through regular practice.

THE PRACTICE OF KABBALAH

Nothing can replace the experience of the Kabbalah in its practical applications. To appreciate this fully, all aspects of the student's being must be involved, not just the intellect. The Kabbalah is relevant to the modern world, both for the growth and development of the individual, and for the growth and development of group and planetary consciousness.

The Hebrew word *Kabbalah* means both to 'receive' and to 'reveal'. This gives us our first insight into the Kabbalah. It is a way of *revelation* (of the 'meaning' of the universe) and at the same time the means of *reception* of its own wisdom. This statement is no paradox when we apply the occult maxim 'as above, so below' to it; for the Kabbalah, the 'revealer' and the 'receiver' are (at least potentially) one and the same.

The Kabbalah is normally classified into five parts:

1. The *Oral* Kabbalah; aspects of the Kabbalah that are received orally, either from a teacher of some kind, from another traveller on the magickal path, from chance remarks made by fellow humans, or from within oneself.

2. The *Written* Kabbalah; this traditionally aims to describe the nature and essential structure of the universe and its destiny. The written Kabbalah also includes all books written from a Kabbalistic viewpoint, whether intentionally on the Kabbalah or not.

3. The *Literal* Kabbalah; this 'section' of the Kabbalah is concerned with the information contained in Kabbalistic teachings, particularly those found in the Bible. It includes Gematria – the science and art of number and letter manipulation, and all forms of evocative reading of 'holy' books using appropriate Kabbalistic codes and correspondences.

4. The *Symbolic* Kabbalah; concerned with understanding, connecting to one's own experience of, and using symbols. It is based primarily upon the Tree of Life diagram.

5. The *Practical* Kabbalah; the utilization of all the various aspects of the Kabbalah to cause change to occur (personally, interpersonally and transpersonally).

This book is a combination of the *Practical* and *Symbolic* Kabbalah through the method of the *Written* Kabbalah, using the *Oral* and *Literal* approaches as appropriate.

The Kabbalah may be seen in many different ways, for its uses are as diverse and wide as the extent of human imagination. The following definitions are by no means exhaustive – the Kabbalah is many other things too. Do not worry if you don't understand any or all of these descriptions. Re-read them later and their meaning will be clearer.

The Kabbalah is:

- a map of physical, etheric, astral and other levels of awareness,
- a way to correlate inner and outer experiences and to express them to oneself and others,
- a way to relate and communicate,
- a way to connect inner awareness to outer awareness, thus creating an active and creative bridge between the two, which expands consciousness,
- a way of relating to the processes of people who are apparently diverse – it is beyond the constraints of religion, or cultural or individual peculiarities of expression,

- a way of formulating ideas with more clarity, and finding simple expression for complex thoughts,

- a way of relating to symbols whose meaning has become obscure, forgotten or misunderstood, by establishing a connection between the essence of forms, sounds, colours, simple ideas, etc. and their spiritual, intellectual, emotional and physical equivalents,

- a way of testing the 'truth' of correspondences and ideas through comparing them with what you already know and understand,

- a means for communication with extra-dimensional entities, transmundane energies or intelligences.

THE NATURE OF THIS STUDY

The following suggestions are practical guidelines for approaching Kabbalistic work and they are not meant as rigid rules. If you prefer to use this book in any other way, or discover a totally different approach to the exercises, then all well and good. Initially, however, I would suggest you follow these guidelines and see how you get on with them:

1. Work through the book from front to back. If you wish to go back to something or study it again in a different sequence you can do that later. For the present, accept that the order of presentation is intentional.

2. Try to read as slowly and carefully as possible – each section, each paragraph, each sentence, even each word! That is a tall order, but the more attention you give to the text, the more your understanding will increase.

3. Copy out in a notebook or your journal (see Appendix 2) anything you find particularly interesting or relevant, or alternatively underline it in the book.

4. If you find any part of the text uninteresting, stop and ask yourself: Why do I find this difficult? What is stopping me from taking in this material? If you cannot overcome your resistance to a particular piece, mark it and proceed. You can always return to it later.

5. Do not try to take in too much at once. Read or practise as little or as much as you feel comfortable with, then take a break of at least ten minutes before continuing.

6. If you don't feel like doing any exercise then *don't*. You can always try again another time. If you meet continued resistance to one particular exercise or set of exercises, try to be aware of how you experience the resistance, rather than trying to force yourself through it.

7. Above all – have fun! Serious study is not only enriched but also improved by laughter, excitement and interest.

As you become really involved in studying this book, a two-way flow is created between you and the text. Be aware of any sensations, feelings, thoughts, insights and resistances that emerge, particularly when doing exercises. If you find yourself flagging, recall your primary *intention* to understand the Kabbalah, and use this energy to carry you through.

The following exercise helps you to contact and formulate your intention with regard to the Kabbalah. Write the results of this exercise in your notebook or diary.

the intention exercise

Follow the usual starting procedure. *You will find this statement at the beginning of most of the exercises in this book. Before continuing, look up Appendix 1 on the starting procedure and make yourself familiar with the processes described. When you are ready, return to the exercise.*

Behind all conscious reasons is an 'inner', 'higher' or 'deeper' purpose.

Allow an image or symbol to emerge in your consciousness that represents your *purpose* for wanting to connect with the Kabbalah.

Don't force it, simply close your eyes and wait for the image to appear.

When you have your image, open your eyes and draw a representation of it. This will help bring the image to life, and act as a reminder of it. (It does not have to be a great piece of art.)

This image represents your *purpose* regarding the Kabbalah. Don't judge it in any way or try to analyse it, simply accept it as a symbol of your 'deeper desire'.

CHOOSING TO BE PRESENT

Whilst you are reading, studying and doing the exercises in this book, as much of your whole person as possible must be present, or involved.

Notice your physical sensations. If you feel uncomfortable sit somewhere else, or in a different posture. Always try to sit comfortably erect without hands or arms crossed. Without forcing your breath, breathe as fully as you can. If something you read makes you notice your body in some way then stop and pay attention to the sensation.

How do you feel as you study this? What feelings and emotions are engendered by the text? You do not have to let these feelings take you over – simply acknowledge that you have them. They do not have you, you have them.

It is the same with thoughts. What are you thinking? Are you concentrating on the text or is your mind wandering? What can you do about this? Distractions are not 'bad' – they are telling you something. Listen to their message, deal with them in whatever way you sense is appropriate.

If you are bored by one section then you would do best to skip on to the next. Perhaps you find something difficult and it would be better for *you* to stick at it, use your power and get through it. Trust your inner guidance and you will reap the fullest benefit from this study.

The following exercise helps make you more 'present'. Some people find it useful to perform it before starting study. It only takes a moment or two. Try it out now, once, and see if you like the feel of it. If you do you can use it whenever you like. If you don't that is fine too. It is only one way; there are many others which you will learn as you continue with this book.

being present

Follow the usual starting procedure (see Appendix 1 – if you haven't looked it up, do so now).

Think of a place that is special for you. It can be a real place you have been or know, or it can be an imaginary place.
   Now close your eyes and for a few moments be there. Really imagine that you are in this place.
   Open your eyes and be 'here', wherever you are. Say to yourself: 'I choose to be here.'

Quite rapidly 'shuttle' between the two places, closing your eyes and being there, opening them and choosing to be here.

What effects do you notice?

Are you feeling more 'here'?

Questions like this are worth answering as you proceed with this study. Write a report in your journal on your answers along with any experiences from the exercise.

CONCENTRATION AND INTEREST

What is concentration?

Think about your answer to this question before continuing. Here are some answers:

Concentration is strenuous.

Concentration is being very deliberate.

Concentration is compulsive.

Concentration is an effort!

In one way or another most of us come to believe that answers like these are right – we 'learn' that concentration is an effort. But it does not have to be. Watch some children at play, concentrating on something – they are so concentrated it can be difficult to draw them away. They can concentrate very effectively, yet it does not appear to be an effort or strain to them. What is special about the concentration of children is that they are really *interested* in and *excited* about what they are doing. It is that simple – if you are interested you can concentrate; if you are not interested, you can't, and would be better off doing something else. Remember as you follow this book on the Kabbalah that you don't have to strain, and as long as your interest is high you'll get through the course with the greatest of ease, and the maximum benefit.

Answer these questions before continuing:

How do you concentrate?

What stops you concentrating?

What resistances do you experience?

Do you get distracted easily?

Where do these distractions come from?

And – most important of all:

Are you willing to concentrate on something that really interests you?

Are you willing to let go of things that don't?

the power of Will

Follow the usual starting procedure.

Consider the following:

> Here is a body erect and motionless. This is your body. Be erect and motionless in your body.

Consider the external forces which are maintaining you:

> the attraction of the earth, the sun, the planets and the stars
>
> the attraction of every mote of dust in your room, one of which, if it could be annihilated, would cause your body to move (albeit imperceptibly)
>
> the resistance of the floor
>
> the pressure of the air
>
> all the other external conditions

Consider also the internal forces which sustain your body:

> the vast and complex machinery of the skeleton
>
> the muscles, blood, the lymph, marrow – all that makes up a body

And consider consciousness:

> the sensations, feelings, thoughts – all that makes you into an individual person and directs your choice to remain in this position

Who chooses to remain here and now, doing this exercise?

You do, through your Will.

> Be aware you have a Will; without it you could not be here, and without it you couldn't choose to move away from your position.

Choose now to move, and be really conscious of how easy it is.
Record your sensations, feelings, thoughts and insights about
this exercise in your journal.

The Sacred Hebrew Alphabet

The Hebrew alphabet is a holy alphabet, as is, for instance, Sanskrit. This
means that as well as being used to 'make up words' each letter also has
a deeper, inner significance. In English the letters U-N-I-T-Y make up the
word 'unity' which can be applied to a particular state of consciousness.
The equivalent Hebrew word is 'achad' made up of the Hebrew letters A-
Ch-D, that is Aleph, Cheth and Daleth. Each of these letters in Hebrew
also has a numerical equivalent and other meanings which can help us
understand more about the word. So the three letters of 'achad' add up
numerically to 13. Apart from many other words – all of which will also
have connections to achad – one other word that adds up to 13 is 'ahbh',
meaning love. So through this numerical analysis, we learn that there is
a connection between 'unity' and 'love'. That in itself may be no
surprise, but many such connections that can be made in this way are
surprising, even sometimes illuminating.

The three letters, aleph, cheth and daleth, can also tell us more
about the word achad through their own individual meanings. Aleph
means an ox, cheth a gate and daleth a door. We may interpret this
many ways, but for instance we could say the message is thus: that unity
is a great strength and comes at the beginning of everything. Indeed, its
strength is so great it needs a gate to keep it from coming through the
door into our dualistic lives, otherwise, like a 'bull in a china shop', it
could destroy our world. Whether that is to be desired or not is a philosophical matter.

To work with the Kabbalah, you do not need to understand Hebrew
at all. If you are interested in the Hebrew alphabet, however, you will
find the letters, their numerical and English equivalents in the correspondence tables in Appendix 4. So, using the tables in the usual way,
you would find, for instance, that the letter Beth is numbered 2, and corresponds to the 'magician' tarot card, the left brain, the colour grey,
frankincense, the beech tree, an owl and so on. The intuitive connections that can be made through this – and the increased awareness that
flows through these connections – can be most illuminating.

You also do not have to overconcern yourself about the pronunciation of Hebrew words. Indeed, no one knows how the ancient Hebrews

pronounced their language (it may have been very different from modern Jewish). So long as you respect the alphabet as sacred, it is enough to follow this basic guideline:

All letters are pronounced as in English except:

H as in English or silent	practise 'hod'
Ch as in Scottish 'loch'	practise 'chockmah'
O or AA (double a) as a long guttural 'a'	practise 'daath'
Tz as a short English 't' then long 'z'	practise 'tzaddi'
Q as English 'k'	practise 'qoph
Th as English 't' (not th)	practise 'malkuth'

KABBALAH AND MAGICK

Whether it is spelt Kabbalah or Qabalah, teachings about the Tree of Life are universally applicable. It used to be the case that some people used 'Kabbalah' to denote the Jewish esoteric approach and 'Qabalah' for that from the Western Mystery Tradition. This always artificial distinction was never valid and has become even less so as the different approaches become better known. In my work I have switched to using Kabbalah rather than Qabalah for the simple pragmatic reason that it is the trend amongst the vast majority of Kabbalists. Also, in English, the word Kabbalah is more elegant than a word spelt with a 'Q' without a 'u' following it.

Throughout this book the word 'Magick' is spelt with a 'k'. This is to distinguish it from 'magic' which is more usually associated with illusion and trickery. Magick (with a 'k') describes the core processes of the Western Mystery Tradition, involved with creating change that is in accordance with the divine or 'True Will' of each individual, and with the evolution of life as a whole.

CHAPTER 2

THE DESIGN OF THE TREE OF LIFE

THE STRUCTURE OF THE TREE

The entire wisdom of the Kabbalah can be summarized in one simple yet unique diagram, the Tree of Life. In Hebrew it is called *Otz Chiim*:

מ	י	י	ח		צ	ע
M	I	I	Ch		Tz	O

There are other versions of the Tree diagram; the one we use is the most popular one, and that which has been found to be the most practical. That is not to say other versions are wrong, rather that they are not as universally applicable as this one. Look at the main Tree of Life diagram (at the beginning of the book) and become aware of its overall shape and structure.

Simple as the Tree of Life looks, it has been described as a *'mighty, all-embracing glyph of the human soul and of the Universe'*.

Owing to its simplicity, it can easily be committed to memory, and it is easy to visualize. From its structure a complete knowledge of the structure of life in all its aspects can be derived. Indeed, the Tree is a map for all levels of experience. It encompasses the outer world, the inner world and the relationship between these two, and includes body, personality, soul and spirit.

Being a map of *all of you* it helps you find your bearing when travelling through life. It is also a map which helps you expand your consciousness, and integrate or ground the new awareness that comes from this expansion.

In the next exercise you are going to build up the Tree from its basic principles. Even if you are already familiar with the Tree's structure, do this experience. It will help you to commit it to memory, and also aid your understanding of the basic attributions of the Tree as they relate to each of us as individual beings.

Before continuing have a piece of paper (A4 or larger) and a pencil or pen ready. Follow the instructions and try to fully understand each point before moving on to the next.

building the tree

Follow the usual starting procedure.

The Kabbalah is an occult system. Occult simply means hidden from our normal everyday perception of the world. On the bottom of your paper, in the middle of the page, draw a circle, thus:

This represents both the external world and the body. Write 'external world/body' in the circle, and the Hebrew word *Malkuth*, which is the name, and 10, which is the number, of this sphere.

Each sphere on the Tree of Life is correctly called a *Sephira*, the plural of which is *Sephiroth*. This word means 'number' or 'emanation', but a good suggestive translation is 'sphere'.

Now, again in the middle of the page, but this time at the top, draw another circle or sphere thus:

This circle represents the 'innermost source' from which all life springs – the 'god-head'. It is the *Self* of the human being, which is individual to each of us and yet common to all. This Sephira is called *Kether* and is number 1. As you learn about each sphere write the information in the circle on your diagram.

We now have two reference points, our physical existence (Malkuth) and our spiritual source (Kether). Our task is to fill in all that comes between, which is equivalent to the inner universe inside each of us, and the outer universe in which we all exist. Do not concern yourself too much with understanding this at the moment; rather, pay attention to connecting with the basic scheme of the Tree.

Starting from the bottom, from the basis of physical existence, the natural focus for our everyday consciousness, we realize that, just as the body is a means for our experience of life, so too are our thoughts and feelings. Ideally the analysing power of the mind and the driving, sensing function of the feelings should act as complementary forces within us, so we will consider these as occupying one plane of being. So put two circles on the page to represent them, each on one side of the lower circle and about one third of the way up the page, thus:

The one on the left represents 'thoughts'; it is called *Hod* and numbered 8. The one on the right represents 'feelings'; it is called *Netzach* and numbered 7. As with all the other spheres, they also correspond to a whole complex of other things, but for the present, pay attention to these particular attributions.

Besides the conscious personality, which is represented by the spheres you have numbered 7, 8 and 10, we also have a 'subconscious' part to our being. It is the seat of the instincts and the autonomic nervous system, as well as being the depository for repressed feelings, which we shall call 'emotions' to distinguish them from 'expressed' feelings. This place we represent with another circle, placed centrally, above sphere number 10, but below the plane of thoughts and feelings, thus:

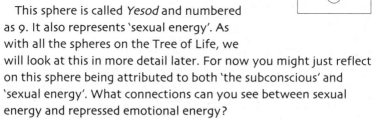

This sphere is called *Yesod* and numbered as 9. It also represents 'sexual energy'. As with all the spheres on the Tree of Life, we will look at this in more detail later. For now you might just reflect on this sphere being attributed to both 'the subconscious' and 'sexual energy'. What connections can you see between sexual energy and repressed emotional energy?

What we have so far is four spheres which represent the whole *personality*. Each of us believes we have a personality. I say 'I have a personality': but *who* has this personality? If you say 'I have a mind, I have feelings, I have a body', who is this 'I' who has these things?

This 'I' is represented on the Tree by another circle, placed centrally, above those representing thoughts and feelings, the same

distance above them as the circle numbered 9
is below them, thus:

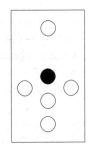

This sphere is numbered 6 and called
Tiphareth. Just as it is in the centre of our
page, so it is the centre of the Tree. It is called
'the centre', 'the personal self', 'the highest
within', or simply 'the real me'. Sometimes it
is described as 'the clearest available space'.
What do you understand by this?

We have now drawn a representation of all of which we are
normally aware. Our consciousness is like an amoeba that moves
around the part of the Tree we have drawn so far. Sometimes it is
totally concentrated on one sphere to the exclusion of others, sometimes it extends 'pseudopods' of consciousness from one sphere to
another. All that the amoeba is aware of is that there is a 'source'
somewhere above or within, and through the personality it experiences the world. The rest of the Tree, as we now build it up,
represents the connection with 'the source',
'God', or whatever you choose to call it.

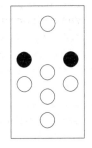

Draw two circles on the same level as each
other, one on either side of the central sphere
of Tiphareth, a little way above it, like this:

These two spheres are: on the left *Geburah*,
numbered 5, and on the right *Chesed*,
numbered 4. They represent the Archetypes,
or abstract principles, of Will (Geburah) and
Love (Chesed). This level also represents 'the
soul', and is equivalent to what is sometimes
called 'the superconscious'. This is not to say
that 'soul' and 'superconscious' are the same thing, but that they
correspond. You will find as your study proceeds that correspondences play an important part in the Kabbalah. These two spheres
of Love and Will complement each other, and it is their interplay
and interaction that is the 'work' of the individual soul. They are
similar to the thoughts and feelings of the personality but on a
'higher' or 'deeper' level. The 'Great Work' may be described, in one
sense, as the total identification of the two lower spheres of Hod
and Netzach with these two spheres, Geburah and Chesed.

Now draw a line above these two circles. This represents a
complete change in dimension, the demarcation between the
individual below the line, and the universal above it. The line is
traditionally known as *The Abyss*. Draw a circle over the middle of

this line with a dotted boundary, thus:

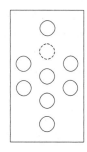

This 'dotted' sphere is 'the Sephira which is not a Sephira' and is called 'Daath'. It has no number. It is of vital importance in the scheme of the Tree but for now simply see it as a kind of 'bridge' between the individual soul and universal spirit.

Above the Abyss, we have the three-in-one trinity of spheres that represents the spirit, so we place two more circles, thus:

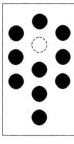

The left one is called Binah and is numbered 3. It represents 'Universal Love' and 'Universal Awareness'. The one on the right is called Chockmah, is numbered 2, and represents 'Universal Will' or 'Purpose'. Sphere 1, Kether, is the Self; spheres 2 and 3 are the Self's Purpose and its Awareness.

You have now drawn a complete Tree of Life, with the ten Sephiroth or spheres numbered 1 to 10, and an eleventh unnumbered sphere in the Abyss.

Finally, draw a line between sphere 6 and the plane of spheres 7 and 8. This is called the Veil of Paroketh and it separates the soul from the personality. Tiphareth, sphere 6, has the function of being the 'I' of the personality, as already described, but also being the part of the soul with which the personality has direct contact.

If you draw a line through the spheres, following the numbers in order, this is called the Lightning Flash of Creation:

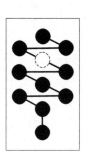

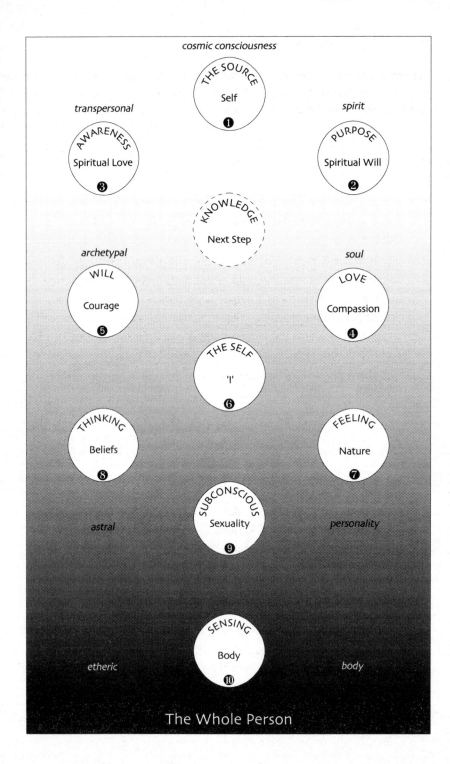

cosmic consciousness

THE SOURCE
Self
❶

transpersonal

AWARENESS
Spiritual Love
❸

spirit

PURPOSE
Spiritual Will
❷

KNOWLEDGE
Next Step

archetypal

WILL
Courage
❺

soul

LOVE
Compassion
❹

THE SELF
'I'
❻

THINKING
Beliefs
❽

FEELING
Nature
❼

SUBCONSCIOUS
Sexuality
❾

astral

personality

SENSING
Body
❿

etheric

body

The Whole Person

ATTRIBUTIONS OF THE SPHERES

There are innumerable correspondences for each of the Sephiroth and we shall be studying many of these later. What we have done so far is built up the basic Tree as it relates to the individual human being; in a sense, the subjective essence of the Tree. But behind this 'outer reality' there are other levels of energy, other planes of being and existence. For now, simply note on your diagram the following attributions.

MALKUTH, sphere 10, represents the *etheric body* (that is 'behind' the 'outer reality' of the physical body). It is the life force of your existence.

YESOD, number 9, represents the *lower astral plane*. The astral substance of this plane is fluid and infinitely elastic; it can take any form. This is how we shape our fantasies and dreams. A dream may originate in any Sephira, but the 'substance' through which you perceive the dream (images, sounds, etc.) is the *Astral Light* of Yesod.

NETZACH and HOD, spheres 7 and 8, represent the *higher astral plane*. This is the astral substance of group or collective consciousness which we can affect and which affects us. It is composed of infinite 'mini-planes', for example: 'the Celtic plane', 'the Alchemical plane', 'the Christian plane', 'the Tibetan plane', and so on.

TIPHARETH, number 6, is the level of the *Guardian Angel*, of which there is one for each human being. In 'initiated' terms, our central purpose in existence is to make a connection with our Guardian Angel. This can also be described as making a connection with the soul. In a later chapter you will be doing just that.

CHESED and GEBURAH, 4 and 5, represent planes of *higher beings*, or *pure beings*; they affect us rather than we affect them (unless we identify with or invoke them, of which more later).

Sephiroth 1, 2 and 3, sometimes called the *Supernals*, represent 'God' or the 'universal source of everything'. Communication or contact with the Supernals is called 'Union with God'. This is the exact translation of *Samadhi*.

DAATH, the unnumbered sphere, is a point of access to other dimensions, and the reverse side of the Tree.

Finally, the spheres of the Tree are associated with various grades of initiation. The most commonly known are those of the Golden Dawn and its successors, which use the following scheme:

10	initiation of earth	neophyte
9, 8, 7	initiations of water, air and fire	intermediate grades
6	initiation to adepthood	the Adept
5, 4	deepening the initiation	Higher Adept
Daath	connecting soul to spirit	Babe of the Abyss
3	connecting to universal love	Master of the Temple
2	connecting to universal will	Magus
1	being one's very own Self	Ipsissimus

THE PILLARS AND THE PLANES

The structure of the Tree of Life can be viewed in many different ways. Firstly, notice that there are three pillars to the Tree – *the Right-Hand Pillar* (Chockmah at the top), *the Left-Hand Pillar* (Binah at the top) and *the Middle Pillar* (Kether at the top). The middle pillar relates to the spinal column; the left-hand pillar relates to the *right-hand* side of the body, whilst the right-hand pillar relates to the *left-hand* side. This corresponds to the fact that the right-hand side of the brain controls the left side of the body, and vice versa. The right-hand, left-hand and middle pillars relate to Ida, Pingala and Shushumna of Tantra.

There are seven planes. These are roughly equivalent to the seven *chakras* or energy centres of the body (but a more accurate, detailed correspondence is given later in the book).

There are three triangles (see overleaf). Notice that the top triangle is upright, whilst the two below are inverted. Malkuth is considered as a 'pendant' to the bottom triangle.

Another interesting pattern involves a hexagram, whilst another involves a hexagram and pentagram:

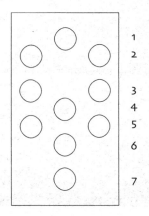

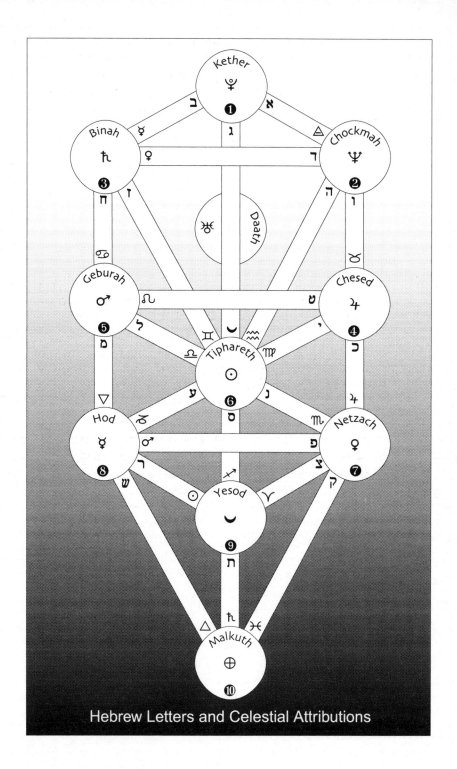

Hebrew Letters and Celestial Attributions

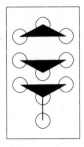

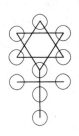

See what other shapes you can find within the structure of the Tree.

One particular set of connections between the spheres are the 22 *Paths*. These are of vital importance, and we will look at them in detail. Look at the paths on the Tree and be aware of the connections they make. For example, the path attributed to the letter 'pe' and the planet Mars, connects the spheres of thoughts and feelings. What does this tell you about this path? Also notice that some spheres are *not* connected by paths. Why do you think this is?

No one way of grouping the ten Sephiroth on the Tree of Life can be said to be right, or wrong; each way serves a different purpose and helps throw light on the whole scheme. In the previous section different ways of looking at the structure of the Tree were described. The Tree may also have different 'structures of meaning' as well as of shape. Both the essence and the form of the Tree may be individualized. For example, the left-hand pillar (Binah at the top), the one that corresponds to the right side of the body, is called *the Pillar of Severity*, whilst the right-hand pillar is called *the Pillar of Mercy*. This helps us understand their respective influence on both the physical anatomy and subtle bodies of each individual.

Each Sephira is positive and masculine in giving energy to the sphere that follows it, whilst it is negative and feminine in receiving energy from the preceding sphere. Therefore each Sephira is bisexual, like a magnet which of necessity has one positive and one negative pole.

The ten Sephiroth may also be seen as seven Palaces. In the first palace are the Supernals; in the seventh Palace are Yesod and Malkuth; the rest of the Sephiroth are attributed one Palace each. This grouping reveals the intimate connection between Yesod and Malkuth, and is one way of enabling sevenfold systems to be understood through the tenfold classification of the Kabbalah.

Another important structural pattern has Kether as Arik Anpin, the Vast Countenance, the Total Creator. This energy then manifests as the Supernal Father, Chockmah, and the Supernal Mother, Binah. Their Union takes place in Daath, and their 'child' is Zaur Anpin, the Lesser Countenance, or Microprosopos, whose centre is in Tiphareth, but who also includes the four Sephiroth surrounding Tiphareth. Malkuth is then the 'Bride' of Microprosopos, and their Union takes place in Yesod.

Perhaps the most illuminating and important of these 'inner structures' is the division of the Tree into four Worlds. This will be described in the next section.

Do not worry if you feel swamped by information at this point; the more you meditate and study the Tree, the more it will become clear to you. It is better to make connections between the various items of knowledge and understanding that you glean from this study rather than trying to memorize too much.

THE KABBALISTIC WORLDS

The Tree of Life can be split into *four Worlds* or Realms of Energy, as shown in the diagram.

ATZILUTH, the first World, is attributed to *Fire*, the *Creative* principle, and consists of Kether and Chockmah.

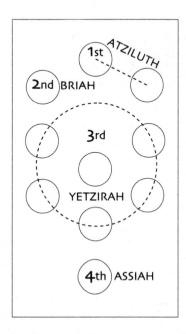

BRIAH, the second World, is attributed to *Water*, the *Receptive* principle, and Binah.

YETZIRAH, the third World, is attributed to *Air*, the *Formative* principle, and the spheres Chesed to Yesod inclusive.

ASSIAH, the fourth World, is attributed to *Earth*, the *Material* principle, and Malkuth.

Another way of looking at these four Worlds is that there is a separate Tree for each of the Worlds. The four Worlds that concern Kabbalists are those that span the extent of human consciousness and are just four in an infinite series of worlds. The other Worlds are the realms of different and alien orders of beings that are (usually) out of the reach of human experience. Sometimes it is more useful to place the four Worlds on to one Tree of Life, sometimes to have a separate Tree for each. As your understanding of the Kabbalah increases, you will find practical value in both schemes.

THE FORMULA OF TETRAGRAMMATON

Tetragrammaton is the fourfold name of God, usually spelt as

H   V   H   Y

that is YHVH, Jehovah, called the 'inexpressible name of God'. Each of the four letters in the name of Tetragrammaton is related to one of the four Kabbalistic Worlds described in the last section. It is said that the true pronunciation of YHVH is the most potent occult secret, because if it is spoken correctly the world will come to an end. Compare this with the Hindu belief that when Shiva awakes, the universe will be destroyed.

YHVH is used as a magickal formula. Its correspondences are as follows:

Y   yod   =   Atziluth/fire/male/active/creative *Force*

H   he   =   Briah/water/female/passive/receptive *Pattern*

V   vau   =   Yetzirah/air/'son'/formative *Activity*

H   he   =   Assiah/earth/'daughter'/material *Form*

The second (or *final He* as it is usually called) is the result of the first three letters acting as one. In other words, the interaction of fire, water and air leads to the formation of earth.

The four letters of Tetragrammaton also correspond to the four suits of the Tarot and the four kinds of court cards, which we will be studying later.

The four letters can also be used pictorially to represent the human body:

THE KABBALISTIC CROSS

The following exercise is useful for three purposes:

1. It connects you to the Tree of Life, and helps you *realize* the Tree within.

2. It aligns your energy, balancing your aura, and is therefore a healing tool.

3. It acts as a protection, a barrier against unwanted intrusions to the aura.

Try to become as familiar as possible with the procedure of this exercise. Practise it often – at least daily until you become familiar enough to do it without prompting. You will find it of great help to you. It is a useful start to any form of magickal or mystical practice, meditation, etc. Indeed, you could make it part of your usual starting procedure for the exercises in this book.

---

the Kabbalistic Cross

Follow the usual starting procedure.

Stand upright, attentive but not stiff.
Touch your forehead (midway between and slightly above the eyebrows) with the forefinger of your right hand. Say:

ATEH

Be aware of the innermost Self residing within you.
Move your finger down in a straight line to touch your genital area.
Say:

MALKUTH

Be aware of your body.
Visualize this straight line down the front of your body, and all the subsequent lines you draw as bright, shining, silver-white light.
Touch your right shoulder. Say:

VE GEBURAH

Be aware of your will power.
Drawing a line across from your right shoulder, touch your left shoulder. Say:

VE GEDULAH

Be aware of your love energy. (Gedulah is another name for Chesed.)
Clasp your two hands together over your heart. Visualize a shining, white cross inscribed over your body. Say:

LE OLAHM

Be aware of exactly where you are (here), exactly at this moment (now).
Extend your arms out so you are standing as a cross, and say:

AMEN

Visualize yourself extending as a silver-white cross in all the four directions (up, down, right, left).

Ateh	pronounced 'ahteh'	means 'for thine'
Malkuth	'malkut'	(is the) 'kingdom'
Ve Geburah	'ver geboorah'	'the power'
Ve Gedulah	'ver gedoolah'	'the glory'
Le Olahm	'le ohlarm'	'for ever & ever'

Pronounce each word very slowly, and really stretch the vowels. The more energy you put into intoning the words, and the more will and imagination you use whilst doing this, the more effective it will be.
Don't rush it – be clear with each stage before you move on to the next. The inner meaning of the procedure is much more important than the outer form.

THE NUMBER SEVEN

There are seven Sephiroth below the Abyss which correspond to many sets of seven items or ideas in lots of different symbol systems. Be aware of these, and the overall importance of the number seven. For example we have seven colours of the rainbow, notes in music, days of the week, cosmic days of creation, stars of the Great Bear, emanations of logoic power (Plato), heavenly men (Vedas), states of activity, ways to transpersonal realization.

In the Bible, the number seven occurs often; for example, the Israelites built seven altars, there are seven oxen or rams for sacrifice, trumpets to be sounded, seals, veiled angels, gifts of the holy spirit, deadly sins.

It is an interesting 'coincidence' that when we put the seven planets around the points of a seven-pointed star, in the order in which they appear on the Tree, and then read around the star following the continuous line joining the points, we find that the planets are now in the order that corresponds to the seven days of the week. This is shown in the following diagram:

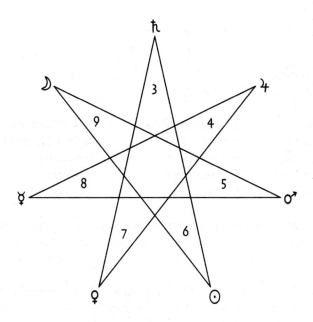

THE PLANETARY SYMBOLS

All the planetary symbols are composed of seven basic components. These are:

the point or dot	the Self, simple consciousness, beingness
the circle	complete awareness, everything
the crescent	receptivity and transmission of energy
the arrow	movement, creativity, response
the horizontal line	female, passive
the vertical line	masculine, active
the cross	union of male and female, balanced manifestation

Each of the planetary symbols can be interpreted according to how it is made up of these component parts. For example, in the symbol for Mercury, there is a crescent, a circle and a cross: receptivity (the crescent), passing down through awareness (the circle) into manifestation (the cross).

It is also interesting to note that the planetary symbols conceal within themselves the numbers of the Sephiroth to which they are attributed:

This is (almost definitely) not intentional, but it is interesting as a comment on the workings of the collective unconscious.

PART II

THE PERSONALITY AND THE TREE OF LIFE

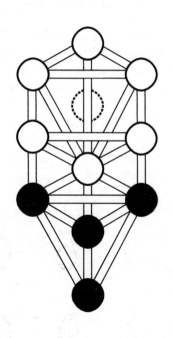

CHAPTER 3

MALKUTH: THE BODY, THE WORLD AND THE TREE

You are now starting a deep study of the Kabbalah. Remember to follow the basic instructions for exercises, to be present with the work, and to be willing to stop if necessary.

Before starting the following exercise, look back over your experience of the exercises you have done already, particularly the *intention* exercise. Try to be aware of how you can interact with these exercises, and take any steps you feel are necessary to improve your situation.

---

the opening exercise

Follow the usual starting procedure.

With your eyes closed, be as relaxed and empty of thoughts, feelings and sensations as possible.

When you feel ready, open your eyes and see the world before you, wherever you are, as a completely new place. Everything and everyone you see before you is not named. You have no mental, emotional or physical constructs with which to identify your environment. You are not attached to *anything*.

Imagine yourself as a new-born being.

Now close your eyes, go back into your inner world, still self-identified, and make a conscious decision that when you open your eyes again you will see everything, and everyone else as equally reborn. Everything has its old familiar name, but is different, new, seen in a new light because of your choice, your will.

Open your eyes.

Be aware of how you needed to use both your will and awareness in this exercise.

Write about your experience in your journal.

THE TENTH SPHERE, MALKUTH

The name of this Sephira is *Malkuth*, which in Hebrew is:

Th   V   K   L   M

The English translation of Malkuth is 'the Kingdom' or 'the Domain'. Malkuth is the 'domain of the body and the senses'. It is also the 'kingdom' of the pure spirit of Kether, which is at the top of the Tree, through being its place of manifestation.

Malkuth has a dual attribution: both to the body (and the senses) and to the 'external world'. More correctly it could be said to represent *the contact between the body and the external world*, experienced primarily through the senses.

---

the exercise of the senses

Before continuing, have laid out before you:
- something edible (either solid or liquid);
- something scented (e.g. a perfume or flower);
- a picture or photo towards which you have strong positive or negative feelings.

Perform the Kabbalistic Cross exercise (or any other exercise you may know for calming and centring yourself).

Pick up your scented object and take a long deep smell of it.

Notice how it affects you: you may think things about the smell; it may evoke memories; it may make you feel good, or sad, or evoke some other emotion. In one way or another the scent has some effect on you.

None of these effects are Malkuth.

Now take another sniff of your scent. This time notice the *smell in itself* – just the smell, no thoughts, no emotions, nothing but the smell. This is the pure experience of Malkuth.

Now clasp your two hands together, in whatever way you wish, and notice the feeling of one hand against the other. You may have effects again, such as perhaps thinking about prayer. Without rejecting these effects, pay *no* attention to them; they are *not* Malkuth. Simply experience the sense of touch. This, alone, is the pure experience of Malkuth.

Clap your hands together and *hear* the sound they make. The sound itself is not Malkuth. Malkuth is the *experience of hearing the sound*, but not the sound.

Now look at your picture or photo. You can experience Malkuth by paying attention to what your eyes see and by not paying attention to the subject of the picture.

Take something to eat or drink, but before you start to consume it, be aware that the *taste in itself* is the experience of Malkuth.

Finally, speak out loud any words and listen to your voice without interpreting what it is saying. Is there any limit to the number of different sounds you can make?

In this exercise there is no implication whatsoever that there is anything wrong with having thoughts, memories, feelings, emotions or sensations. Similarly this is no implication that you ought to ignore, suppress or repress these reactions. All of these things belong to other parts of the Tree. The purpose of not paying attention to them was to enable you to experience Malkuth *on its own*.

By now you should have the habit of generally writing about your experiences of these exercises in your diary or workbook. Whilst this is not essential, it is highly recommended.

the temple of Malkuth

Follow the usual starting procedure.

Imagine yourself in the middle of a vast plain that reaches as far as the horizon in every direction. As you turn and look all around, it appears as though you are standing at the very centre of a circle:

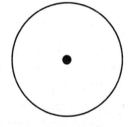

The consciousness that you are at the centre of a circle can remain even when you fill up that plain with cities, roads, gardens, rubbish heaps, brick walls or whatever happens to surround you in your environment. That horizon, although not directly seen, is still present – and if you move in any direction, however small or large a distance, you always remain in the centre of that circle.

This is an important exercise in consciousness. It is a practical, living way of experiencing the truth that *you are always the centre*. Wherever you are, you are the centre of the circle of your consciousness, both in the inner world and the outer.

This circle, of which you are the centre, may be interfaced, crossed, knotted up with and overlapping myriads of other circles belonging to other people, animals, plants, inanimate objects – in fact everything; but your own circle is always uniquely yours. If I were standing next to you looking into deepest space at a far distant star, although we could not directly perceive it, our perception of that star would be altered by the few feet between us. I call this colour before me 'green' and so do you – but do we really see the same thing? Even if we do, could we prove it?

Malkuth has appropriately been called *The Temple*. It is *one temple* composed of *two* parts: an inner temple (when you have your eyes closed), an outer temple (when you have your eyes open).

You may wish to create a particular 'environmental' temple (be it a magician's temple, a living room or whatever) but your true outer temple (eyes open) is that circle (or perhaps more correctly, sphere) of which you are always the centre. Your true inner temple (eyes closed) is everything within you, including both things of which you are aware *and* unaware. All boundaries are artificial.

the awareness continuum

Follow the usual starting procedure.

Using the words: 'Now I am aware ...' to start each time, voice whatever you are aware of and watch how your awareness changes all the time, for example:

> Now I am aware of typing these words ... now I am aware of being comfortably warm ... now I am aware of a car going past

> outside ... now I am aware of a gurgling in my stomach ... now
> I am aware of a slight ache between my shoulders ... now I am
> aware of feeling happy ... now I am aware of the rattling keys
> as I type ... now I am aware of ...

Try this awareness continuum for yourself – keep it up for around
five minutes.

Now do it again for a few minutes, this time noticing what stops
your awareness. Are there moments when nothing seems to come?
Do you feel silly doing it – or does it seem pointless?

Now do it once more, remembering to start each time with: 'Now
I am aware ...' This time pay attention to how your awareness
changes from inside to outside, and vice versa.

This awareness continuum is composed of our intuitions, thoughts,
feelings, emotions, sensations, imaginings ... all the functions of our
total being.

Malkuth could be described as the place where everything happens.
It has been called *The Gate*, both the gate through which we physically
manifest all aspects of ourselves, and the gate through which we come
into manifestation. Malkuth, then, is the 'primary' existence, or the 'first
body'. Later we will learn of the 'second' and 'third' bodies of Hod and
Netzach.

CORRESPONDENCES TO MALKUTH

As we investigate the workings of each Sephira on the Tree of Life, we
will look at some of the main correspondences. A correspondence is
something that 'goes with' what the sphere represents. For instance, as
Malkuth represents the earth, all earth gods and goddesses (for example
Ceres) will correspond to it. Similarly the magic circle corresponds to
Malkuth, as do your feet. Although the number of correspondences
covered in this book will be limited, these alone run into dozens. There
are countless others. Crowley's *777*, Fortune's *The Mystical Qabalah*, and
Knight's *Practical Guide to Qabalistic Symbolism* are all good sources of correspondences, but the best source is experience of practical work with
the Tree of Life. The correspondence tables in this book are based on years
of research by many students of the Kabbalah. As you progress with
studying the Kabbalah you will find your own 'personal' correspondences
for every sphere and path upon the Tree. It is a good idea to keep a
notebook for all the correspondences that you discover, either personally

or through your study of this course and other sources of Kabbalistic teaching.

It is of primary importance to test the validity of all correspondences. Ways of doing this will unfold with the course, but nothing can test a correspondence's validity better than your own feelings and intuitions about it. If it seems 'right' to you, and fits in with your perception of the universe (inner and/or outer) then take it on board; if not, let it go.

Mal in Hebrew means 'royal' and *kuth* 'vulva'. So *Malkuth*, as the 'royal vulva' is the gate to manifestation. A Magical Image associated with Malkuth is the meadow of delights, the earth goddess in her realm of manifestation. Malkuth is sometimes called *Kallah,* meaning 'the bride', and is also sometimes called 'the virgin'.

Attributed to each Sephira is what is traditionally called a Virtue and a Vice. Sometimes there are more than one of each. The Virtues that correspond to Malkuth are discrimination and scepticism, whilst the Vices are inertia and avarice. Before going any further, consider these Vices and Virtues and see how they are appropriate for you regarding what you already know of Malkuth.

In the body, as well as representing the whole body as the temple, Malkuth is attributed to the feet (as organs of manifestation) and the anus (as an organ of discrimination).

Malkuth is also attributed to the *Muladhara* Chakra, the lowest of the seven major chakras. This 'energy zone' is associated with the base of the spine. In a later chapter we will look more deeply into the correspondences between the chakras and the Tree of Life.

Do not attempt to memorize these correspondences. It is okay to do so if you want to, of course, but the most useful correspondences are the ones that you almost instinctively or intuitively sense to be right. These ones do not need to be memorized: once known, they are never forgotten.

Also do not get swamped by correspondences. This section has only itemized a few major ones. For the moment strive mainly to get a sense of their *meaning*. Try to understand them and feel them, but do not worry if you forget them.

Malkuth is associated with the four elements in their primary manifestation, and is therefore described as 'the sphere of the elements'. These four elements are:

fire, water, air, earth

They are perhaps more appropriately called 'the elements of the wise', for although they do represent what they are particularly called, they represent much more than this. Everything in the whole world is composed of a particular combination of these elements. So for example, iron might be earthy in its hardness, airy in its conductiveness, fiery in its magnetism. A cloud could be said to be fiery in its ability to turn into a storm cloud, watery in its ability to produce rain, airy for its lightness, and earthy for its ability to blot out the blue sky. (You might disagree with these correspondences to a cloud – good! The more you make up your own correspondences the better.) Try working out the elemental composition of other items from your life. It is not always possible to work out these combinations, but it is a useful exercise to try.

The symbols commonly associated with the four elements are:

F   A   W   E

As well as being coloured blue ('our blue planet'), Malkuth is represented with four colours that relate to the four elements. They are:

russet   for fire

citrine   for air

olive   for water

black   for earth

As you probably know, the primary colours are red, yellow and blue. It is interesting to note:

russet is all the primary colours with added red

citrine is all the primary colours with added yellow

olive is all the primary colours with added blue

black is the absorption of all the colours, rejecting nothing

The number of Malkuth is 10. Ten is the Decad, composed of 1+2+3+4=10. Ten is also, as its symbol shows (10) one returning to nothing.

The initiate sees the world (i.e. Malkuth) as resplendent (brilliant, shining, illuminated) and the 'Sepher Yetzirah' calls Malkuth the 'resplendent intelligence'. The 'Sepher Yetzirah' (The Book of Formation) is a traditional Kabbalistic text, and the source of many original correspondences. Sometimes pieces from it are quoted as being 'the Yetziratic Text'.

The magickal symbols and Weapons that correspond to Malkuth are the circle and triangle, the equal armed cross, and the body itself.

The Vision attributed to Malkuth is the 'vision of the Holy Guardian Angel'.

The Holy Guardian Angel resides in Tiphareth, the 'sun' at the centre of the Tree. The vision of this sun or Guardian Angel is *seen* – but not attained – in Malkuth. Later in this book you will learn how to have knowledge of and conversation with your Holy Guardian Angel.

Every sphere has numerous gods and goddesses associated with it. The primary ones attributed to Malkuth are Osiris (Egyptian), Persephone (Greek) and Ceres (Roman). All gods and goddesses relate, through their different aspects, to many or all of the spheres. Like humans, they are 'complete' in their nature. Angels and archangels, on the other hand, specifically relate to particular spheres. (See correspondence tables.)

Once again, remember not to try to memorize these correspondences, but rather meditate upon and consider them deeply, and see how they make sense for you and your experience. They will then not be dead, intellectual symbols, but thriving, growing fruits on your personal, living Tree of Life.

THE TREE AND THE TAROT

The study and practice of the Tarot is a great aid to enmeshing oneself in the living Kabbalistic system. In Chapter 13 we will look at the Tree of Life and the Tarot in detail. For now, however, you will see that as we progress up the Tree of Life, an understanding of the Tarot helps you understand the Tree, and vice versa.

The Minor Arcana of the Tarot, sometimes called the 'small' or 'suit' cards, correspond by their number to the Tree. So, for example, the four 7s go with Netzach (number 7), the 3s go with Binah (number 3), and so on. The Major Arcana, called the 'Atus of Thoth', the 22 primary cards of the Tarot, correspond to the 22 paths joining the spheres, whilst the court cards have special associations with certain spheres.

Regarding the court cards, the Princesses are of particular interest to us here because they correspond to Malkuth. They can be considered (for now) to represent the materialization of energy.

The court cards also correspond to the four elements, and to the letters of Tetragrammaton, YHVH, thus:

Knights (Kings)	Y	fire
Queens (Queens)	H	water
Princes (Knights)	V	air
Princesses (Pages)	H	earth

If we consider the union of the male and female to produce the son and daughter, as represented in this formula of Tetragrammaton, we have:

$$Y + H = V + H$$

In this the final H represents the Princesses, associated with Malkuth. This formula could also be written as:

$$Y + H = V + E$$

where 'E' represents the energy produced from the union of the Y + H. This 'E' is also represented by the Princesses.

The four suits of the Tarot also correspond to the elements:

fire	wands	will, creative energy
water	cups	love, receptive energy
air	swords	intellect, formative energy
earth	discs	material, manifesting energy

The four 10s of the Tarot are the final manifestation of the energies of the elements. They correspond to Malkuth.

If you want to study the Tarot in depth, which is highly recommended, it would be a good idea for you to acquire a set of Tarot cards. These days many different packs are available from a variety of outlets (see Further Reading).

THE WHOLE PERSON

Study the various associations and correspondences on the diagram of the whole person (on page 20), and try to commit as much of it as possible to memory. Don't worry if you find that difficult, it will sink in as your work progresses.

THE UNWRITTEN KABBALAH

The essence of the so-called 'unwritten' Kabbalah is the knowledge of the correspondences as they appertain to the various spheres and paths on the Tree. These correspondences include many that you have already met in this description of Malkuth, and include the Tarot cards, the visions, vices and virtues, the signs of the zodiac, the planets, the elements, archangels, colours, herbs, trees, flowers, and so on.

Each path can be seen as a dynamic connection between the Sephiroth, or spheres, that it connects. It is best understood by taking into account the nature of the spheres it joins. So the path between Hod and Netzach, say, is concerned with the relationship between the mind and feelings. Each of the individual Sephiroth, however, cannot be understood so simply. For one thing, they have to be comprehended within the four Worlds (see previous section on the four Kabbalistic Worlds), and their nature in having a 'front' or positive side, and a 'back' or negative side to their make-up must be understood. Also they are both male (in their creative aspects) and female (in their receptive aspects). Taking all these attributes into account, all seen together and interrelated, we then can look at what each Sephira actually consists of: that is, primarily, its function as an 'energy zone' or 'chakra'; secondly, its function as the origin of beings of other dimensions; thirdly, as the consciousness of a certain function; and fourthly as a particular aspect of energy in manifestation.

the ten secret joys of the master

Follow the usual starting procedure.

Read the following text from the writings of Aleister Crowley very carefully, then choose one of the statements which correspond to the spheres numbered thus on the Tree:

1. Thou art that which thou choosest to think thyself, immune to all, for it is nothing but a *point of view*.
2. Thy name, which is thy word, is the substance of thy will, whose mode of action constitutes existence. *Chance*.
3. That which thou createst is thine understanding of thy *love*.
4. The Necessity of the Universe is a Measure of thy *Righteousness*.
5. The Movement of the Universe is the Fulfilment of thine *Energy*.
6. The Order of the Universe is the Expression of thy Rapture of *Beauty*.
7. The Sensibility of the Universe is the Triumph of thine *Imagination*.
8. The Mutability of the Universe is the Splendour of thine *Ingenuity*.
9. The Stability of the Universe is Change, the Assurance of thy *Truth*.

10. The Perfection of the Universe is the Realization of the Ideal of thy *Passion*.

Meditate upon your chosen sentence, reflecting upon each of the words in the sentence individually, then the meaning of the sentence as a whole.

Put the word in *italics* from the sentence into a circle in the middle of a large, blank sheet of paper and meditate upon this word. As associations come to mind add rays to the circle:

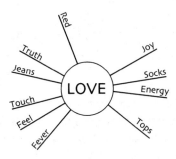

Stay tuned in to the central word; that is, after each association go back to the original word. So in the above example, after writing 'red' I went back to 'love' to meditate upon that, and didn't follow the track from 'red' which could have led elsewhere, for example to lips, postboxes, buses, etc.!

Don't censor or judge. For example, in the above diagram 'socks' is as appropriate as, say, 'energy'.

Copy your diagram into your diary, and write about anything you felt whilst doing the exercise.

If you picked statement number 6, for example, then 'Beauty' would have been in your circle. You could then say, through the system of correspondences, that everything on the rays coming from the circle is associated with 'Beauty', and these are correspondences *for you* particularly, to the sphere number 6 – that is, Tiphareth.

Without doing more than one of these meditations per day, go through each of the statements in the text and so build up your understanding of all the ten spheres on the Tree of Life.

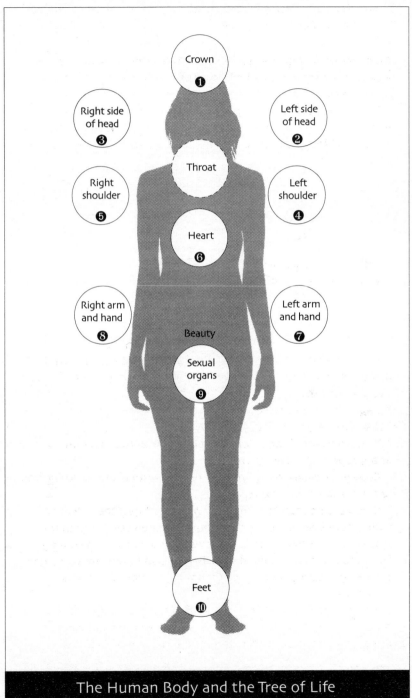

The Human Body and the Tree of Life

THE HUMAN BODY AND THE UNIVERSE

As we have already seen, Malkuth corresponds to the body and to the external world, or the universe. You have also learned that there is a real, living correspondence between the two. It is important that you understand this correspondence and start relating your inner world, and your body, to your outer world, and your universe. You will find, in the correspondence tables, detailed attributions of the physical structure of the body, and inner body components. As your study progresses, you will become familiar with these connections. Spend some time before moving on to the next chapter studying the Correspondence Tables, particularly *Physical Structure and Inner Body Components*. These two correspondence tables are fairly self-explanatory. Do not make any attempt to learn them: for now simply try the following exercise:

body awareness

Sit quietly for a while and locate a place in your body that draws your attention – it may be because it feels tense, ill, or in discomfort; it may be because it feels good, warm; or it may just draw your attention for some unconscious reason.

Once you have located a specific area in your body, use the correspondence tables to discover to where on the Tree of Life this place corresponds. For example, if you chose 'solar plexus' you would find this relates to the path joining 6 to 9 (i.e. Tiphareth to Yesod) and is number 25 in the left-hand 'key number' column.

Now look at the other columns in the tables, and find other correspondences to this place. You can do this most easily through simply reading across the 'key number'. In my example, you would find, for instance, that the key number 25 corresponds to the colour 'mauve' and the 'Art' or 'Temperance' tarot cards, and the Hebrew letter Samekh, meaning a 'support', with a numerical value of 60.

The purpose of this exercise is to increase your awareness of the tables, and help you find your way round them. At this point you do not need to do anything with the correspondences you find, but if the place in your body that you located feels tense or in some pain, you may find it helps to visualize the corresponding colour as energy entering that region of your body.

CHAPTER 4

YESOD: THE POWER OF THE PAST

THE NINTH SPHERE, YESOD

The name of this Sephira (or sphere) is *Yesod*, which in Hebrew is:

ד ו ס י

D V S Y

Yesod is situated on the middle pillar, directly above Malkuth but below the plane that incorporates Hod (thinking) and Netzach (feeling).

All the spheres of the middle pillar have a dual attribution. As you will recall, Malkuth, on the middle pillar, was attributed to both the physical body/senses *and* the external world. Yesod is attributed to:

the lower unconscious

and

life/sexual energy

Yesod means 'Foundation', and it may be looked at as the foundation of our life work in that it:

- encompasses the 'stuff' we have picked up in our past and are carrying within us,
- is the perfect transmitter from higher spheres of potential or 'future' energy with which we create ourselves *and* our world.

The particular energy which we are discussing can be termed 'the lower unconscious', 'the subconscious', 'the driver', the 'unconscious' and so on. When it is related to the Freudian 'subconscious' it particularly relates to the part of the subconscious that is involved with the *past*.

You can think of all the spheres of the Tree down as far as Tiphareth as representing the *future*, the potential within us. Netzach, Hod and Malkuth represent the *present*. Always carried within the present is the *past* – that is, Yesod. The past affects the present. Who we are at any one moment is conditioned by what has happened to us and what we have learned so far. Energies that we have learned to use freely and appropriately are amalgamated into and become part of our total being as we are *now*. But many experiences we have in life – for example grief, fears, emotional turmoils, and so on – we do *not* accept as part of us. Instead we suppress and/or repress the energies concerned. It is this energy, pushed down in this way, that controls us and 'keeps us in our place'.

This suppressed/repressed material, together with all our basic survival drives, is the stuff of Yesod as the lower unconscious. If all our energies are working harmoniously, then Yesod is a truly positive Foundation for 'higher' forces to manifest within us. But the suppressed and repressed material – which we all have – causes *unbalance*.

Abraham Maslow viewed our needs as being of two kinds – the 'deficiency needs' and the 'being needs'. If deficiency needs, which are basically our needs for food, shelter, etc., are met, then we can start fulfilling our being needs, which are the needs for qualities such as love, truth, beauty, knowledge and so on. If your deficiency needs were not met you would be unlikely to be reading this – more likely you would be in the kitchen preparing some food (assuming you are fortunate – you could also be in a severe drought somewhere starving to death). Yesod performs the function of 'driving' us to fulfil those deficiency needs, then supplies us with the basic material to manifest our being needs.

The process of suppression/repression described above is in no way 'bad', or negative. This unbalanced energy is what we have to work with in our lives and through which we may – by its release and transformation – increase our knowledge, understanding and wisdom. (Knowledge is Daath, Understanding is Binah, Wisdom is Chockmah.)

Sex, too, is the 'balancer' or 'unbalancer' in our lives. The power of sexual energy for good or bad is well known to us all. The Kabbalah places a vital importance on the correct understanding and use of sexual/bipolar energies. We will be looking into this subject later in this book. For now, consider Yesod, in its attribution to sexual or life energy, to be the 'manifestor' or 'creator' of new energy patterns. Sex is a primary manifestor of potential or future energies, the transmission of which is the primary function of this sphere.

It can be said that 'the new is born out of the foundation of the old'. Yesod gives each of us the opportunity to make ourselves whole.

balancing the opposites

This exercise calls for the use of Tarot cards. If you do not yet have a pack, you can use any pictures or photographs, choosing one with which you feel positively identified at the moment of doing the exercise, and one to which you feel negatively disposed. For example, one may be the photo of a loved person, the other an advert or perhaps the picture of a politician.

If you are using Tarot cards lay out the full pack face down, then turn them all up so you can see their faces. Take some time looking over the cards and choose one card with which you feel identified, to which you have a positive reaction; then a second card towards which you feel negative, that you don't like at this present moment.

The rest of the exercise is now for everyone.

Follow the usual starting procedure.

Place the two cards/photos in front of you and turn the negative one face down. Spend some time looking at and identifying with the *positive* one.

Identify some central figure within the scene depicted (it may be a person, animal, or inanimate object, it makes no difference). *Be that figure* and talk as if you are that figure. *Out loud* describe yourself using the personal pronoun 'I'.

Describe yourself physically (for example 'I am red, I live at the foot of a mountain' etc.); then describe yourself emotionally; then mentally; finally describe yourself spiritually.

Lay the positive card face down and turn up the *negative* card. Follow the same procedure, remembering to use the personal pronoun 'I' when describing yourself.

Swap the cards again so you are holding the positive card before you and repeat the procedure but *this time pay particular attention to the negative aspects of this card*, the card you originally chose as positive.

Finally, take the negative card and repeat the exercise, *paying particular attention to the positive aspects* of the 'negative' card.

Having performed the exercise four times (positive card: positive and negative attributes; negative card: positive and negative attributes), you are aware how within the positive there is negative and vice versa. This is a way of unleashing energy and creating balance.

Nothing is all-good or all-bad, there is at the very least the seed of the opposite pole within each, and often much more.

The past holds the present as it is; the future is potential change.

You can repeat this exercise often with your Tarot cards, and then it has a secondary function of helping you in your understanding of the Tarot (and through this, the Tree of Life).

Yesod binds our personality and is the creator of rigid character. Our work is to release our personality and become free characters through which soul and spirit may manifest. (Do not worry if you have problems accepting such terms as soul and spirit, or if you wonder what they mean – we shall be looking into these terms in depth later.)

Yesod can be described as the fulcrum between Hod (thinking) and Netzach (feeling).

THE SPHERE OF THE MOON

Yesod is attributed to the Moon. The moon has no light of its own, but is a reflector of light from the sun to the earth (during the night). Similarly, Yesod reflects light from the sun of Tiphareth to the earth of Malkuth (although Yesod, unlike the moon, does have its own light source, too).

The moon shows only one face to us and there is a continuous dark side we never see. This is also true of Yesod, which has a dark side or reverse side (as is true of all the spheres).

The face of Yesod which we see (the transmitter of light) is its function as the sphere of sexual energy; as the continuously unseen, dark side it is the sphere of the lower unconscious. This distinction helps us to understand also the difference between feelings and emotions. Sometimes you find these terms used interchangeably, but emotions are *reactive* (dark side) and feelings are *expressive* (light side).

The moon has four phases: waxing, full, waning, and absent (compare this with the four stages of the sun: sunrise, midday, sunset, midnight/hidden sun). The waxing and full moon can be attributed to Yesod as the sexual sphere and the waning and dark moon to Yesod as the sphere of the lower unconscious.

The 'high' moon (lower and full) receives light and *retransmits* it. The 'low' moon (waning and dark) receives light and *absorbs* it – it is a closed system wherein our energies can stagnate, unless we consciously work on ourselves, and release this energy. Consider the two moon goddesses: *Diana*, the huntress, and *Hecate*, the hag. Consider also the importance of both in order to create a whole system.

CORRESPONDENCES TO YESOD

A magickal image associated with Yesod is of a beautiful, sexually aroused person. Yesod corresponds in the body to the genitals (male and female – the erect penis being equivalent to the sexually excited clitoris).

The traditional Virtue of Yesod is independence, whilst the Vices are idleness, sloth and stagnation.

The Yetziratic Text calls Yesod the 'Pure intelligence', pure in the sense of it being at the culmination of the creative process. The spiritual experience associated with Yesod is 'the Vision of the Machinery of the Universe'. Contemplate this vision in terms of what you have already learned about this sphere.

Perfumes and *sandals* are associated with Yesod. Perfumes are used in ritual to give a material base for forces to manifest in (the smoke itself), and to play on particular emotions, memories, and so on. If therefore, the appropriate perfume/scent is used, it will trigger the corresponding emotions/memories, feelings/reactions as required for the aim of that particular ritual to be fulfilled.

The sandals may be seen in two ways: as the part of each individual most directly treading the path; and as the foundation of the whole being, the connector of the individual to the world. Compare this with the view of reflexology, which believes that in the sole of the foot the whole being is mapped out.

A substance associated with Yesod is the *orchid root*. Powdered orchid root is extremely sustaining to the human system, and it has been said it could be used as a complete food.

The four Tarot cards associated with Yesod are the four 9s:

9 of wands	strength	(Moon in Sagittarius)
9 of cups	happiness	(Jupiter in Cancer)
9 of swords	cruelty	(Mars in Gemini)
9 of discs	gain	(Venus in Virgo)

Even if you are not using Tarot cards yet, it is worth spending some time reflecting upon their titles and, if you are interested in astrology, on their astrological correspondences.

COLOURS AND THE TREE OF LIFE

There are four scales of colour, one for each of the Kabbalistic Worlds:

Scale	World	Letter of Tetragrammaton
King	Atziluth	Y
Queen	Briah	H
Emperor	Yetzirah	V
Empress	Assiah	H

You can use the four scales when working operations through the four Worlds, but for all practical purposes the scheme of colour is as shown in the diagram. This scheme is based on traditional correspondences and the perception of people sensitive to colours in the human subtle bodies. So long as you remember that balance is important you cannot go far wrong.

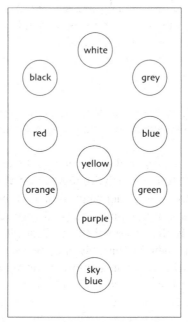

There is significance to all the colours on the Tree of Life. The top triangle represents the spirit that is everywhere, inside and outside everything, around everything, and is the totality of everything. The middle triangle represents the soul, our primary level of manifestation, whilst the bottom triangle represents the personality, the vehicle for soul. We are not personalities that have souls, we are souls that have personalities. The soul is primary, the personality secondary. So the middle triangle is coloured red, blue and yellow, the primary colours. If you mix these together, you get orange, green and purple, the colours of the lower triangle.

Sometimes it is asked, if the three spheres at the top of the Tree of Life represent our connection to illumination, why are they represented by black, grey and white? The spirit that is everywhere and everything is said in the Kabbalah to be beyond anything that can be physically manifest, so it is beyond manifest light. The obvious choice of colour for the top sphere is white for its light illuminates the rest of the Tree. If it is white, however, because in the spiritual realm everything always includes its opposite, there has to be a black sphere, too. If you've got white and black you can mix them together and get grey. That's the colours of the spheres in the top triangle. Of course, another thing Kabbalists believe is that everything you say about the spiritual triad is untrue, because partial. Everything you say about it is described in the words of our realm, our world, and it is something beyond that. So it isn't really white and grey and black at all!

THE ASTRAL LIGHT

The *Astral Light* has been called by many other names such as – the aethyr of the wise, akasha (in one sense of the word), élan vital, and orgone energy.

The astral can be considered as the energy double of the material. It is, in one sense, 'the stuff of which dreams are made'. Dreams originate on other spheres of the Tree, either singly or in combination, but *the substance* from which their images are made is the astral light, which is the energy of Yesod. It is the same substance that gives light and life to anything you imagine, whether visually or using the other senses.

The astral light, which is equivalent to the astral 'plane', is the realm of astral projection or travel. Astral projection works through the combination of *will* and *imagination* creating the required and appropriate images. These 'come to life' in the astral light of Yesod. Although the 'quality of feeling' about it may be different, the images created in visual imagination, day-dreams, night-dreams, guided fantasy or directed day-dreaming are all – in terms of their relevance and their substance – identical with the images of astral travelling.

Books which describe astral travelling as a process of the 'double' leaving the body (usually through the top of the head and attached by a silver or gold thread or cord) are actually describing the process of splitting the *etheric* double from the physical form, and not astral travel. The process of separating the etheric double from the body is dangerous; astral 'separation' is rarely if ever harmful.

Various groups over the whole history of humankind have concentrated their energies, imagination and will on various symbols or symbolic systems – both mystical and magickal in emphasis – and have created 'permanent' astral planes; that is, places where the astral light has been imprinted with the symbols of a certain belief. For example, on the astral plane various 'sub-planes' may be found: an alchemical plane, a Christian plane (or many such!), a fairy plane, a Celtic plane, a Tibetan plane, and so on. Whilst these are more collective than individual in character, it is through Yesod that an individual may contact these planes.

the moon grotto

Follow the usual starting procedure.

It is night-time. Visualize yourself as walking down a steep but easy path to the edge of a river. You can hear the water gently lapping against the shore as you approach.

At the river's edge you find a small boat. Climb into the boat, untie it, and allow it to float downstream, taking you on a mystical journey in the night.

Imagine you are going deeper and deeper into the night, aware only of the rocking motion of the boat and the sound of water gently lapping the sides. Relax and enjoy your dark journey.

After some while the boat gently comes to a shore and beaches itself. You can step out of the boat on to a small island. As you do so the cloud cover parts and a full, bright moon lights up the scene before you. Look at the island in front of you. A little way ahead is a cave or grotto, brightly lit by the moon.

This cave is a special place, the home of a moon goddess who can heal you, and teach you the art of moon magic. Walk up to the cave and see the goddess step out to greet you.

Listen to what she has to say. Her words are words of wisdom. Ask her about your problems and worries. Ask her for instruction in magic.

This is an important time you are spending with the moon

goddess. Relish it! When you are ready, bid her farewell and, using your little boat, go back upstream to where you started – your usual waking reality. Open your eyes and feel refreshed, relaxed and centred.

Write in your diary about your experience.

You can return to see the moon goddess any time you wish.

A particularly good and appropriate time is at the full moon.

THE PATHS AND THE TREE OF LIFE

As you have studied this chapter your focus has shifted from Malkuth to Yesod. This is equivalent to passing through the 32nd path, the pathway that connects the earth to the astral, Malkuth to Yesod. The paths connect the spheres on the Tree. Looking at the Tree from the bottom to the top, they are the paths we climb to attain the knowledge and under-standing of the higher spheres. Looking at the Tree from the top to the bottom, they are the paths which transmit spiritual energy through the whole system.

The paths are the *experience of connection*. They are the subjective experience of the objective reality of the spheres. For example, the path connecting Malkuth to Yesod is the path for going *up*, or *deeper* into the Tree, and also the path that transmits (a) the pure energy of Yesod into Malkuth, and (b) the repressions associated with Yesod down into the body (in the form of tensions, emotional armouring, and so on).

The paths that cross the Abyss have a special function in represent-ing the *Qualities* of the Self radiating down into the soul of the individual. They are of the level of the radiation of Archetypes through the soul. In the section on soul Qualities later in the book this will be explained in more detail.

It is worth meditating upon each path, until what they connect, and how they do it, becomes clear.

active path meditation

Follow the usual starting procedure.

If you meditate upon any path of the Tree of Life and the associated symbols, it helps to *harmonize* and *balance* the connection between the two associated spheres.

Use the table of correspondences (Appendix 4) to choose several potent symbols associated with the 32nd path (Malkuth to Yesod) and meditate upon these symbols in any way you like. Visualize them, consider them, make pictures of them to put on your wall, see the connection between them, and so on.

Also cherish them as they aid your first step into the Kabbalistic system of knowledge, understanding and wisdom.

Repeat this, as you work up the Tree, with all the other paths connecting the various spheres.

meditation for inner peace

As you continue your Kabbalistic work you may find times when you feel disturbed or low in energy. This exercise may help you to balance yourself and find inner peace and certainty.

Follow the usual starting procedure.

Pay attention to your breathing, not forcing it, simply watching the rhythmic flow in and out of your body at its natural pace.

Affirm silently to yourself: 'My body is at peace.'

Be aware of any sensations in your body – do *not* try to suppress them.

Then affirm silently: 'My emotions and feelings are at peace.'

Again do not try to suppress any emotions that arise – simply be aware of them and let them pass.

Then affirm silently: 'My thoughts are at peace.'

Let any thoughts that arise be noted but do not become attached to them.

Visualize your being as perfectly silent and at peace in a perfectly silent and peaceful world.

Affirm silently to yourself:

'I do have sensations, emotions, feelings, thoughts, but I, as an individual spark of the Self, am eternally at peace and at one with the universal rhythm.'

Realize the truth of this statement.

Record in your diary any impressions, difficulties or results in performing this exercise.

THE MEANING OF SYMBOLS

In a symbol lies concealment or revelation

CARLYLE

Symbols are a means of releasing energy from the unconscious. By gradually integrating conscious with unconscious content within the psyche, they affect the quality of your personal life, bringing value and meaning to it.

Symbols cannot be understood intellectually, but must also arouse feelings to be truly understood and integrated.

They cannot be understood outside their context. For example, a car on a racetrack and a car on a country lane not only involve different concepts of 'car' but also arouse quite different feelings.

Whether a symbol reveals of conceals depends not on the symbol itself but on our attitude towards it. If we stop at its appearance, its form, then it veils and hides. If we understand its meaning and succeed in grasping what it signifies then it is a means of revelation.

Symbolism, the study of symbols, is concerned with *wholes*, perceived by intuition, that is, whole patterns and whole sequences, and the interaction of the parts within the context. Symbols allow us to connect with the macrocosm. In the world of symbols you can connect your heart with the sun, and realize your identity with the farthest stars, even with the whole of creation.

Symbols describe pictorially and vividly what is of greatest concern to us on this planet, both individually and collectively – that is, our own inner being and its relationship with the outside world.

Symbols destroy the distinction between inside and outside. Our inner vision seeks expression, and the apparently 'outer' world seeks meaning – symbols both mediate between and combine the two.

You will already have looked at the correspondence tables in Appendix 5. (If you have not, do so now before continuing.) These tables are of vital importance to a thorough study and experience of the practical Kabbalah. They will be referred to often during this book, and from now on you should make it your business to study them. Do not try to memorize them parrot-fashion, but rather constantly familiarize yourself with them and their connections. This is vital; the more you use them, the more the correspondences connect and attune themselves to your personal psyche.

The correspondences are not arbitrary. They are based upon:

- observations and experience throughout many centuries
- rational connections
- personal and group investigations

Although they are not worth learning by rote, some are worth paying particular attention to in your initial phase of study, and worth committing to memory if you are so inclined. These are: the celestial attributions, the numerical values, the Tarot trumps, the titles, and the Hebrew letters.

Remember that although these correspondences are, in the most part, 'universally' true, correspondences that matter are those that resonate with you as an individual. If through your practical study you find other correspondences work better for you then throw these out of the window and create your own tables. This is particularly true of the paths, which are subjective in nature.

The Tarot cards are very powerful symbols corresponding to both the spheres and the paths of the Tree and this is why it is so strongly recommended you have a pack. The 78 cards may be seen as *living entities* that inhabit the Tree of Life, and whose substance is created from the symbols that correspond to their location. By getting to know these entities you improve your knowledge of the whole Tree.

CHAPTER 5

HOD: THE CENTRE OF THE MIND

THE EIGHTH SPHERE, HOD

The name of this Sephira (or sphere) is *Hod*, which in Hebrew is:

$$\text{ד} \quad \text{ו} \quad \text{ה}$$

D   V   H

Hod is situated on the plane between Yesod and Tiphareth, on the left-hand side of the tree (which corresponds to the right side of the body). It forms a 'pair' of Sephiroth on this plane, the other being Netzach, on the right-hand side of the Tree.

Hod is attributed to the mind. The mind can alternatively be called the intellect, the intellectual mind, the concrete mind, the *thoughts*. Hod means 'glory', the glory of the illuminated or light-filled mind.

'Mind' can mean many different things. For example, some people use 'mind' to mean what we would term in the Kabbalah, either the Supernal Triad (that is, Kether, Chockmah and Binah), or the whole Tree. 'Mind' is also sometimes used to mean 'the connecting faculty', the consciousness of awareness itself. The term as applied here to Hod means the 'concrete mind, intellectual mind, thoughts' as opposed to the 'abstract' mind, which includes 'higher' elements of Hod together with aspects of Sephiroth 4, 5, 6 and 7.

the mind door

Follow the usual starting procedure.

Have only dim light in your room (candle light is ideal).

Sitting or lying comfortably, close your eyes and breathe deeply. You can always use your breath to calm and centre yourself.

Imagine a door before you, a door of any type you care to imagine. On this door are the words 'Hod' and 'mind'. Visualize these words clearly on the door in bright, white light.

For now do not go through this door but open it and see what is on the other side. Allow whatever images emerge to appear before you. Do not judge or censor them.

If you wish, and only if you wish, you may go through the door and step into the world you see there. If you decide to do this, only go a little way into this world. You can always return at another time if you wish.

Whether you go into the world behind the door or not, when you have finished, *firmly* and *wilfully* close the door shut.

Record in your diary what you have experienced.

You can use this exercise in many different ways – as many different ways as there are different words, pictures and/or symbols you can visualize on the door.

CORRESPONDENCES TO HOD

Thoth, Mercury and Hermes, insofar as they are messengers and communicators, are deities that may be associated with Hod. All these gods are associated with *communication*. Communication may be defined as imparting, exchanging and/or connecting information. Hod is concerned with both inner and outer aspects of communication; that is, the communication between the parts of your total self, and your communication with 'other selves'.

Hod is the sphere of *mental magick*, the magick of grimoires (that is, grammars) and spells (that is, spelling).

The polarity between thoughts and feelings, well known to us from the constant effects we all experience as a result of their interaction, will be discussed further in the next chapter. Keep in mind for now that where two Sephiroth appear on the same plane (as is the case with Hod and Netzach) they are properly studied together, as one is inexorably linked to the other. Also at this stage pay attention to understanding the difference between the *feelings* of Netzach, which come from inside, and the *emotions* of Yesod which react to outside. There are also two levels of thoughts; those from inside and those which are reactions to outside.

The Yetziratic Text calls Hod the 'perfect intelligence'. The traditional Virtue associated with Hod is truthfulness, whereas the Vices are falsehood and dishonesty. Mental rigidity may be added to these.

The colour associated with Hod is orange. The spiritual experience is called the 'Vision of Splendour', where 'splendour' is a word describing brilliance, light and illumination.

Associated with Hod are the words, names, verses and spells of traditional magick. All mantras in their physical essence (if not in their intended effect) also belong to Hod.

The Tarot cards associated with Hod are the four 8s. These are:

8 of wands	swiftness
8 of cups	indolence
8 of swords	interference
8 of discs	prudence

It is a useful exercise to reflect upon the qualities of fire, water, air and earth, how they may be applied to the mind of Hod, and how these Tarot titles may describe aspects of this correspondence.

8 of wands	fiery mind	(Mercury in Sagittarius)
8 of cups	watery mind	(Saturn in Cancer)
8 of swords	airy mind	(Jupiter in Gemini)
8 of discs	earthy mind	(Sun in Virgo)

What do you understand by the terms 'fiery mind', 'watery mind' and so on? Before continuing consider the question:

If thought precedes action, what precedes thought?

mind charting

For this exercise you will need some sheets of paper, the larger the better but at least A4 size, and some writing materials, preferably colours.

Follow the usual starting procedure.

Take one of the statements from the list below and write it in a circle in the middle of your paper. Look at the statement in the circle and allow your mind to wander into associations. For example, if you had 'fish' in your circle, you might get a whole range of associations coming into your mind, from 'chips' to 'Christ'. You may also get associations that you do not understand at all – do not censor, include these too.

With each association, as it occurs, draw a line out from the central circle, and write the appropriate words on the line. As your circle gets more and more spokes radiating out from it, allow your associations to run on to the words and images on the spokes also – add other lines coming out from the first ones. You can create a 'complex' of association from the first single statement.

Try the experiment for at least two of the statements, then for one other statement you take yourself from a favourite book.

As well as recording the results of this exercise in your diary, answer the question: 'What did I learn about myself through doing this exercise?'

THE STATEMENTS

1. Pure folly is the key to initiation.
2. The soft conquers the hard.
3. Walk silently but never alone.
4. This is my wisdom face.
5. The place of original magic.
6. Enter paradise, here today.
7. There is nothing that is not a flower.
8. To be the singer and the song.
9. Blessings and curses are not different.
10. Life is only real, then when I am.
11. In problems discover gifts.
12. The word made flesh.
13. Mirror mirror on the wall.
14. Do what thou wilt.
15. This is my life, now.

HOD AND THE BODY

Hod, as the thinking, intellectual mind, is usually associated with the physical brain, but the whole truth is not that simple. Hod, as has been mentioned, is in constant interplay with Netzach, the feelings. This *polarity* is situated and experienced at the *solar plexus*. When we have pains, feelings, energies, or other effects in our solar plexus or upper stomach region we tend to consider them as the effect of feelings and emotions. Fear in the pit of the stomach, the sobbing belly of grief, butterflies in the tum, the fiery solar plexus of repression, are all such effects. The Kabbalah says these *experienced* sensations are the result of the *interaction* of feelings and thoughts.

In a later chapter we will be studying the chakras, or energy centres of the body. The chakras are connected to the spine, and both Hod and Netzach are connected at the same place, behind the solar plexus. This again confirms the interconnectedness of these two Sephiroth. By way of metaphor it can be considered that our large, bulbous brains are merely a 'growth' on the top of the spinal column to accommodate our vastly increased Hod.

Hod is also associated with the right arm and right kidney.

THE INDIVIDUATION OF CONSCIOUSNESS

The four Sephiroth – Netzach, Hod, Yesod and Malkuth – are all associated with the individual personality. The first of these spheres is Netzach, number 7; Hod, number 8, comes next. The sequence is not arbitrary. As 'consciousness' individuates in this bottom part of the Tree, at Netzach it is fluid, individualizing but still in touch with group consciousness. As it moves into Hod it becomes harder, more concrete, and the process of individuation is complete.

A balanced personality is fluid and free, however individuated. It is in touch with the collective, at least through Netzach, feelings. Compare this with the unbalanced personality which becomes hard, rigid, and incapable of creative growth; this 'unbalanced' personality is not in touch with either itself or other consciousness levels. It is what is termed the 'character' of a person. Beware of character-forming habits!

An analogy for the process of individuation lies in the total interrelatedness and yet vastly different emphasis of *art* and *philosophy*. Art is fluid, connected to group consciousness and feelings-orientated. Philosophy, on the other hand, is concrete, connected to individual consciousness, and thought-orientated.

SELF AWARENESS
(both 7 and 8)

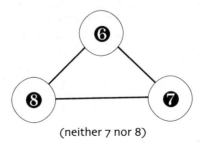

(neither 7 nor 8)

That is not to say that philosophy is unbalanced, or that one is better than the other. Both are equally needed, for themselves, and by the other. And both need the centralizing influence of Tiphareth, the 'I' that knows itself.

the three symbols visualization

Follow the usual starting procedure.

Choose any three items from either the Netzach or the Hod lines in the correspondence tables (see Appendix 4, row 7 or 8).
   Relax your body, close your eyes, and visualize a door before you with 'Netzach' or 'Hod' written on it (whichever you have chosen).
   Pay attention to the door (noting what kind of door it is, its style, colour, shape, size, etc.).
   Imagine you walk up to, open and pass through the door into another world. Before you is a scene from that world that incorporates in some way your three *chosen items* from the corre-spondence tables.
   Do not judge or analyse this scene, simply watch it as it is or as it unfolds before you.
   Pay particular attention to the contents of the scene *other* than the ones you chose.
   Returning through the door when you feel ready, remember to close the door behind you securely. In your own time open your eyes.
   Take a large sheet of paper and either draw, crayon or paint the scene you have witnessed. (It does *not* have to be a great work of art!)

THE HEBREW NAMES OF THE NUMBERS AND LETTERS

You can find this information in the correspondence tables (Appendix 4). Look at the columns headed:

- Hebrew Letters
- Hebrew Names of Letters
- English Equivalent
- Numerical Value
- English Letters

There is no need for you to learn these by rote, but at this stage you should now pay attention to these particular correspondences. Study them in detail and see if you can make any connections between them. You will be using Hod to do this! It is also necessary for you to familiarize yourself with these columns before attempting Gematria, which is described in a subsequent section.

The translation of the letters helps us to remember them. For example, if we remember that 'zain' is a sword, its shape is easier to recall. The following suggestions may help you to understand the Hebrew letters and remember them:

letter		meaning	connections
aleph	א	ox	shape of a yoke
beth	ב	house	shows roof, floor and one wall
gimel	ג	camel	reminds us of its position on the Tree (crossing the desert of the Abyss)
daleth	ד	door	shape of the porch of a doorway
he	ה	window	the gap is the window
vau	ו	nail	directly hieroglyphic
zain	ז	sword	the hilt and the blade
cheth	ח	fence	cross bar on uprights
teth	ט	serpent	obvious from the shape
yod	י	hand/sperm	smallest letter

kaph	כ	palm of hand	suggests a fist
lamed	ל	ox-goad	shape obvious
mem	מ	water	looks like a wave
nun	נ	fish	imagination stretched for this one!
samekh	ס	prop	shaped like a pillow
ayin	ע	eye	shape of two eyes and a nose
pe	פ	mouth	shape obvious; the yod in the middle is the tongue
tzaddi	צ	fish-hook	obvious shape
qoph	ק	back of head	suggestive shape
resh	ר	head	side view of a head
shin	ש	tooth	three fangs of molar
tau	ת	tau cross	shaped accordingly

The Hebrew letters are split into three types, the 'mother', 'single' and 'double' letters. Analysed in this way they reveal an interestingly coherent scheme of associations.

The mother letters:

the three	ש	fire	head	summer
elements	מ	water	stomach	winter
	א	air	chest	spring/autumn

The double letters:

the seven	ב	Mercury	above	life/death
planets	ג	Moon	below	peace/war
	ד	Venus	east	knowledge/ignorance
	כ	Jupiter	west	wealth/poverty
	פ	Mars	north	grace/restriction
	ר	Sun	south	fertility/sterility
	ת	Saturn	middle	power/slavery

The single letters:

the 12 signs	ה	Aries	north-east	sight
of the zodiac	ו	Taurus	south-east	hearing
	ז	Gemini	east	smell
	ח	Cancer	east	speech
	ט	Leo	north	taste/digestion
	י	Virgo	north	sex
	ל	Libra	south-west	work activity
	נ	Scorpio	north-west	movement
	ס	Sagittarius	west	firmness/anger
	ע	Capricorn	west	lightness/mirth
	צ	Aquarius	south	imagination
	ק	Pisces	south	sleep

GEMATRIA, TEMURAH AND NOTARIQON

Gematria is based upon the relative numerical value of words. Words of the same numerical value are considered to be explanatory of each other, and this theory is extended to phrases. Thus the letter shin, sh, is 300, and is equivalent to the number attained by adding up the value of the letters of the words RVCh ALHIM, Ruach Elohim – the Spirit of the Gods. Similarly, the words AChD, Achad – Unity and AHBH, Ahebah – Love, each equal 13 (for A:1, Ch:8, D:4 = 13 and A:1, H:5, B:2, H:5 = 13). Therefore, by Gematria, we find that Love and Unity are equivalent!

In Genesis 49:10 we find the phrase 'Shiloh shall come', Yeba Shiloh, IBA ShILH, which equals 358. This is also the number of MShICH, the Messiah.

In Genesis 18:2 we find VHNH ShLShH, Vehenna Shalisha, which means 'and lo, three men'. This is equivalent numerically to the phrase ALV MIKAL GBRIAL V RPAL, Elo Mikhael Gabriel Ve-Raphael; that is, 'these are Michael, Gabriel and Raphael' (each phrase is 701). So the 'three men' of the first phrase conceals (by Gematric correspondence) the names of the three archangels.

Whenever difficulty arises between two phrases or words which add up to the same numerical value but do not initially seem to correspond, the key is often found through meditation. There will be an identity. Thus

ALP, Aleph – the Unity, is 111; also APL – thick darkness, and ASN – sudden death, both add up to 111 also. This can be interpreted as revealing the annihilation of the individual in the Unity, and the darkness which is the threshold of that Unity.

Gematria may seem to be nothing but nonsense at first sight, taking liberties with names, letters and numbers. You could probably do the same with words and phrases out of an Agatha Christie novel! But in point of fact, just as a koan in Zen Buddhism is meaningful but not necessarily rational – a statement made from a mystical level of consciousness – so Gematria may also be seen in this light and used to induce a similar type of illumination. The excitement of making a connection between two or more apparently disconnected words or phrases has to be experienced to be understood.

The process of reducing a word or phrase to a number, then testing this against one's previous knowledge of that number, is both a test for your Kabbalistic skills *and*, more importantly, a stimulus for the surrender of the rational mind to the mystical experience in which One is seen to be All, and vice versa.

You can use the same numerical values for the English alphabet and have a reasonable, working English Gematria. But be careful – there are possibly other attributions and there can be no finality in this work. It is making the connections that is important.

You can use attributions, Tarot cards – indeed anything meaningful to you – to assist your Gematric connections. For example, in English the words 'infinite space' add up to 289 which is 17 x 17; this then affirms that infinite space contains a multitude of stars as 17 is the number of the Tarot card 'Star'. Or in English again 'Ankh-af-na-khonsu' and 'Hoor' (the god Horus) both add up to 345. This is the number of Mosheh (Moses) and also of AL ShDI, God Almighty. So an identity can be made between Horus and the scribe of his 'book', and the Jewish 'God' and his scribe Moses. It is valid to cross over languages, correspondences, etc., so long as you make connections and consequently experience the 'excitement' engendered by these sorts of connections. If the connections given here seem meaningless to you, all the more reason for you to try out your own.

Temurah and Notariqon are far less useful than Gematria, and are not really worth pursuing unless they particularly appeal to you. Temurah is based upon a system of permutations, with letters being substituted for other letters. Notariqon has two forms: the first, in which every letter from a word is taken to be the initial of another word; the second, exactly the opposite, taking the first letter of the words of a phrase to make a word (rather like an acrostic). So, for example, with the first kind of Notariqon every letter of BRAShITH, the first word in Genesis, is the initial of another word – the phrase usually quoted being BRAShITH RAH ALHIM ShIQBLV IShRAEL ThVRH: 'In the beginning Elohim saw that Israel would accept the law.' There could be many other possible answers to this. Of the second type a good example is ChKMH NSThRH, the secret wisdom. The initials of these two words are ChN, the word meaning 'grace'. So Notariqon (and Temurah) can lead to interesting results, but generally a thorough knowledge and practice of Gematria is sufficient for the practical Kabbalist.

THE POWER OF SOUND

The sphere of Hod is concerned with mental magick, and the spoken word (in the form of spells, grimoires, mantras, and so on) is the basis of this kind of magick. Sound can be considered to be like an ocean of vibration that pervades everything. It has always done so and as far as we know, this will not change. 'In the beginning was the word ...' and in the end will be the word also. Even in the quietest places, although you might not be able to hear it, there will be some external sound – and internal sound is incessant. Put your fingers in your ears and listen for a while ...

This 'ocean of sound' varies from the *music of the spheres* to the *cacophony of the modern world*. It has been proven that harsh, loud, prolonged sound can affect (usually adversely) the nerves and various parts of the body. It is also believed that low, continuous sub-aural sounds can do the same. By analogy it is easy to suggest that harmonious sounds may affect the individual beneficially. In an average city the normal sound level is around 50 db, in the country around 10 db. If this seems meaningless then consider that a horn blown about 10 feet away from you is equivalent to 90 db and causes the amount of blood pumping through the heart to double.

Each letter of the alphabet (any alphabet, English as much as any so-called sacred alphabet) has an effect on the body when sounded. The way the sound is pitched also changes the effect of the letter. Different notes are found to make different patterns when resonated through iron filings.

Harmony and balance may be achieved through using sounds that are beneficial to hear, to 'receive' inside. The best-known example is, of course, *om*.

sound exercises

OM

Follow the usual starting procedure.

Make the sound *om* (pronounced owm) particularly stretching the sound of the vowel. As you make the sound, gaze steadily without blinking at some fixed point (such as a candle flame) that is level with your eyes, and about 4–5 feet away. When you have finished making the sound, listen attentively for sounds in your ears (particularly the right ear).

Repeat the procedure several times, listening closely each time.

Finally repeat the procedure but with your eyes closed. What do you hear now?

CLOSING THE OPENINGS

Follow the usual starting procedure.

Close all the openings of the head and listen. (The openings referred to are the eyes, ears, nose and mouth. Close eyes and mouth, put thumbs in ears then pinch nose closed with fingers. Remember to breathe between attempts!)

AUM

The sound mentioned above, *om*, is better understood through its component parts, that is *a u m: a* is the start of the breath in the lungs, *u* is the sound made as it passes the throat, and *m* is the sound on the lips; one may add *gn*, which is the resonating sound as the mantra continues, or the sound of the indrawn breath through the nose. The whole formula then becomes *aumgn*, and resumes the whole of creation.

Follow the usual starting procedure.

Make the sound *aumgn*, being aware of the component parts *a, u, m, gn*.

Take in a deep breath. Visualize the *a* at the beginning of the mantra to be in your heart, as a shining white light.

As you breathe out, let the *a* change to a *u* (pronounced oo) sound as it passes through your throat. Imagine the sound as a wave of white energy coming up from your heart.

Then as the sound reaches your lips, let it become an *m* sound. Do not stop there but let this sound turn into a resonating, nasal *gn* (pronounced nnnn) sound, and as it does so imagine the energy that has come up from your heart rising through your nose and eyes.

You can finish the exercise here. Alternatively you can then project the energy out as healing energy, either to a specific person (in your presence or far away) or to the earth as a whole. Alternatively, you can allow the visualized energy to rise up to your third eye/ajna chakra (midway between the eyebrows, in the middle of the head) and visualize there a symbol or sigil for a desire.

AL AND LA

The two words *Al* and *La* represent God/All and Goddess/Nothing, Form *(Al)* and Force *(La)*, the infinitely small and the infinitely large, and the point and the circle. Put together they make *Alla*, a name of God (equivalent to Allah).

Listen to the sound of your breath as it passes through your nose, mouth and throat. On every in-breath, you make the sound *Al* and on every out-breath, the sound *La* (the *l* sound being the stopping place where the breath turns from inwards to outwards).

It could be said that everyone breathing, by the very fact that they are breathing, is continuously voicing the name of God, Alla.

Do not confuse the essential nature of 'Alla', which is a perfectly balanced manifestation of the male/female principles, with 'Allah', which although it is absolutely equivalent in essence, has come to refer to a much more specifically male-orientated God by many people.

Hod is the locus of mental magick, involved primarily with words and sounds. The above exercises will help you connect with some of your own Hod-related powers. Used wisely and with love, these powers can not only aid your own development but also help raise the consciousness of the planet as a whole.

Chapter 6

NETZACH: THE CENTRE OF FEELINGS

THE SEVENTH SPHERE, NETZACH

The name of this Sephira is *Netzach*, which in Hebrew is:

ח צ נ

Ch   Tz   N

Netzach is situated on the plane between Yesod and Tiphareth, on the right-hand side of the Tree (which corresponds to the left-hand side of the body). It forms a 'pair' of Sephiroth on this the fifth plane (the other being Hod, with which you worked in the last chapter).

Netzach is attributed to the *feelings*, which need to be distinguished (in theory if not so easily in practice) from the emotions. Feelings come *from within* and include positive and negative energies, for example love and hate, joy and sorrow. The emotions are always reactive, that is, they arise as the result of some happening *outside* you, and are a result of your *internal reaction* to this incident. Emotions are attributable to what might be called 'lower' aspects of Netzach, along with 'higher' aspects of Yesod. This is not to say feelings are 'better' than emotions; they are different, but equally valuable as part of your total make-up.

Netzach means 'Victory', the victory of the actual over the potential (the move of the Lightning Flash from the 6th to the 7th sphere on the Tree), and the victory of undifferentiated or collective energy over individual energy (the move from the 8th to the 7th sphere on the journey back up the Tree).

As already described in the last chapter, Netzach forms a *polarity* with Hod, the other sphere on the same plane of the Tree. All our everyday and ongoing growth situations can be expressed in terms of the interaction between these two spheres. Consider your own experience of 'thoughts' and 'feelings'. To which of these are you most attached?

Remember that growth comes from *inclusion*. If, for example, you consider yourself to be more mentally attached (or identified) and that you pay less attention to your feelings, do not suppress or depress your mental strength to correct the balance, but increase your feelings side until it is of equal strength. Obviously the opposite is true if you are primarily feelings attached. The importance of this concept cannot be overemphasized.

THE CHALICE

A symbol traditionally associated with Netzach is the Chalice, Magick Cup or Grail. Imagine you could use whatever materials you like, and had all the necessary skills to do it – what kind of chalice would you construct?

Do this now: really imagine the chalice you would make if you could create one in any size, pattern, shape, colour or form you like.

The chalice is a symbol of Netzach. It can be said that the chalice *you* have created is a symbolic representation of your current relationship with this sphere. As you change, so your chalice will change too.

---

the chalice

Before continuing follow the usual starting procedure.

Imagine you are in a field at the bottom of a hill. With you is your chalice, just as you constructed earlier. Look at the chalice, and clearly visualize its form and shape. Then look around you; be aware of everything you can see, everything you can smell, touch, taste and hear. Perhaps the grass is long, perhaps there is bird song, perhaps you can see early morning dew glistening on the meadow – let the image of your meadow form around you.

You are going to take your chalice to the top of the nearby hill.

So, in your own time, walk across your field to where a path slopes upwards towards the hill. Walk this path, taking your time to be really aware of what is around you. When you get near the top, stop for a rest, and look back over the path you have travelled, and down to the meadow below.

When you are ready, walk to the very top of the hill. There you will find a standing stone, about the height of your waist. Place your chalice on top of this stone. Be aware that the energy of the sun, shining on your chalice, charges it, and lightens it. Be aware that the earth energy coming up through the stone also charges your chalice. Your chalice is receptive to the energies of the earth, the air, water and fire. Allow your chalice to change shape, or acquire new parts, or simply become radiant as it receives all this positive energy.

When you are ready, thank the sun and thank the stone, then return to the meadow, taking your chalice with you. When you are back, really pay attention to feeling your feet on the solid ground, then open your eyes and write about your experience in your diary.

THE VENUS CONNECTION

Netzach is attributed to Venus. It is also attributed to the 'higher feelings' (to distinguish from emotions). These 'higher feelings' are a manifestation of love.

Note that Netzach (number 7) is connected to Chesed (number 4), which is attributed to Love.

Similarly it could be said that 'higher' mentation is a form of will, as Hod (number 8) is connected to Geburah (number 5), which is Will.

An important aspect of Kabbalistic growth is to make the *cross connections* from Will to Feelings and from Love to Thoughts:

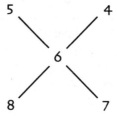

Consider this crossing of the energies in terms of the Tree of Life diagram, and be aware you could make these cross connections through Tiphareth – the centre, the heart, the 'I'.

CORRESPONDENCES TO NETZACH

The traditional Virtue of Netzach is unselfishness, altruism, the love of 'good-for-all'. The Vice on the other hand is lust, being ruled by the 'lower' emotions.

Netzach corresponds in the body to the solar plexus (along with Hod – see last chapter if you don't recall this) and to the left arm and left kidney.

The colour of Netzach is emerald green.

The Yetziratic Text calls it the sphere of 'Occult Intelligence', occult because it is hidden intelligence compared with the 'open', 'resplendent' intelligence of Hod.

The vision of Netzach is the 'vision of Triumphant Beauty'. It is closely associated with the highest forms of art, in any form.

A symbol of Netzach is the lamp which is carried (as opposed to the lamp which hangs over the head, or other lamps such as those around the circumference of the circle).

Deities typical of Netzach are those associated with love and intense feeling, such as Aphrodite (Greek), Hathoor (Egyptian) and Venus (Roman).

The Tarot cards connected with Netzach are the four 7s:

7 of wands	valour	(Mars in Leo)
7 of cups	debauch	(Venus in Scorpio)
7 of swords	futility	(Moon in Aquarius)
7 of discs	failure	(Saturn in Taurus)

CONTACTING NETZACH

A good way to contact Netzach is through *art* in all its manifestations, whether it be painting, dance, music, or any other form of creative art. You can become involved in art in two different ways: as a creator or as a spectator. This is a clear example of how the *creative* and *receptive* principles can be applied to one sphere on the Tree. Both ways are equally valid in terms of contacting Netzach, or any other sphere.

How do you apply the principles of being creative and/or receptive to Hod?

On the level of the personality, it is easier to make a creative connection to Hod and a receptive connection to Netzach. This is why crossing the energies is so important, for it allows the opposite polarities to be more active in the personality.

Particularly apt for Netzach is the process of *surrendering* to the energy – not forcing anything, being quietly receptive to the flow, and allowing it to happen. Surrendering to the energy of Netzach leads to *clarity*, particularly with respect to the appreciation of beauty. This is why being in nature appeals to so many people. It connects them to Netzach.

When you have finished this section take a walk somewhere nice (even if you live in a big city there is a park somewhere nearby), and pay attention to just *being* there, appreciating all that is around you. You can create a world of beauty anywhere. Try it.

---

surrender

Follow the usual starting procedure.

Imagine you are on a beach – a long, empty, warm, beautiful beach. Really take time to picture yourself there, and notice what you feel and what you sense. What can you see? hear? smell? taste?

Walk slowly into the sea, deeper and deeper until you have to start swimming, then let yourself go and swim out into the deeper water.

Really experience the sensation of swimming out to sea, for no purpose other than for the enjoyment of it, the experience in itself being all there is, all you need at this moment.

Then relax and simply float on the salt water, which holds you buoyant and safe.

Surrender yourself in any way you desire to the embrace of the sea.

Write about your experience in your diary, asking yourself the questions: Can I surrender like this, and if so, how easily? What does this tell me?

THE EXPRESSION OF EXPERIENCE

It is important in studying magick in any form to pay attention to the language we use. In the last chapter it was mentioned that your grammar is your grimoire, and a connection was made between spelling (or the words that make up spelling) and casting a spell. To use words that you *choose* to use is a vital part of being a magician. It is particularly vital with a 'language' like the Kabbalah, where the change of one letter can change the whole meaning.

Language is vital to our communication about ourselves – both to other people *and* to ourselves. Reification of a language involves finding and using the correct word for each idea, concept, being and/or thing in existence. If you know the name of something, you control it; if you do not, it controls you.

It is essential to understand one's own inner Kabbalah, and this can only be achieved through the use of precise language, whether the language be written in the symbols we call words, or in *any* other symbols.

Own as belonging to you what you say and what you are talking about – for example, instead of saying: 'it makes me feel ...' or 'my foot hurts', try saying: 'I feel ...' and 'I hurt in my foot' or whatever.

Clarify what you say in terms of how you are really experiencing it. For example, you may say, 'I feel that you should do some more work' – but *how* and *where* do you 'feel' such a thing? What you probably mean is 'I think ...' or 'I imagine ...' Do you see the difference?

Paying attention to *owning and clarifying* your experiences are two ways of starting the process of controlling and directing how you talk both to others and to yourself.

the walking meditation

Follow the usual starting procedure.

Imagine that the Self of Kether resides somewhere within your body – at the top of your head, in your feet, in your heart, left thumb – anywhere!

Locate a place where the Self resides in you, and try to imagine that place as specifically as you can.

Now centre all your attention on that location in your body. Imagine that all the qualities of life – joy, peace, truth, love, etc. – emanate from that place.

Realize that although everything you know, feel and sense radiates from this place, the location itself is perfectly centred, calm, clear, pure, silent – totally without any content whatsoever.

Holding your awareness of this place inside you and attending to this alone, *stand up* and start walking.

Any time you feel you are losing awareness of this place, *stop*, stand still and re-centre and focus yourself before continuing to walk.

Stop this exercise when you feel ready.

In the following days bring this awareness into your everyday life by centring yourself in this way when walking from room to room, in the street, in a park – wherever you are.

Mostly: enjoy yourself doing it!

PATHS CONNECTED TO HOD AND NETZACH

At the moment you are studying Hod and Netzach. The following exercise can usefully be performed on any plane of the Tree, whether it is a single sphere plane or one with a pair of spheres. All you have to do is 'extract out' the paths connected to your sphere(s), and contemplate these in isolation from the remainder of the Tree.

At first simply *reflect* upon the connections that are made – for example, with Hod and Netzach, you might notice the balance between the *nun* and *ayin* paths connecting these spheres to Tiphareth. What are the similarities and differences between these paths? What do they mean taken together rather than in isolation? Can you connect them to the *pe* path connecting Hod and Netzach? Why are 'The Tower' and Mars attributed to this path? Would these attributions fit better elsewhere and if so why? Try other attributions on this path – do they work? What is the connection between the Mars correspondence on this path and the Mars correspondence to Geburah? – and so on. Really reflect upon all the knowledge you have about these paths, and the connections you can make.

Then follow the usual starting procedure, sit with a map of your chosen area of the Tree before you, and let all the knowledge drift away. Still your mind, and simply *receive* any images, thoughts, feelings you might get about this area of the Tree.

Record these impressions, along with your reflections, in your diary. What difference, if any, is there between the knowledge you reflected upon and the insights you received about your chosen sphere(s)?

RAISING ENERGY

'Exalt thyself in prayer'; 'Enflame thyself'

There are many different ways of raising energy or 'enflaming' yourself in order to exalt your consciousness, when appropriate, so you can more readily tune into and perform your chosen task(s). As you will soon be starting Part III of this book, which is concerned with more transpersonal realms than those which you have been studying so far, now is a good time to look at these ways of raising energy. They include:

1. Total concentration.
2. Sex.
3. Merging (absolute compassion for all sentient life).
4. Aesthetic ecstasy (artistic appreciation).
5. Music (rhythm, drumming, jazz; also includes mantras, sounds).
6. Speed (including dance).
7. Drugs.
8. Shock (including emotions such as surprise, grief, ecstasy).
9. Devotion (to any 'deity' whatsoever).

THE BANISHING RITUAL OF THE PENTAGRAM

You will, hopefully, have been doing some centring and banishing work already, for example performing the Kabbalistic Cross. The following technique can be used at the beginning of an exercise or ritual. It both centres you and banishes all unwanted thoughts, emotions and sensations for the duration of the ritual or exercise. By banishing unwanted items, you make more space for the 'wanted items' or desired results to manifest. The Banishing Ritual of the Pentagram, which incorporates the Kabbalistic Cross, is also a way of clearing a space of unwanted 'psychic' energies and/or impressions. Performed with true intention its effects last for at least hours, often days or weeks, and sometimes even months. If you are doing it in your own room or temple and you do not perform other particularly unresonant acts in this room, you will probably only need to do the ritual occasionally. Otherwise it is recommended you perform it fairly regularly.

the pentagram ritual

Facing East – perform the Kabbalistic Cross.
Using the forefinger of the right hand inscribe in imagination
the shape of a flaming pentagram in the air in front of you.
Point to the middle of the pentagram and say in your most
sonorous voice: IHVH (pronounced yyoh-hey-wow-hey).
Turn around, or walk around the room, holding your hand outstretched as before, inscribing the line of a shining white circle as
you go.

Facing South – inscribe a flaming pentagram and say: ADNI
(pronounced ahhh-don-ayyy).

Facing West – the same and say: EHEIEH (pronounced ehhh-hey-
eee-yeh).

Facing North – the same and say: GAIA (pronounced gai-yaaaah).

Return to the East, so that you have now traced an enclosing circle
of light around you, with four flaming pentagrams at the four
quarters. Take a while to really visualize this as strongly as you can.
Then stand with your arms outstretched as a cross, and say:

> 'Before me Raphael
>
> Behind me Gabriel
>
> At my right hand Michael
>
> At the left hand Auriel
>
> Around me flame the pentagrams
>
> Above and within me shines the hexagram'

Imagine a shining hexagram above your head, energy radiating
down from it through your whole body.

Finally perform the Kabbalistic Cross once again.

For banishing, the direction to inscribe the pentagram is thus:

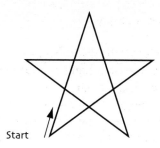

Start

This is the one you normally use. To change this ritual to an 'invoking ritual of the pentagram' you would inscribe the pentagram in reverse, thus:

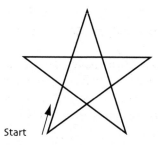

Start

You never perform the 'invoking pentagram' without having already done a banishing ritual before it. The invoking pentagram is then followed by the main part of the ritual, and then by a final banishing ritual.

PART III

SOUL, SPIRIT AND THE
TREE OF LIFE

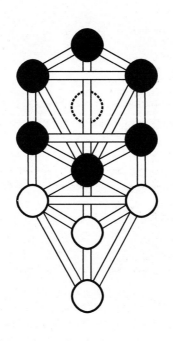

CHAPTER 7

TIPHARETH: THE HEART CENTRE

The name of this sphere is *Tiphareth*, which in Hebrew is:

ת פ א ר ת

Th   R   A   P   Th

Tiphareth is situated on the central pillar, on the fourth plane, at the centre of the whole Tree. It forms an ascending triangle with Netzach and Hod, and a descending triangle with Geburah and Chesed.

Tiphareth is attributed to the centre of the whole person, the 'personal self', 'personal identity', 'ego', 'centre', or (sometimes) 'soul'. It is given many different names which are used by different people in different ways. For example, it is 'ego' in one sense of the word but not in another. For this reason, we prefer to attribute it to *pure self-awareness*, or quite simply the 'I'. This is the 'I' that has a personality consisting of Netzach – Feeling, Hod – Thinking, Yesod – Subconscious and Malkuth – Sensing.

Tiphareth means 'Beauty and Harmony', the beauty created when everything is synthesized into a complete *whole*, the harmony that results from living life from a clearly defined centre.

Tiphareth is attributed to both the *sun* – the centre of the solar system, and the *heart* – the 'centre' of the human system. This dual attribution confers an identity between the heart and the sun – or, put another way, between the microcosm and the macrocosm.

The sun can be described as the point around which everything else clusters or revolves. So can the heart.

When you are 'living within your personality' (which is represented by all the spheres studied so far) you are *attached to* or *identified with* the contents of your awareness – you are sensing, feeling, thinking, or a combination thereof. Some people tend to be more identified with their thoughts, and look upon the mind as the central pivot of their existence. Others are more identified with their feelings, and look upon these as the experience of prime importance. A few people are primarily identified with their bodies.

There is nothing 'wrong' with being identified in this way – indeed it is absolutely necessary in order to be able to experience and express oneself in the world through the medium of these 'vehicles of identification'. What is needed, however, in order to be whole or balanced, is:

1. A balanced attachment; not one-sided towards the mind or overdeveloped towards the feelings, but equally able to identify with either of these 'vehicles of manifestation' as appropriate.

2. The ability to withdraw from these identifications *altogether*, and be in a clear space, dis-identified from the personality. From this clear space it is then possible to make clear choices to re-identify as seems appropriate. Tiphareth (the sun and the heart) is the place where this clarity is discovered. It is the 'I' that can say of itself: 'I am I, a centre of pure self-consciousness and of self-directed choosing'. The will of the individual in this centred, clear space is to identify with the lower spheres in order to gain experience and express itself, and to contact the higher spheres in order to manifest the Qualities of the soul.

solar and terrestrial consciousness

Follow the usual starting procedure.

Standing on the earth you have the experience (whatever your knowledge tells you) that the sun is 'born' every morning, rises, grows, reaches a peak (at midday) – then declines, sets and 'dies', to be reborn again the next day. Until very recently (in terms of human history) we all believed this to be the case.

To change this terrestrially based consciousness into *solar* consciousness we need only take one small step:

View the solar system as if you are now standing on the sun (rather than the earth).

Your experience changes. Now you are constantly alight, there is no birth or death or rebirth – there is the constant factor of being at the centre of all awareness and experience. Everything changes all the time, but the solar 'I' remains omniscient, omnipotent and omnipresent.

You can experience life from this centre, this 'I', the I of the sun and heart.

This is the experience of Tiphareth – solar consciousness.

CORRESPONDENCES TO TIPHARETH

The traditional Virtue associated with Tiphareth is devotion to the Great Work. This Great Work is what was described by Jesus of Nazareth as 'Know Thyself'. Your True Will, or purpose in life, is your goal, and the Great Work is everything you do that takes you a step closer to the completion of that purpose. This is everything you do with awareness, consciousness and choice.

The traditional Vices are pride and selfishness; not the Self that illuminates the being with light, life, liberty and love – but the 'dark self' that turns everything inwards, takes but never gives, a distortion of the true Self that lives in a mesh of tangled selfishness.

The Holy Guardian Angel is attributed to Tiphareth. You will learn more of this in the next chapter.

The colour of Tiphareth is golden yellow.

An image associated with Tiphareth is that of a majestic king, who in the old age (of terrestrially based consciousness) was usually depicted as a venerable, bearded adult male, but now (in this new age of solar consciousness) is more correctly depicted as a radiantly beautiful, smiling, hermaphrodite child.

The Yetziratic Text describes Tiphareth as the 'mediating Intelligence', mediating between the soul and the personality. Other names given to Tiphareth are: Adam, Man, Son, King. It is worth meditating upon these names, and why they are applied to Tiphareth, in the light of what you have already learned about this sphere.

Adam is, in Hebrew, MDA: A, as the first letter, indicates the beginning of something; DM is the Hebrew word for 'blood', so Adam (ADM) means 'the first blood'.

The spiritual vision attributed to this sphere is the 'Vision of Harmony', the harmony created when all the 'parts' come together into a 'whole', or cluster around a stable centre.

Tiphareth corresponds with the lamen, the Rosy Cross, the

'Christian' Cross (all three usually worn over the heart), and the Cube.
The Tarot cards related to this sphere are the four 6s:

6 wands	victory	(Jupiter in Leo)
6 cups	pleasure	(Sun in Scorpio)
6 swords	science	(Mercury in Aquarius)
6 discs	success	(Moon in Taurus)

They all display harmony in their design.
The four Princes of the Tarot are also assigned to Tiphareth.

self-awareness

The exercise which follows should be done without interruption.
Follow the usual starting procedure, then go through the words of
the exercise once slowly, paying attention to the concepts as
presented and attempting to feel the meaning of the exercise. Then
settle yourself in a comfortable but attentive position, breathe in a
relaxed way and do the exercise a second time, this time stopping to
complete the instructions as you go. (Alternatively you could get
someone else to read you the exercise very slowly, or use a tape
recorder.) It is a particularly important exercise, so please pay
particular attention to performing it with the right attitude and in
the right space.

Be aware of your body:
- what sensations are you experiencing?
- do you feel any tensions?
- what position is your body in?
- be aware of the exact position that your body is in
- be aware of the floor/chair beneath you
- be aware of the air around you

Now be aware of what is going on inside your body.

Be as fully aware of your body as you are able to be.

Now imagine a sphere around this body awareness, and that you step out of it.

Before you is a sphere that encloses all your body awareness. Vividly imagine this sphere before you.

Now become aware of your emotions and feelings:
- do you have emotional reactions to these questions?
- what feelings do you experience?
- are you happy or sad?
- how do you feel?

Be aware of how your feelings are changing all the time.

Be as fully aware of your feelings as you are able.

Now imagine a sphere around this awareness of feelings, and that you step out of it.

Before you is a sphere that encloses all your awareness of your feelings. Vividly imagine this sphere of feelings.

Now become aware of your thoughts:
- thoughts about this exercise
- other thoughts that come in and out of awareness
- watch these thoughts for a while

Be aware of how these thoughts come and go almost as if they are independent of you.

Be as fully aware of these thought processes as you are able.

Now imagine a sphere around this awareness of thoughts, and that you step out of it.

See these three spheres of awareness before you:
- the sphere of body awareness   (equivalent to Malkuth)
- the sphere of feelings awareness   (equivalent to Netzach)
- the sphere of thought awareness   (equivalent to Hod)

These three spheres constitute your personality. You have a body, feelings and thoughts to enable you to experience the world and to express yourself.

You can choose to go into any of these spheres of awareness when it is appropriate for you to do so.

You can also choose to be separate or not-attached to these contents of your personality.

Again become aware of the three spheres before you.

Now ask yourself:

- *who am I?*
- *who is it that has these spheres of body, feelings and thoughts?*
- *who connects these vehicles of expression?*
- *who is this 'I' that experiences incessant change?*

Allow yourself to experience this 'I' fully.

Be aware that you are a self-conscious being.

Say to yourself:

I am I, a centre of pure self awareness ... I can choose to identify with the contents of my personality, or equally choose to simply be self-aware.

Perform the Kabbalistic Cross.

Take some time after this exercise to bring yourself back into everyday consciousness.

Write about your experience in your diary.

The three spheres of body, feelings and thought awareness were the Sephiroth Malkuth, Netzach and Hod. This self-awareness, this 'I', is Tiphareth.

PATHS CONNECTED TO TIPHARETH

If you look at the diagram of the Tree of Life (page 2), you can see there are eight paths directly connected to Tiphareth: five that descend from above and three that ascend from below. In a later section there will be more on the five paths that come down into Tiphareth. For now meditate upon all eight of these paths, and consider the structure as shown in the diagram.

Kether is the Spiritual or Transpersonal Self, which we can simply call the Self. From the mundane point of view it is universal; on its own level it is a 'being', a stable centre of life from which radiate energies. Kether is often called 'God'.

Tiphareth is the personal self, the self-conscious 'I', a projection, reflection or spark of the Self into normal levels of human consciousness.

The relationship between the Self, residing in Kether, and an individual self, represented by Tiphareth, can be compared to the relationship between the Sun and a planet, but this is only a partial, approximate analogy. From the Sun many powerful radiations emanate which affect the planet and all living things on it – indeed they would not exist without these energies. They produce the conditions necessary for evolution, development and growth. In the same way the Self projects a small portion of self-consciousness, Tiphareth, which may grow in self-awareness, intelligence, power to act, and so on, under the combined influence of nourishment from that which is below (the personality and the environment) and from the impact of the energies radiating from above. Tiphareth, the personal self, may become aware of Kether, the Self, in two basic ways:

1. By opening itself *consciously* to, and *recognizing* the radiation from, Kether;

2. By *rising* towards and eventually contacting and merging (at least partially) with Kether.

Many people have testified that the Self can be experienced as a living reality, even more as a living 'being'. The actual experience is indescribable. To call Kether a 'being' (or anything else) is merely a way of trying to communicate the experience. The experience is perhaps most clearly exhibited in the changes brought about in the life of the Adept. A clear and full experience of Kether gives such a strong sense of Self identity that it is felt as something pure, permanent, unchangeable and indestructible. In comparison, all other experiences seem impermanent and of lesser significance.

Some of the Qualities manifested by Kether are: pure initiative, total free will, creative impulse, wisdom, altruistic love, and a sense of power that is both totally peaceful and dynamically surging. Some of the effects of the realization of Kether are: a sense of inner guidance, of strength, purpose, true will, responsibility and joy.

Remember: Kether is the Self. Chockmah, Binah, Chesed and Geburah are the spheres through which Kether radiates its energy into Tiphareth, which is the personal centre or self, which in turn then channels energy into the personality represented by the spheres from Netzach to Malkuth.

SELF-IDENTIFICATION

The experience of self-consciousness, of having an 'I', distinguishes our consciousness from that of the majority of other sentient beings on our planet. This self-consciousness, however, is usually experienced not as pure self-consciousness, but rather mixed with and veiled by the contents of consciousness – that is, everything we are sensing, feeling and/or thinking at any time. We usually live our lives *identified with* these contents of our consciousness. To make self-consciousness an explicit, experiential fact in our lives we need first to *dis*-identify from the 'contents' of consciousness.

Most people tend to be generally more identified either with their thoughts or their feelings sphere, and can thus be described as mentally or emotionally identified. Such identification can be useful at times, even necessary, but to live a balanced life we need both to cultivate the sphere in which we are deficient, and to be able to dis-identify from all these spheres of experience and expression. Thus people who are predomi-nantly identified with their thoughts – who are, in other words, mentally identified, need to increase their awareness, experience and expression of their feelings side, rather than diminish or decrease their mind aware-ness. If we picture the situation as one where the two spheres of Hod and Netzach, Mind and Feelings, are unequally developed and of unequal size, the process is to increase the size of the smaller one so that it matches the size of the larger one. This is balance through upward growth and increase, rather than through decrease, which is both unnec-essary and inefficient.

You have already had some experience of dis-identifying from the personality in the 'three spheres' exercise earlier in this chapter. If we combine this need for dis-identification with the process of identification with the Self, we can perform two useful and growth-orientated func-tions at the same time. Through *deliberate* dis-identification from the personality and identification with the Self, we gain freedom and the power of choice to be identified with, or dis-identified from, any aspect of our personality according to what is most appropriate for any given situation. Thus we may learn to master and utilize our whole personality in an inclusive and harmonious synthesis. The following exercise, which does just this, is borrowed from psychosynthesis. It is intended as a tool for achieving the consciousness of the Self. Follow the procedure of the exercise carefully. You will find it is similar to the 'three spheres' exercise, and is here presented as an alternative way of achieving what is basically the same end. The importance of learning ways of dis-identification cannot be overstressed.

self-identification

Follow the usual starting procedure.

Affirm to yourself the following:

> I have a body and I am more than my body. My body may find itself in different conditions of health or sickness, it may be rested or tired, but that has nothing to do with my Self, my real I. I value my body as my precious instrument of experience and action in the world, but it is only an instrument. I treat it well, I seek to keep it in good health, but it is not my Self. *I have a body, and I am more than my body.*

Close your eyes, recall what this affirmation says, then focus your attention on the central concept: 'I have a body and I am more than my body.' Attempt as much as you can to realize this as an experienced fact in your consciousness.

Now proceed with the following two affirmations, treating them in the same way, realizing the central concept in each as an experienced fact:

> I have emotions, and I am more than my emotions. My emotions are diversified, changing, sometimes contradictory. They may swing from love to hatred, from calm to anger, from joy to sorrow, and yet my essence – my true nature – does not change. I remain. Though a wave of anger may temporarily submerge me, I know that in time it will pass; therefore I am not this anger. Since I can observe and understand my emotions, and can gradually learn to direct, utilize and integrate them harmoniously, it is clear that they are not my Self. *I have emotions, and I am more than my emotions.*

I have a mind and I am more than my mind. My mind is a valuable tool of discovery and expression, but it is not the essence of my being. Its contents are constantly changing as it embraces new ideas, knowledge and experience, and as it makes new connections. Sometimes it seems to refuse to obey me. Therefore it cannot be me, my Self. It is an organ of knowledge in regard to both the outer and inner worlds, but it is not my Self. *I have a mind, and I am more than my mind.*

Next comes the phase of identification. Affirm clearly and slowly to yourself:

After this dis-identification of my Self, the I, from the contents of consciousness, emotions, sensations, thoughts – I recognize and affirm that I am a centre of pure self-consciousness. I am a centre of will, capable of observing, directing and using all my psychological processes and my physical body.

Focus your attention on the central realization:

I am a centre of pure self-consciousness and of will.

Attempt as much as you can to realize this as an *experienced* fact in your awareness.

When you have practised this exercise a few times, you can use it in a much shorter form. You can personalize it too, if you wish, so long as you keep to the four main, central affirmations:

I have a body and sensations, and I am more than my body and sensations.

I have feelings and emotions, and I am more than my feelings and emotions.

I have a mind and thoughts, and I am more than my mind and thoughts.

I am I, a centre of pure self-consciousness and of will.

This exercise is effective if practised daily, preferably during the first few hours of the day. It can then be considered as a second, symbolic re-awakening.

INFLUENCES FROM ABOVE

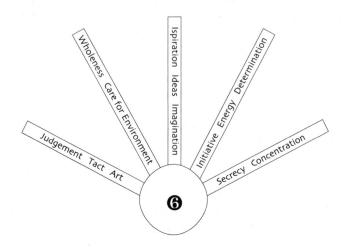

These five paths which converge on Tiphareth are the paths associated with the radiation from the Self to the personality, through Tiphareth, of the Qualities of the Self.

The diagram shows the influence of the forces of the five paths upon the human heart, which is Tiphareth on the Tree of Life.

The three paths which originate above the Abyss bring their benefits only upon the Adept who is centred upon Tiphareth. There can only be *true* inspiration, initiative and intellectual wholeness for one who has Knowledge and Conversation with the Holy Guardian Angel.

The paths from Chesed and Geburah are more practical influences and their qualities are well shown by their respective Tarot attributions, the Hermit and Adjustment (or Justice).

These five paths are associated with the following Hebrew letters:

the Priestess path	gimel
the Star path	he
the Lovers path	zain
the Hermit path	Yod
the Adjustment/Justice path	lamed

If we add up these letters according to their usual values (G=3, H=5, Z=7, Y=10, L=30) we have a total of 55.

Fifty-five is the sum of the numbers from one to ten, representing the complete Tree of Life. Fifty-five is the Mystic Number of Malkuth, affirming this completeness.

the sorcerer exercise

This is an extremely easy exercise, but one of great importance. Practise this exercise as often as you can.

Perform the usual starting procedure.

Close your eyes and affirm to yourself:

> I am a sorcerer. Everything I see I create. I have created, and will continue to create my own world.

Open your eyes, look around you and realize the truth of the affirmation.

CHAPTER 8

AT THE CENTRE OF ALL

THE CREATION OF THE TREE

So far we have been looking at the Tree of Life from the bottom upwards. This is the route we, as incarnated beings, follow in our initiation and growth. The Tree was 'created', however, from the top downwards, as is shown by the numeration of the spheres from 1 to 10. How it was 'created' need not concern us unduly, but being able to see the process in this direction is vital. When we see the Tree from top to bottom we can see the 'thrust' of creation, the creative drive in action. It is important as you continue your study of the Tree to see it *both ways*, top to bottom and bottom to top.

The creation or construction of the Tree, from top to bottom, follows the course of the *Lightning Flash* which starts in Kether and moves through the spheres in their usual order, to reach Malkuth. The Veils above the Tree represent an absence of anything concrete, *nothing* in its most positive sense. This area of the Tree is *veiled*, which suggests that these are the furthest reaches of *human* knowledge and understanding. It takes a long time to achieve a full understanding of *this side* of the Veils, perhaps many lifetimes. What is beyond these Veils is something to consider later, after we have mastered the manifest Tree.

The first step in the process of creation is understood through the concept of *position*. A *point* appears which has neither parts nor magnitude, but only position. It is positive yet undefinable. This is Kether. It is the number 1, which is indivisible, incapable of multiplication or division by itself.

Position does not mean much unless there is something else, some other position with which to compare it. The only way to create this is to have a second point, which then forms (between the two points) a *line*. The only way that the original 1 of Kether can become more is through duplication of itself (by a kind of reflection). This second point,

Chockmah, is given the number 2, and corresponds to the will or purpose of the original point to duplicate itself.

This created line does not in any way allow for measurement. All that is known so far is that there are two points at an indeterminable distance from each other. In order to discriminate between them at all there must be a third point, Binah, the number 3. Three points can create a surface, a *triangle*. Now we can define any of these points in terms of its position relative to the other two. Thus an awareness (that is, Spiritual Awareness) is born. Love is attributed to the third point, as being the agency of true understanding. These three points create the 'Supernal Triangle'.

Between the Supernal Triangle and the rest of the Tree is the *Abyss*. This is the gulf between potential and actual, universal and individual, the 'creator' and its creation, the noumenal and the phenomenal. At this potential stage, where only the Supernal Triangle exists, there are three distinct points (the Self, its will and awareness) but there is no idea of where any of them are; they are unmanifest. A fourth point (not in the plane of the triangle inscribed by the first three points) must arise, which formulates the idea of matter by creating a three-dimensional solid.

Now the original point can be defined by three other co-ordinates. Solidity exists, manifestation has taken place. The potential has become actual; from an original nothing, something has now emerged. This is Chesed on the Tree of Life.

This initial 'matter' is exceedingly tenuous, for the only property of any given point is its position relative to other points. No change is possible, nothing can happen. A fifth (point) positive idea must be postulated therefore, which is that of 'motion' (Geburah, the number 5). Only in motion/time can events occur. Not only is the concrete idea of a point now possible, but this point can become self-conscious, because it can define itself in terms of time and motion – it has a past, present and future. Here is Tiphareth, the number 6, the centre of the system, pure self-awareness, capable of experience.

By the creation of the solid, at Chesed, a three-dimensional reality came into existence, space was created. When time arises, at Geburah, we then have in manifest existence, the true Space-Time Continuum.

Notice how the spheres 4, 5 and 6 are an inverted triangle, as if they are a reflection *beyond the Abyss* of the upright triangle of the Supernals. But notice also how Will (spheres 2 and 5) and Awareness (or Love) (spheres 3 and 4) have changed columns, or sides. So as well as the second trinity of spheres being inverted, on its head so to speak, it has also spiralled round.

This spiralling process reminds us of the double spiral of DNA, and also of the relationship between the right- and left-hand side of the body, controlled by the opposite sides of the brain.

This self-aware point, number 6, Tiphareth, has the will to know itself further, and thus the creation of the remainder of the Tree proceeds, forming vehicles for experience and expression. These are the feelings, mind and body, carrying within their own substance, the past (Yesod) that controls their character-function in relation to the external world. This is the personality with which the Self cloaks itself. The spheres numbered 7, 8, 9 and 10 are the original point's experience of their attributions. Sometimes 7, 8 and 9 are related to sulphur, mercury and salt, and to Satchitananda, which is Being (Sat), Knowledge (chit) and Bliss (ananda).

Notice how 7, 8 and 9 are a reflection of the triangle of 4, 5 and 6 on a lower plane (as 4, 5, 6 were a reflection of 1, 2, 3) *but now without spiralling or inversion.*

In Malkuth, number 10, the point's idea of itself is fulfilled and there is complete material manifestation.

To describe 'reality' in a form of knowledge, Kabbalists devised this description of the creative process, using the ten ideas ascribed to the ten spheres as the *shortest way* to describe nothing becoming something which is aware of itself.

THE QUALITIES OF THE SOUL

The second triangle on the Tree, that of Chesed, Geburah and Tiphareth, is equivalent to the Soul. The 'soul' is the bridge between the spirit and the personality. Pure spiritual energy is individualized through the soul before it enters the personality. This is partly to protect the personality from too great an influx of undiluted spiritual energy which could 'blow it out' and partly to individualize the energy for the lessons of the incarnation of that particular soul.

This spiritual energy, when it is individualized in the soul, is still very pure, and can be called the *Qualities* of the Soul. These Qualities are related to Archetypes, and are often termed the 'Qualities of Life'. They are beyond description but we can give them names which help us understand them, including: Joy, Truth, Peace, Beauty, Courage, Creativity, Power, Enthusiasm, Eternity, Universality, Freedom, Goodwill, Wonder, Harmony, Humour, Bliss, Light, Love, Order, Patience, Reality, Trust, Service, Silence, Synthesis, Wholeness, Vitality ...

These soul energies or Qualities flow into the personality and there become diffused and 'distorted'. This does not imply anything 'wrong' or 'bad': it is necessary in order that the soul may grow through a variety of experiences – for example, the Quality of pure Will might become distorted in the personality into blind anger, Love into possessiveness, Truth into partial truth or even deceit.

A major part of the work of the Adept is watching for these 'distortions' of soul energies as they appear and then transforming them into purer energy. For example, the 'distortion' of anger may be due to a feeling of frustration over not succeeding in something. Conventional morality might suggest that this anger should be suppressed, as it is seen as being negative and harmful. The Kabbalistic Adept, however, will not do this. He or she will look at the anger, give it rein, allow it to build up and express itself – but in some harmless way (not through beating someone's head in, for example, but rather discharging it through a harmless medium, such as a cushion). Then the Adept looks for the Quality at the heart of this anger and experiences it in a fuller sense. He or she will find out what is needed to allow this purer energy to express itself in a more creative way, and then create the conditions for this to be possible. So an apparently 'negative emotion' is transformed into a life-enriching creative energy.

One way of strengthening the flow of spiritual energy into the soul (and thence to the personality) is through constant contacts with Tiphareth. Thus the importance of both dis-identification and Self-identification. Along with strengthening the centre, and channelling energy through the soul, there is also a need to work actively on clarifying the personality. This may be achieved through the kinds of exercises you have met so far in this book, and that you will be undertaking as your Kabbalistic work continues.

evoking and developing desired qualities

This experience enables you to create inner and outer conditions through which you can connect with and nurture a desired quality. The more frequently and regularly you perform it for any chosen quality, the stronger the quality becomes. You can use the exercise for any quality; as an example, we will use *Joy*, a quality associated particularly with Chesed and generally with the whole Tree. It is important, however, when you perform the exercise to choose *from within yourself* the quality with which you wish to work. Choose qualities which will further your Great Work.

Follow the usual starting procedure.

Think about Joy (or substitute your chosen quality). Hold the concept of Joy in your mind and reflect upon it. Ask yourself questions about this quality: what is it? what is its nature? what is its meaning? and so on. Record your ideas, and any images that emerge.

Be still and receptive. What does the quality mean to you now?

Realize the value of Joy, its purpose, its use in your life and on the planet as a whole. What differences would there be if Joy was in abundance?

Desire Joy.

Allow Joy to be in your body, assume a posture that expresses this quality. Relax all your tensions, let them drift away. Breathe slowly. Allow Joy to express itself on your face. Visualize yourself with that expression.

Evoke the quality of Joy. Imagine you are in a place where you feel Joy; a quiet beach, with a loved one, in a temple of Joy – wherever you choose. Try to really feel it. Repeat the word Joy several times. Let the quality permeate you, to the point of identification if possible. Allow yourself to be Joy.

Resolve to remain infused with Joy, to be the living embodiment of Joy, to radiate Joy.

Draw on a piece of paper or card the word Joy, using the colours and lettering that best convey the quality to you. Place this sign where you can see it daily, as often as possible. You can make several such signs and place them strategically around your home. Whenever you notice a sign, recall within yourself the feeling of Joy.

You can develop this exercise into a much more intense, prolonged ritual by performing it daily and at the same time gathering together poetry, writings, pictures, symbols, artwork, dance, anything that symbolizes your chosen quality to you. By surrounding yourself with these symbols, especially whilst performing the exercise, you can help deepen your sense of the quality. This is essentially identical with the use of correspondences in ritual magick.

If you find that attempting to evoke the desired quality brings the opposite (for example, if instead of Joy you get Sorrow), this is usually a sign that there is a block of negative emotions stopping the development of the desired quality. If the negative feeling is strong, then stop the exercise and explore the negative feelings that emerged, and, without becoming entrapped in them, allow them to express themselves symbolically. Then let go of them and resume the exercise, realizing that as you now evoke the quality it can fill the empty space left vacant by the released negative emotion.

CO-CREATION AND THE HUMAN AGES

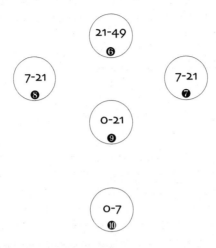

We tend to think of ourselves as being a personality that has a 'higher' self. *From this moment on, start considering yourself as the Self which has a personality*. The Self is a living reality, however you experience it. You are the Self, you have a personality so that you can experience the infinite diversity in this mundane world.

Look at the above diagram. Each of the lower spheres is attributed to an age range. Thus Malkuth is attributed to the years 0 (birth) to 7, Netzach and Hod to the years 7 to 21, and so on. This does not mean that the development of any sphere happens only during these years, but rather that the primary focus of development is through these years. The years as such are only approximate. It is not a rigid rule and varies from person to person, but the sequence remains constant.

As you can see, the work of the Soul (spheres 4, 5, 6) is attributed to the years 21–49+. Everything is seen in seven-year stages. Compare the diagram above with the one overleaf.

You see that after 49, there are still three sets of seven years left to make up the 'average allotted lifespan' of 70 years. These are a reflection of the first three sets of seven years, and allow the individual who has not completely worked through these spheres a kind of 'further opportunity' (you could *not* call it a second chance!) to deal with these vehicles of manifestation. Note how 'dis-eases' of the mind tend to occur in the period 49–56 (various mental crises for example), 'dis-eases' of the feelings between 56 and 63 (for example, heart attack), and 'dis-eases' of the body in the period 63–70 (for example, at '70', or at whatever age it actually occurs, the 'end' is bodily death).

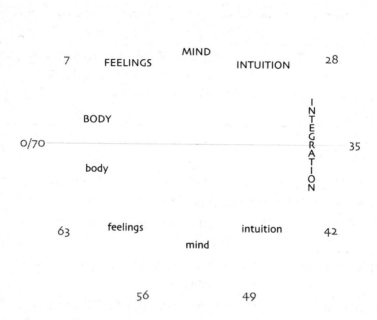

'Co-creation' is the process implicit in this whereby after our 'initial creation' in birth, out of the Self – we 'ascend' in our growth and development back towards the Self, thus co-creating, along with the Self, the totality of our experience.

FIVE WORLDS AND NINE PLANES

The diagram on page 102 reveals a new way of looking at the scheme of the Tree of Life. Using the following notes, study the diagram carefully and apply your existing Kabbalistic knowledge to its understanding.

The five spheres (lettered a to e) correspond to:

(a) The Self connected to Universal/Cosmic Consciousness.

(b) The microcosm completed. The next step for humankind as a whole.

(c) The microcosm in perfection, centred upon Tiphareth, connected to Daath and Yesod.

(d) The personality, centred upon Yesod, but inclusive of Tiphareth.

(e) Astral, etheric and demonic interactions.

The planes are found within the five spheres:

1. The 3 veils — the universal self, the crescent of Nuit (the Egyptian goddess of the moon).

2. Spheres 1, 2, 3 and Daath (D) — the spiritual vesica (the shape created by the overlapping of two circles), the Self transcendent and immanent.

3. Daath — the next step, the immanent Self.

4. Daath (D) and spheres 4, 5, 6 — the soul vesica.

5. Sphere 6 — the centre of pure self-consciousness.

6. Spheres 6, 7, 8, 9 — the personality vesica.

7. Sphere 9 — the sexual vesica, and the lower unconscious.

8. Spheres 9 and 10 — the physical vesica, including the astral and etheric vehicles.

9. Sphere 10 — the body and external world, the receptive crescent to match the creative crescent of plane 2, for 'as above, so below'.

CONVERSATION WITH THE GUARDIAN ANGEL

Conversation with the Guardian Angel is also sometimes called Knowledge and Conversation with the Holy Guardian Angel (abbreviated to KCHGA) or simply the Inner Dialogue. This 'inner dialogue' is not the incessant chatter of the thoughts (which indeed needs to be turned off for true inner guidance to be heard), but rather the dialogue between the centred personality and the focus of the soul. This is represented by a symbol such as a dove, light, an angel, a radiant, wise, old person and so on. The 'Guardian Angel' is such a symbol. The angel may be described as a 'link with the spiritual realms' or 'the transmitter of the next step'. The Guardian Angel resides in Tiphareth and conversation with this angel is the primary work of this sphere. In the next section you will find more about the angel and a way of contacting him/her (the angel may be either sex – or both).

The work of contacting and conversing with your Guardian Angel is vital to your progress. Aleister Crowley said it was a matter of utmost and

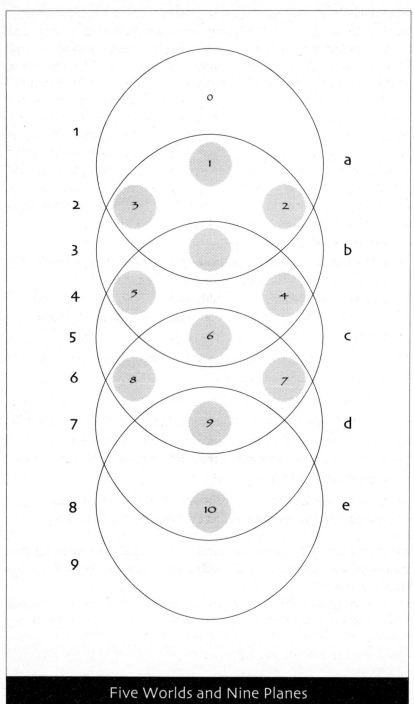

Five Worlds and Nine Planes

primary importance to the individual to have this conversation and that nothing else compares with it in importance. Gurdjieff described the same process as 'catching a soul' and also gave it primary importance. All religions, except those based primarily on faith, believe this *contact* to be vital. It is a way of forging a link between the temporal and the eternal.

When you perform the exercise, you may ask how you can be sure that what you contact is your Guardian Angel. It could be another being, masquerading (so to speak) as this source of 'divine wisdom'. Whatever this other entity might be – a dark demon, your own superconscious or a 'topdog' sub-personality – the following points can help you check the validity of your contact. Remember that your *sense* of what is right or wrong for you is of primary importance. Only you can decide whether a message or piece of advice is meaningful for you.

Checks on contact:

1. All messages from the Guardian Angel are ultimately *positive* rather than negative towards the self. They are never judgemental or a 'put-down' (although they can be serious and severe) but reflect the attitude of a kind, loving father or mother rather than of a pompous or uncaring authoritarian figure.

2. Use Netzach and Malkuth. Does it *feel* right? Do you *sense* it is real contact with your real Angel?

3. Use Hod and Malkuth. The virtue of Malkuth is discrimination (in a sensory sense) and the mind is the best 'weapon' for discriminating.

4. Is there non-verbal re-inforcement? Does the scene look right? Do you sense the rightness of the symbols involved? Is the expression of your Angel right?

5 All such messages (when understood – they may not be clear immediately) are expanding and extending to the personality.

The three key words involved in checking the validity of a message from your Angel are *discrimination* (Malkuth), *interpretation* (Hod) and *sense of rightness* (Netzach).

It is also worth remembering that the Angel might tell you its name. If you hear your Angel's name, *never* share it with anyone else – it is the prime secret of your life and a word of the greatest *power*. This is because by knowing your Angel's name you can then summon him/her at will.

We all have a source of wisdom and understanding that knows who we are, where we have been and where we are going. It is in tune with our unfolding purpose or True Will and clearly senses the next steps to be taken in order to pursue that aim. As we contact it we can better recognize the difficulties we are having in our growth and, with its help, we can guide our awareness and will towards the resolution of these difficulties. Rightly used it can help us direct our energies towards achieving integration in our personality and towards unifying the personality, soul and spirit into one living reality.

Many images are associated with this source of inner guidance. In usual occult parlance, as you have already seen, it is called the Holy Guardian Angel, Augoeides or Daemon. Other common images are the sun, a diamond, a fountain, a star, an angel, an eagle, a dove, a phoenix, Christ, Buddha, a Wise Old Man or Woman. Different images emerge to meet different needs and according to the development, culture and conditioning of the individual. In general terms it is often found that a 'masculine' image is encouraging, stimulating and inspiring whilst a 'feminine' image is nurturing, supportive and allowing. This is not always the case, however.

conversation with the guardian angel

There are many complicated rituals and procedures for contacting the Guardian Angel or Wise Old Person. The simplest procedure, however, is that which follows – an advantageous technique in being not only simple but also very effective.

Follow the usual starting procedure.

Close your eyes, take a few deep breaths and let appear in your imagination the face of your Angel, whose eyes express great love for you.

Engage him/her in dialogue and, in whatever way seems best, use the presence and guidance to help you understand better whatever questions, directions, choices, problems and so on, that you are dealing with at this moment. This dialogue can be verbal or non-verbal, taking place on a visual and symbolic level of communication and understanding.

Spend as much time as you need with your Angel then thank the image for having appeared to you, return to normal consciousness and write down what has happened.

Note well that the only advice that it is really appropriate to ask your Angel about concerns the *next step(s)* in your process of development.

You may not, particularly after some practice, need to actually imagine an Angel – he or she may be heard as a sort of inner voice, or even a direct 'knowing' what is the best thing for you to be doing in any given situation.

Your Angel does not always have to be of the same sex.

Remember to check the validity of all messages.

You can adapt this simple procedure to dialogue with anything else from a particular god-form to a part of your body. Try this: have an inner dialogue with various parts of your body – external and internal – and see what they have to tell you.

THE ENLIGHTENED BEING

The diagram below shows the results of placing the spheres of the Tree on concentric circles, the 'universal' aspects at the centre, radiating outwards. Notice how by changing the direction of the circle, after the Supernal Triad (that is, in place of the Abyss) we effectively line up the spiritual and soul aspects of the spheres. Thus Chockmah (Spiritual Will), Geburah (Will) and Hod (Mind/Thoughts) fall into the same segment.

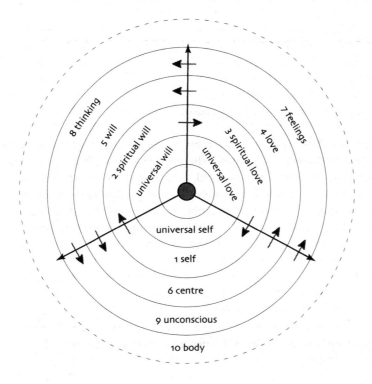

Hence the description of this diagram as 'The Enlightened Being'. It could just as well be called 'The Moment of Full Integration'.

A POETICAL SUMMARY OF CREATION

The following chapter from Aleister Crowley's *The Book of Lies* is the most succinct summary of the whole Tree and is both a stimulus to the imagination and an aid to memory.

0. *The Ante-Primal Triad which is 'not-God'.*

Nothing is.

Nothing becomes.

Nothing is not.

The First Triad which is God.

1. I AM.

2. I utter the Word.

3. I hear the Word.

The Abyss.
The Word is broken up.
There is Knowledge.
Knowledge is Relation.
These fragments are Creation.
The broken manifests Light.

The Second Triad which is God.

4. God the Father and Mother is concealed in Generation.

5. God is concealed in the whirling energy of Nature.

6. God is manifest in gathering, harmony, consideration, the Mirror of the Sun and of the Heart.

The Third Triad.

7. Bearing, Preparing.

8. Wavering, flowing, flashing.

9. Stability, begetting.

The Tenth Emanation.

10. The World.

THE PRINCIPLES OF CHANGE AND MAINTENANCE

In the next chapter you will learn about *Will* and *Love*, the two primary Archetypes, related respectively to Geburah and Chesed. They constitute the *action* of the soul in manifesting itself. They create a horizontal polarity across the Tree from sphere 4 to 5. These two directions (left and right) are balanced by the two other directions (up and down) in the form of a vertical polarity on the Tree between the Archetypes of Change (up) and Maintenance (down). These Archetypes or Principles of Change and Maintenance make, with the two Archetypes or Principles of Love and Will, the Four Directions of Growth (see diagram below).

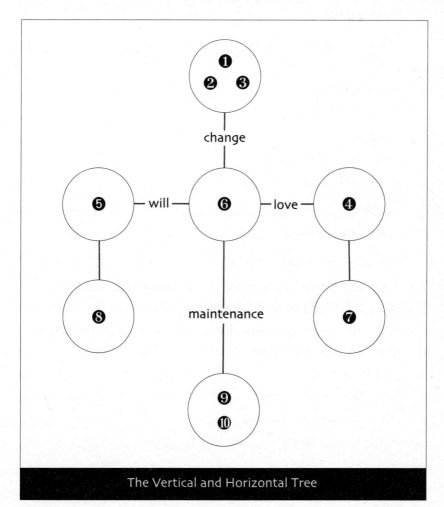

The Vertical and Horizontal Tree

As you have already learned, Qualities may be (at least relatively) 'clear' or 'distorted' in their manifestation – as, for example, 'Will' may be manifest as clear purpose or as blind rage; 'Love' as altruism or possessiveness, and so on. The two vertically polarized Qualities of Change and Maintenance are no exception and may also be manifest in a clear or distorted way. The following table shows some of the conditions exhibited by their manifestation and gives an indication of the difference in their positive or negative aspects.

	Change	*Maintenance*
clear	progress	eternity
	evolution	timelessness
	transformation	rhythm
	dis-identification from form	patience
	freedom	regeneration
distorted	destruction	strangling of life
	fear of limitations	fear of unknown
	purposeless change	inertia, laziness
	energy dissipation	'closed-mindedness'
	no boundaries	cowardice
	insensibility to needs	rigidity

Each of us tends to be drawn to one side of any polarity, to be more on the 'Will' side than the 'Love' side or vice versa. So it is with Change and Maintenance. As the table shows, both have clear *and* distorted qualities. It is for us individually to balance ourselves in a way that excludes neither, but includes the best of both.

the cloak of negativity

Follow the usual starting procedure.

Imagine you are wearing a dark, heavy, black cloak. This dark, hooded, black cloak is the cloak of your negativity, fears and any negative emotions, thoughts, sensations. Really feel the heaviness of this cloak.

Now become aware that this negative cloak is gradually lifting up and away from your body, taking with it all your negativity.

Imagine the cloak slowly vanishing. When it has completely gone, you are free to clothe yourself in a new cloak of your own choice, a cloak of love, joy, protection, or any other qualities you choose.

Vividly imagine this new cloak you are wearing, this cloak of light you have chosen. Realize it as a symbol of your soul.

CHAPTER 9

CHESED AND GEBURAH: THE CENTRES OF LOVE AND WILL

THE FOURTH AND FIFTH SPHERES

The name of the fifth sphere is *Geburah*, which in Hebrew is:

ה　ר　ו　ב　ג
H　R　V　B　G

Geburah is situated on the third plane, on the left-hand pillar (the right side of the body).

Geburah is attributed to 'personal' (as opposed to 'spiritual' or 'transpersonal') *will* or *power*.

The name of the fourth sphere is *Chesed*, which in Hebrew is:

ד　ס　ח
D　S　Ch

Chesed is situated on the third plane, forming a polarity with Geburah, but on the right-hand pillar (the left-hand side of the body).

Chesed is attributed to 'personal' *Love* or *Awareness*.

Geburah means 'Strength' or 'Severity' whilst Chesed means 'Mercy' (or 'Love').

These two Sephiroth correspond to the polarity of *Love and Will*. These are basic Archetypes or principles, and *every* issue in life can be viewed as an expression of the relationship between Love and Will.

This level of the Tree also corresponds to the *soul*, and equally, every issue in life can be seen as the result of the expression and experience of the soul.

This is not to say that Love and Will are equivalent to the soul. Their relationship is better seen as one where the soul 'uses' the Archetypes of Love and Will as its primary tools for growth. Their interplay is then an expression in itself of the emerging and unfolding soul. An imbalance between Love and Will will cause problems in the personality; the soul, directing the relationship between the Archetypes, will see this problem as an opportunity for growth.

In the last chapter you learned to view the relationship of spirit, soul and personality from a different direction, performing a kind of 'flip-over' where instead of being a personality that has a soul, you view yourself as a soul that has a personality. Another way of saying this is that the 'Archetype', 'pattern' or 'principle' from this level creates experience, *as opposed to* the experience creating the Archetype, pattern or principle.

As an example, if part of your personality is dependent upon the love of others and exhibits a desire to please, this does not affect your soul directly; it is your soul that creates or 'sets up' the conditions in you so that the personality exhibits these features. The soul does this to give itself the opportunity to grow through learning how to resolve these issues (through the interactions of the personality).

Sometimes Geburah can be investigated through your relationship with your father (and Chesed through your mother). This is not always clear-cut, however, and may even be reversed in some people. Your soul creates the conditions for your relationship with your father and mother. This is not to say that your father and mother do not have an effect in themselves on your development, but that you play a more central part in these relationships than you might initially realize. It is saying, quite simply, that you choose your own father and mother!

useless will exercises

Keep the faculty of effort alive in you by a little gratuitous exercise every day. That is, be systematically heroic in little, unnecessary points; do every day or two something for no other reason than it is difficult, so that, when the hour of dire need draws nigh, it may find you not unnerved and untrained to stand the test. Asceticism of this sort is like the insurance a man pays on his house and goods. The tax does him no good at the time, and possibly may not bring him a return. But if the fire does come his having paid it, it will be his salvation from ruin. So with the man who has daily inured himself to habits of concentrated attention, energetic volition, and self-denial in unnecessary things. He will stand like a tower when everything rocks around him, and his softer fellow-mortals are winnowed like chaff in the blast.

WILLIAM JAMES

Later in this chapter you will find numerous exercises for the training of the will. The following exercises, the 'Useless Will Exercises', are recommended, for they will stand you in good stead when you find yourself needing strong will.

The technique involves performing actions which have no use whatsoever in themselves, but are performed for the sole purpose of training the will. They can be compared to muscular exercises in gymnastics which have no use except the developing of muscles and the enhancing of neuro-muscular co-ordination and physical well-being in general.

Examples of Useless Will Exercises:

1. Pick five objects at random in a room. Spend exactly five minutes, no more and no less, wilfully walking around the room touching each of these objects in strict rotation as you pass.

2. Take a full matchbox. Wilfully and deliberately remove the matches from the box one by one, counting them carefully. When the box is empty reverse the process until the box is full again.

3. Stand on a chair and count to 100 very slowly and deliberately. When 100 is reached reverse the counting until you reach 1 again.

It is best to devise your own 'Useless Will Exercises', and remember:

Pure Will, unassuaged of purpose, delivered from the lust of result, is every way perfect.

When you have finished performing 'Useless Will Exercises' note any reactions you may have had – particularly resistances and blocks to achieving the end of the exercise.

CORRESPONDENCES TO CHESED AND GEBURAH

The attributions of Chesed and Geburah are best viewed together because, in a primary sense at least, they are inseparable.

Geburah	*Chesed*
Attributed to Will/Power	Attributed to Love/Awareness
Doing	Being
Mars	Jupiter
Right Shoulder (and Adrenal)	Left Shoulder (and Adrenal)
Red	Blue
Vision of Power	Vision of Love
Virtues: Energy, Courage	Spiritual Alignment
Vices: Cruelty, Restriction	Bigotry, Hypocrisy
Sword and Spear	Orb, Wand and Sceptre

With both these spheres you can have 'too little' or 'too much' of the energy. Too much Geburah leads to cruelty, selfish imposition of one's will and an overblown view of oneself, whilst too little Geburah leads to laziness, lack of energy and restriction. Too much Chesed leads to sloppiness, lack of energy and restriction. Too much Chesed leads to sloppiness, blind love and bigotry, whilst too little Chesed leads to separateness, loneliness, anguish and possibly too great an importance attached to the opposite pole of will.

The path that connects these spheres on the Tree is related to the Tarot card called Lust (or Strength in traditional packs) – this is not mundane lust, which would be a traditional vice, but the lust of Love under Will. This is the lust for life engendered by a perfectly *dynamic balance* between the two spheres.

The four 5s of the Tarot are attributed to Geburah and the four 4s to Chesed:

wands:	5 – strife	4 – completion
cups:	5 – disappointment	4 – luxury
swords:	5 – defeat	4 – truce
discs:	5 – worry	4 – power

Other names given to Geburah include *Din*, which means 'Justice', and *Pachad* which means 'Fear'. It is interesting to analyse this word for 'fear': *achd* means 'Unity or Oneness'. By placing the letter 'P' – that of martial energy – in front of this word it becomes *Pachd*: Fear. This suggests that fear comes from being too alone with one's power, not being connected.

Another name given to Chesed is *Gedulah* (which you have been using in the Kabbalistic Cross). Gedulah means 'Glory', particularly the Glory of Love.

THE PRINCIPLE OF ADJUSTMENT

Balance is not static, it constantly adjusts itself. So, for example, a see-saw with people of similar weights on either end (see diagram above), will not balance in one place and remain static there – it will be constantly moving, a little bit this way, a little bit that way, maintaining a dynamic balance.

In another sense, balance is achieved only through a third factor, which in our see-saw example is the fulcrum. The balance is achieved dynamically through inclusion. If you want to balance two polarities, a kind of balance might be achieved by finding the midway point between them, but this is neither one nor the other. A dynamic balance will only be found in a separate place where they are both included. So then the second diagram becomes:

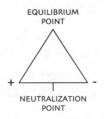

EQUILIBRIUM
POINT

+   -

NEUTRALIZATION
POINT

In a sense Tiphareth is the balancing point for Netzach and Hod. In the case of Chesed and Geburah, however, Tiphareth and Daath can be seen as the third point. Consider this diagram:

The balance between Chesed and Geburah in terms of Tiphareth is a balance of the heart and soul. The three spheres involved create a downward pointing triangle. In terms of Daath, however, the balance is being made through connection to the spiritual realms, and the three spheres form an upward pointing triangle. These two triangles together form a hexagram, or six-pointed star, which is a perfect symbol for total balance between spirit and soul, or to put it another way, between 'universal' and 'individual' energies.

To create this balance which incorporates both the spirit and soul again involves a kind of 'flip-over' from the descending triangle centred on Tiphareth to the ascending one focused on Daath. Then, as Daath is attributed to the throat (see next chapter), this leads to *clear expression* of one's spirituality.

THE MAGICKAL LINK AND THE GROUNDING OF ENERGY

To bring anything into manifestation there are always four stages to the process:

1. *Banishing*   relates to Hod particularly, and means that all other ideas apart from the matter at hand must be banished – one-pointedness and single-mindedness.

2. *Purifying*   relates to Netzach, and refers to purification of the feelings and emotions.

3. *Consecrating*   relates to Tiphareth, and is the dedication of the magician to a single purpose.

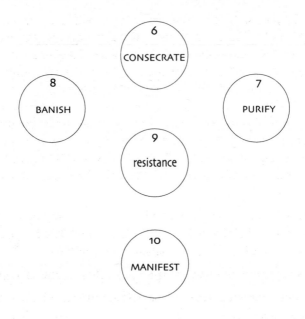

4. *Grounding*   or 'bringing' into manifestation', relates to Malkuth. There is no point in banishing thoughts, purifying feelings, consecrating the purpose and oneself, if you do not ground the energy, and bring about the desired change. This can be done effectively through a 'magickal link'.

Magick can be defined as *any* act brought to pass by will. In every operation of magick the link must be properly made; that is, the appropriate means used in the appropriate measure and applied in ways pertinent to the purpose, through an 'agency' that connects the 'willer' to the desired object.

As an example, a fisherman may have an unswerving desire to catch a fish. You could even imagine a fish with a similarly strong desire to be caught(!). But unless the link is made (in this example, the fishing line and hook) the will of both will be unfulfilled for ever.

Imagine I want a fruit bar from a local shop. I know the means for getting there (walking), the right direction (turn left, right, then right again), the correct pressure to apply in the right direction (that is, forward at 4 mph in a determined manner) – all the details are there for me to fulfil my will and purchase a fruit bar, except the magick link. Unless when I get to the shop I can make a magickal link with the shop-keeper, I won't get the bar. In this case the magickal link will be a talisman (of a particular kind, usually called 'money'!).

There are two kinds of magickal link – those that take place 'inside you' and those that happen 'outside you'. Inner links are those made within your own body. They are the easiest in the sense that everything needed is contained within the system, and perhaps the hardest in that internal inertia has to be overcome. Consider the forces which maintain your body:

- the attraction of the earth, sun, planets, stars, every mote of dust in the room (one of which – if it could be annihilated – would cause your body to move, however imperceptibly)
- the resistance of the floor, air-pressure, all the external conditions
- internal sustaining forces: the skeleton, muscles, blood, lymph, marrow, and so on
- the consciousness: mind, feelings and body
- and the will, directing your choice to be here and now in this position, in this place, reading this book. Without your will you would not be able to do anything. If your will disappeared right now you would be forever chained to the place and position you are now in!

However, despite this condition, for any 'purpose' you choose with inner work, whether it is spiritual or material in orientation, you have all the necessary energies within. With outer links this is not so – there has to be a connector between you and the object of your will, such as the fishing line and hook or the money in the previous examples.

Sometimes *inner force* itself can make the link; for example, if you express your true love for someone a link might be made, assuming that person feels the strength of your love and it connects with their love for you. All the Qualities of the Soul (truth, joy, beauty, and so on), *if they are made manifest in the personality,* become links in themselves.

In one way or another, with both internal and external work, the *link* has to be made. This cannot be stressed too often. The most frequently used method of creating a link is through *grounding*, which gives the energy you wish to manifest a 'place' in which to manifest itself.

Say you have an experience, for instance a 'peak' or 'high' experience that you wish to ground. If you don't ground it, the 'high' will remain ethereal and not manifest in you (and around you) and the energy will eventually dissipate. Awareness, in whatever form, needs to be integrated into the whole person. There are several easy ways to ground energy:

1. Simply by expressing the experience.

2. Writing, drawing, constructing sigils.

3. Evening reviews or morning previews (going over the past or coming day and looking at how you performed, not as a judgemental exercise but in order that you might function more effectively through knowledge of how you habitually perform).

4. Construction of talismans (or using existing ones as in the money example above).

5. 'Acting as if' – in other words acting as if the desired end had already happened.

6. Meditation, either on the object of the will itself or a symbol you have constructed to represent the will.

7. Evocative word cards – sometimes called 'self-advertising' – you write your desire (in words or symbols) on postcards and stick them up around your home in places where you will frequently see them – just as with commercial advertising, constant exposure has an effect on the unconscious.

8. Free drawing or automatic drawing.

9. Creating a suitable (psychological) environment.

10. Creating a 'mantra' based on the desire or experience and continually chanting it silently or vocally to yourself.

What gets in the way of grounding?

1. *Lack of will* – absence of a strong or skilful will. This can be overcome by strengthening the will (see 'Training the Will' exercises later).

2. *Fears* – fear of responsibility, of loosing individuality, of impotence, of being a victim, of power, of misusing power, of disrupting your life, of loneliness, of inadequacy, of being rejected, of being on the wrong tack, and so on. Even fear of success!

3. *Rationalizations* (for example, 'yes ... but') – talking yourself out of it, in some way or another devaluing your experience through analysing it.

4. *Distractions* – from inside yourself or from outside sources. The only way really to deal with this is to get in touch with your purposes and ask yourself what your priorities are.

LOVE, WILL AND THE PERSONALITY

In the section on Change and Maintenance you learnt of the vertical polarity within the Tree of Life. Love and Will, Chesed and Geburah, form a horizontal polarity. These two spheres may be seen 'in action' in the personality through the study of one's own attitudes and experiences. These energies, just like the energies of Change and Maintenance, may be seen as *clear* or *distorted*. Study the following table then follow the directions as given. (Note that, in the mid-range, 'clear' and 'distorted' qualities meld into one another and are difficult to distinguish; those given here are examples of the extremes involved.)

Look at the table overleaf and, considering it very carefully, give yourself a score of +1 for every positive/clear expression of Love you feel applies to you; then –1 for every distorted aspect of Love. Then do the same for Will.

It may seem obvious but it is worth stating that there is no point in doing a self-evaluation like this unless you are as *honest* as you can possibly be with yourself. Also do not take it too seriously – humour can be a great aid to self-evaluation!

As an example, someone might have felt they were 'including', sensitive and receptive but also exhibited dependence, attachment, loneliness, the desire to please and the inability to say no. Their positive Love score would be +3 and their negative score –5.

When you have completed this work, calculate an overall score for the two poles. For example the person above will have an overall score of –2 for Love.

Make sure you have done this before reading any further!

An 'ideal' person (if such a person could exist) would have a score of +7 for both Love and Will, which is unlikely, as is –7 for both spheres. By way of example, we will continue looking at our imaginary person who has a score of –2 for Love. Let us say he or she scored –1 for Will. Then we could say that both poles tend towards distortion, slightly more so on the Love side. This expresses the person's relationship to the Archetypes

CLEAR

Chesed	Geburah
Love	*Will*
altruism	assertion of self
co-operation	being the cause
brotherhood	activity
caring	strength
including	order
sensitivity	self-determination
receptiveness	focused awareness
dependence	manipulation
attachment	selfishness
conformity	competitiveness
desire to please	separateness
loneliness	pride
fear of being alone	ambition
inability to say no	fear of impotence

DISTORTED

Clear and Distorted Qualities

of Love and Will and, through them, to the soul. Another person might have, say, +3 for Love and –4 for Will. We would say this person is well advanced in clarifying their Love but distinctly more distorted in terms of their Will.

So what can you do about it? The keys to working on yourself in terms of the polarity of Love and Will can be expressed simply:

Elevate the opposite : Refine the distortions

So in our example of the very unbalanced person, what this person needs to do is to refine the distortions that hold the Will side of her energy back and to elevate this to the same level as the Love. In other words, you would not want to obtain balance through bringing the Love down to the level of the Will – for example, to make both Love and Will –4; rather, you should elevate the Will up to the level of +3.

There is nothing 'wrong' suggested in the word 'distortion' as it is used here; even if you got a score of –7 for both poles it would only mean this is the current state of your soul in how it is *choosing* to experience life. It would probably mean you have a lot to learn about this polarity, which is both an incentive and an exciting promise! Indeed, having +7 for both poles might suggest you have no work left to do; anyone getting +7 on both these poles would be unlikely to be doing this or any other course!

For the moment the most practical thing you can do is watch yourself in how you relate to Love and Will and how you express them to others, and make continued contact with your centre in Tiphareth.

THE HIGHER RESOLVING FACTOR

We have already seen how to achieve a vital balance between any two polarities or duality by finding a 'third place' which incorporates both, rather than one that negates both. This may be graphically illustrated thus:

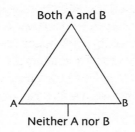

'A' and 'B' represent the two opposite poles of any duality. True balance is then represented by the apex of the triangle labelled 'both A and B', this state being achieved through *synthesis* and *inclusion*. This third place is called the 'Higher resolving factor'; 'higher' to distinguish it from the 'lower' balance of 'neither A nor B' which is not a true balance, being based upon exclusion.

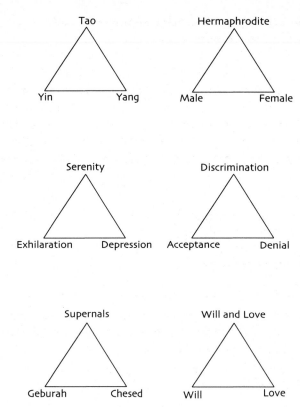

Many examples may be given of the higher resolving factor – indeed, as many as there are dualities in existence. Some of these are shown above.

polarity triangles

Create at least five of these triangles with a pair of polarities at the lower angles, and a *named* higher resolving factor. Thus in the above examples, 'Will and Love' is not sufficient as a name for the higher resolving factor between Will and Love. It needs to be named. What would you call it?

Finally consider the names given to higher resolving factors, both in the examples and in the ones you have created. These 'resolving factors' are almost certainly half a duality in themselves!

THE BALANCE OF LOVE AND WILL – REFLECTIVE, RECEPTIVE AND CREATIVE MEDITATION

We will now do some meditation on the balance between the Archetypes of Love and Will. You have already done some of the meditative techniques suggested in this section but now they are undertaken sequentially in a process called 'reflective, receptive and creative meditation', a particular form of meditation that allows for many levels of the being to operate during the meditative process.

meditation exercises

Follow the usual starting procedure.

REFLECTIVE MEDITATION

Reflective meditation could also be described as 'directed thinking'. Take a sheet of paper and put a circle in the middle, with the words 'the balance of Love and Will' in it, thus:

The
balance
of Love and
Will

Now, quite simply, think about this subject – the 'balance of Love and Will'. Any words, images, ideas and so on, that come to you as you think as one-pointedly as possible about this subject, put on lines radiating out from this circle (refer to previous exercises if you are unsure about this process).

When you feel you have exhausted your thoughts on the subject, *continue for at least another five minutes*. This allows you to delve deeper than you normally might, accessing deeper recesses of your mind. Your knowledge on the subject, through this kind of reflection, is stretched.

RECEPTIVE MEDITATION

In receptive meditation you tune into the unconscious and receive intuition, inspiration, messages or stimuli about your chosen subject. The most important requisite for this kind of meditation is *silence*, as without it you cannot hear what your 'inner world' is saying to you.

Find a silent space, inside and outside.

Holding the concept of the 'balance of Love and Will' in your mind, try not to think of anything. Be one-pointed in your determination to shut off all extraneous thoughts, sensations and feelings. Just *be*.

Don't do anything, just see what you receive. Meditate like this for at least fifteen minutes.

Before continuing, record anything that came to you during reception.

CREATIVE MEDITATION

Now consider what you have learned about the 'balance of Love and Will' from both the reflective and receptive stages of your meditation, in particular how you could put these ideas or insights into *action*. Try to find which of these ideas are the most important or relevant to you right now.

Choose one item from your meditation that you would like to put into action.

Consider this one concept. Try to find a way of acting upon it. Be precise and practical in this. For example, if you were using 'will-to-good' as your concept you would need to find ways of concretizing your action in bringing this quality more into manifestation. Even the simplest act, rightly performed with intention, can be effective.

THE GODS OF THE SPHERES

You have already learned that all gods and goddesses relate, through their different aspects, to many or all of the spheres. The names of gods and goddesses represent magickal formulae, the use of which sets relevant energies in motion. Most god-names are complex, involving attributions with more than one sphere, sometimes several. This is partly due to the complex nature of the god-force described by the name, and partly due to the popularity of many of these gods in the past and their identification with the interests of each set of worshippers. A god-name should be taken to mean all the related ideas necessary to make up the complete description of that particular god-force, each individual attribution representing a part of its totality.

Create your own correspondences of god-forces that you understand are related to each sphere. Do not worry about mixing gods from various cultures, or even making up god-names with meaning only to you. The practical importance is to create a practical *working* correspondence of god-names/forces for your own work relating to each sphere and path on the Tree. Do not expect to be able to do this at one sitting or perhaps to ever complete it. It will be a long-term on-going process.

As you create your own personally relevant correspondences, contact them individually to see if your attributions stand up to practical experience.

The best ways to contact these god-forces are:

1. Invocation: 'enflame yourself', turn off the inner dialogue and one-pointedly hold in consciousness the image and the name of the required god. Enflame yourself through dance, music, words and so on (as mentioned in Chapter 6).

2. Rising on the planes to the corresponding sphere.

3. Reciting the mantra or the name of the required god.

4. Assuming the form of the god and acting this out.

Gods are natural phenomena caused by activities of some sort which we recognize in ourselves (for example, the anger of the gods, the will of the gods, the gods' endless love, the thoughts of the gods, and so on) *but* on a 'higher' plane, invisible to our usual perceptions. There is a direct correspondence between gods and humans or, in other words, between the macrocosm and the microcosm. One is of the *same nature* as the other, but one does not equal the other. As above so below, but after a different manner.

There are various names for the same forms of energy, various god-names for one force. Invocation is calling up the god energy inside you; evocation is calling it up outside of you. The name of a god is the magickal formula which can set its energy in motion. It is important, therefore, to find the 'right' or 'true' formula. The Hebrew names are fairly straightforward formulae (see Appendix 4), but the best ones are devised by the Adept through practical experience.

Attributions can be confusing; for example, *Isis* can be attributed to Binah in her form as the mother, to Tiphareth for her harmonizing features, to Netzach as Venus, to Yesod as the moon, to Malkuth as a virgin, and so on. Moreover, each of these spheres may also contain other gods. This does *not* mean the gods are the same, but they are as 'complete' as we humans are. Gods and goddesses are *living entities*, or may be seen as such. They should therefore be treated with the same respect you would give to your very best friends. Then, like best friends, they will assist you in your journey through life and be available in times of great need.

WILL, LOVE AND IMAGINATION — THE VITAL ELEMENTS OF MAGICK

Study the diagram of the 'Will Tree' opposite.

Will power or *energy* may be attributed to the whole Tree, as well as to a particular sphere of the Tree. Or, to see it another way, the diagram represents the 'full Tree' embedded within the one particular sphere of Will Energy, that is, Geburah. Remember that all spheres on the Tree contain another whole Tree within themselves.

In work with the Will both the *magickal link* (see previous section) and *right proportions* are necessary. By 'right proportions' we mean the process of using the right amount of Will for the situation. Too much could be like taking a pneumatic drill for punching a hole in paper; too little could be like using a spoon to move a mountain!

Love is equally important to magick. Primarily it is the motivating force of the universe as we know it, and to be a truly great Adept the individual has to align him or herself with this dynamic energy we call *Love*. Binah is attributed to both Spiritual Love and Spiritual Awareness; it is just as true below the Abyss as above that 'Love *is* Awareness'.

You have not yet seen an attribution of *Imagination* on the Tree, which is because it is not attributable to one sphere, but is in one sense equivalent to the whole of the third world of Yetzirah, spheres 4 to 9 inclusive. In fact, Imagination is a vital aspect of all the spheres on the Tree.

Will and Imagination are the two faculties most used in magickal work. Imagination is not just fantasy and day-dreaming; it is the *image-making faculty*, the power to create anything we wish, through images. It is necessary to all creative processes, whether artistic or scientific. The power of the Will has already been well documented in this book. The development of both these faculties is the most important part of the training of any Adept, whatever his or her goal in life. The following two sections describe a series of exercises for the training of Imagination and Will. They are exercises which can be usefully carried on over a long period of time. They cannot be overworked as they may be interchanged and used in varying ways to add variety to the work.

There are no exercises given as such for the development of Love. This is not to suggest that it is any less important than the other two

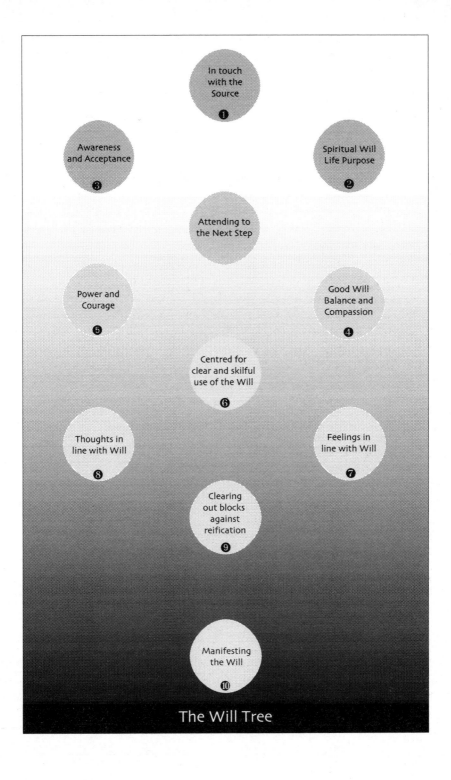

The Will Tree

elements dealt with here. In many ways it can be considered as more important, for Will and Imagination without Love are abominations, examples of which we can all too readily recall from the history of our planet. You cannot really be given a set of exercises, however, for the development of Love, for its true development and growth in your work will only come from *within yourself*. You have already learned how to develop an astral temple; perhaps you might like to create a Temple of Love in your sphere of working? In whatever way you deal with this do not lose sight of Love as the energy that underlies all your work. A little goodwill is worth a whole heap of badwill to the magician.

training the will

exercise 1

Follow the usual starting procedure.

When you are ready, reflect upon the unfortunate circumstances that have happened to both yourself and other people as a result of 'inadequate' Will energy. Consider both personal affairs and events beyond your personal sphere.

Choose one of these events which is both personal and particularly striking, where lack of Will has caused real problems. Really picture this event … try to be aware of as much detail as possible … examine the scene carefully … allow feelings that are aroused to affect you intensely …

Now picture all the differences there would have been if you had been filled with Will energy … visualize the scene with everything happening as you *will* it to happen …

Be as intensely aware as possible of the advantage of having Will energy available to you to use when and how you need it.

Reflect on the advantages of training the Will.

exercise 2

Follow the usual starting procedure.

Stand facing a mirror. See your reflection as vividly as possible as being filled with very strong, clear Will energy …

Take time to fill the image before you completely with as much strong and skilful Will as you can imagine …

Now be aware that the image is you …

Using the imagination rather than a mirror makes it possible to adapt this exercise to meet particular needs, to visualize the successful attainment of any desired purpose.

exercise 3

You learned of 'Useless Will Exercises' earlier in this chapter. Devise some Useless Will exercises of your own and create a programme to experiment with them for a given period.

exercise 4

Select a fictional book to read that you feel will assist your growth. Read this book very slowly, with undivided attention. Mark in the book or copy out impressive passages. Re-read these first whenever you next pick up the book.

exercise 5

Be aware of training your Will in everyday life situations. 'Make haste slowly', deliberately set up willed actions, perform distasteful or boring duties cheerfully and with interest.

exercise 6

Every movement you make is an act of Will. Be aware of this. Perform some physical acts with the exclusive purpose of training the Will.

training the imagination

VISUAL
exercise 1

Follow the usual starting procedure.

Imagine you write a single digit number on a blackboard ... then add another number in front of or behind the original number (for example, if you originally chose 5 and now choose 8 you could have 85 or 58).
Continue this procedure making the number larger and larger.

Remember to visualize the number on a blackboard.

Finish the exercise when you can no longer visualize your number.

Perform this exercise as often as you like. It is a useful test of your progress in training the visual imagination (the test being how many digits you can visualize at once).

exercise 2

The five *tattva* symbols are a black oval, a red triangle, a blue circle, a white crescent and a yellow square. Use these symbols to train your visualization. At first work with a single tattva symbol – try imagining a yellow square on its own, for example, held in the mind's eye continuously for one minute. You will notice how the shape and colour changes as you try to hold it steady. Do not try to force anything; each time it changes simply recall your will to visualize the shape and bring back the original.

When you are capable of holding a chosen tattva symbol in consciousness, progress to visualizing two at once – for instance, a white crescent on top of a blue circle, a blue circle on top of a yellow square and so on.

Note: In the above two exercises notice the connection between exercise 1 which uses *form* – connected to the thinking function of Hod – and exercise 2 which uses *colour* – connected to the feeling function of Netzach.

AUDITORY
exercise 3

Follow the usual starting procedure.

Remember a time when you were at the sea … Allow yourself to visualize the scene and then pay attention to the sound of the sea. In your imagination close your eyes and let the sound of the sea fill you … listen to the sound of the sea as if nothing else existed.

Evoke other sounds from nature and repeat the exercise with these memories, for example a waterfall or the wind in the trees.

Try the experiment with man-made sounds, including music.

To elaborate the training you can pay attention to the elements of music and sounds: the rhythm, melody, harmony, pitch and timbre (quality).

exercise 4

When you are being disturbed by a particular noise, practise excluding that sound from your consciousness. You may also practise this with remembered sounds.

exercise 5

At any time, but particularly when you are out in the countryside or when listening to music you like, practise 'auditory registration'. This means you consciously 'make a tape copy' in your mind of the sound. File these sounds and play the tape back as you will.

'Mental photography' is a version of this exercise, taking pictures of particular scenes with an imaginary camera. With this kind of sound recording and photography the sound and pictures *always* come out exactly as you want them!

OTHER SENSES

For the other senses adapt the procedures already given. For example, for tactile sense training you might practise passing your hand over an object and immediately afterwards evoking the sensation, or for the olfactory sense you could build up a library of your favourite smells, to evoke as you wish. Using your Will and Imagination to devise tasks like this is a useful exercise in itself.

CHAPTER 10

DAATH: THE SPHERE WITHOUT A NUMBER

THE CENTRE OF BECOMING

Daath is *not* situated on the Tree of Life, thus it is given the title 'The Sephira that is not a Sephira'. It is (usually) given no number, there is no plane equivalent to it, and although it is situated in the middle of the Abyss, above Tiphareth and below Kether, it has in fact no position in terms of the other Sephiroth. If the diagram of the Tree is seen as a two-dimensional representation of a three-dimensional existence, then Daath represents at one and the same time *no dimensions and all dimensions*.

In Hebrew Daath is spelt:

$$\text{ת} \quad \text{ע} \quad \text{ד}$$
Th   O   D

Daath means *Knowledge* – knowledge without understanding (the understanding of Binah).

Daath is sometimes called the 'child' of Chockmah and Binah, and sometimes the 'false head'. Its position coincides with the head of the serpent that spirals up the Tree from Malkuth, attempting to get to the very crown of the Tree. This serpent is unable to break the veil of the Abyss and reaches no further than Daath, Knowledge. People who make knowledge their god are worshipping the false 'god-head' of Daath (even though they often call themselves aetheists).

Traditionally Daath is seen in a very negative light, certainly in exoteric lore anyway, but as with all duality (and Daath is still in the realm of duality being below the supernal triad) there is also a positive side to it. Daath is related, through its correspondence with the throat, to the *expression of Spiritual Knowledge*. This expression can either be clear or distorted depending on how 'open' the Daath expression centre is in the individual. Daath is also the centre of generation and re-generation.

The two diagrams illustrate the central importance of Daath within the Tree of Life diagram.

Whilst Daath's negative qualities – as the false god-head – are dispersion

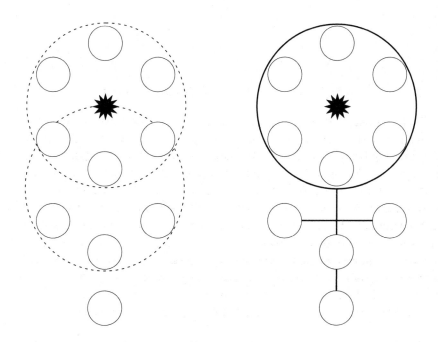

and restriction, its positive quality is clear expression. Expression from Daath may be clear or distorted as it comes through the individual. It is made clear through the balance (in the dynamic sense explained in the last chapter) of Love and Will, that is Chesed and Geburah.

We said that Chesed (Love/Awareness) could be related to *being*, and that Geburah (Will/Power) could be related to *doing*. Daath as the higher resolving factor which includes both being and doing can be termed – *becoming*.

Our True Will and ultimate purpose in life is something we need to contact and understand, but from day to day, moment to moment, the important factor for all of us is the *next step* we shall take towards that ultimate goal. Daath, as the 'child' of Chockmah and Binah, is the indicator of this next step.

Sometimes, because there are ten other spheres, Daath is attributed to the number 11 or at least called 'the eleventh sphere'. This is appropriate because 11 is the number of magick, of 'energy tending to change'. Number 11 is the first step after the full cycle of ten is complete: this also complies with the attribution of Daath as the 'next step indicator'.

Daath is sometimes given the number 8, as it is the eighth sphere, if you start from the bottom of the Tree and work your way up. This is also appropriate because 8 is equivalent to 'height' (h : eight) and Daath can be considered as the 'height of the Soul'; positive when it is connected to the spirit of the Supernal triad, negative when it is made its own god.

CORRESPONDENCES TO DAATH

Daath as 'the Sephira that is not a Sephira' is also sometimes called the 'false' Sephira. Knowledge without understanding is false. There is no path from Chockmah to Geburah or from Binah to Chesed. Why do you think this is, in the light of what has already been said of Daath?

Daath is the gate of access to the reverse side of the Tree, which is the zone of the Qliphoth – demons, dis-ease and so on. This zone is also equated in an occult manner to a 'state that is not a state' (sorry! – there is no better way to describe it in words) that has been called by various authors, the 'naugal', 'universe B' (the front side being 'universe A'), or the 'tunnels of Set' (as opposed to those of Horus which illuminate the front side of the Tree. Set being Horus's dark brother).

THE ABYSS

The Abyss, in which Daath resides, is the gulf or chasm between the noumenal (that is, spirit) and the phenomenal (everything except spirit). The Abyss exists between what is real and what is illusionary, between the ideal and the actual, the potential and the manifest. Above the Abyss *all opposites are reconciled* – there is no duality above the Abyss. Below it everything is duality. The Abyss can also be described as the gulf separating the individual soul from its source.

It is said that unresolved and irrational elements of the individual 'exist' within the Abyss, which cannot therefore truly be crossed without these elements being completely resolved. It is also said that to cross the Abyss the Adept must leave *everything* behind, give up all that he or she is.

In the Abyss a great demon called *Choronzon* is met. It is the archdemon of dispersion of the individual's false knowledge and is therefore sometimes described as the 'consumer' of human consciousness.

THE CHAKRAS AND THE TREE OF LIFE

The chakras are energy centres in the human body – there are seven major ones. A chakra may be either closed or open and when it is open it gives the individual powers of perception and creativity. Chakra literally means 'wheel' – wheels or centres of energy within the subtle body of each individual.

There are more chakras than the seven 'major' ones, sometimes termed 'minor' chakras (a comment on their position within the body rather than on their relative importance). We will not deal with these minor chakras here, but it is worth looking at your own body and how you sense each part of it to see if you can find the location of any of these other centres. For example, if we look at just one arm we could locate minor chakras thus (the numbers corresponding to the spheres on the Tree):

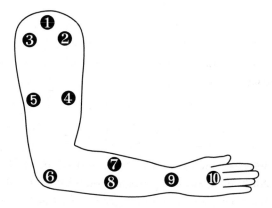

How about all seven chakras within a hand, a finger, a fingertip?

There are other ways of relating chakras to the body than those given here, but this is the most actively practical attribution. It also increases our understanding of the relationship between the Sephiroth.

Look carefully at the diagram of the chakras attributed to the Tree of Life (page 137). As you do so consider these comments on each of the seven chakras:

Manipura

The solar plexus chakra is dual in nature since the left-hand and right-hand columns of the Tree have to be balanced for it to be effectively and fully open. In other words, if the mind and feelings are not balanced there will be distortion of manipura energy.

Ajna

The 'third eye chakra' is also of dual nature, but on a higher or deeper level. Balance of the left-hand and right-hand pillars is again necessary for its full opening, which represents 'Love under Will' in its clearest aspect.

Anahata

The heart chakra has a dual nature 'hidden behind it', that is, Chesed and Geburah. The heart chakra is really a trinity. The solar plexus and ajna chakras will function even if there is not balance, albeit distortedly. The heart chakra is more of an 'on/off' affair – it is open if there is balanced energy between Love and Will and closed if there is not.

Visuddhi

The throat chakra only opens when the anahata chakra is open, hence its 'dotted' representation and its equivalence with Daath. The throat chakra has to be open for energy to be channelled effectively and fully both to ajna and sahasara.

Muladhara, Svadisthana, Visuddhi, Sahasara

These four chakras are each attributed to a single Sephira. But these too have a dual nature. Whereas with the other three the concern is with *inner* balance, these four chakras are concerned with *outer* balance. Muladhara – survival in the world; Svadisthana – interplay and interpersonal relationships, particularly sexually oriented; Visuddhi – the outer, creative aspect of harmony and balance within; Sahasara – the realization of unity within and without.

Note that in some systems of chakra classification, two chakras are given at the level of the navel, the one on the left corresponding to lunar energy and the one on the right to solar energy. This is an interesting correlation with Hod and Netzach.

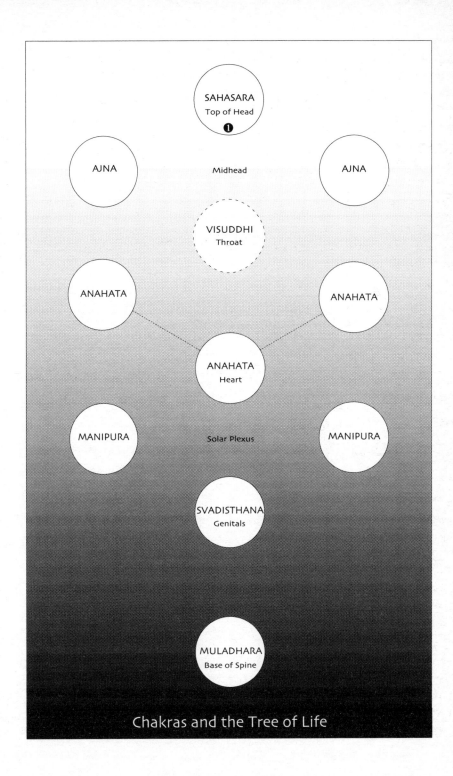

Chakras and the Tree of Life

CONTACTING THE WHEELS OF ENERGY

With each of the following descriptions, vividly visualize and feel the energy as described for each chakra location.

Sahasara — Blood pulses in the brain at the very top of the skull; draw all your body forces there.

Ajna — There are pulsations in the brain, behind the frontal bone in the middle of the forehead.

Visuddhi — Concentrating on the region of the throat, imagine the sound of 'U' (as the middle letter of A-U-M) there.

Anahata — Concentrate on the heart, perceive your heart beats. Imagine the blood circulation throughout the whole body.

Manipura — In the area of the solar plexus, perceive blood pulsations. Imagine the energy of assimilation.

Svadisthana — Contract your perineum, concentrate on the sensations perceived at the base of the penis or clitoris. Imagine sexual dynamism.

Muladhara — Concentrate on the zone activated by contraction of the anus and perineum. Imagine the life energy that informs the human species, particularly you as a manifest individual.

---

contacting energy

This is a simple exercise for contacting any of the chakras. Following the above instructions first will help to enrich your experience.

Follow the usual starting procedure.

Tune into your body and receptively allow one chakra to call your attention, to 'make itself heard'. Alternatively choose the chakra you wish to contact and concentrate your energy there.

Give a voice to this chakra. Allow it to speak to you. Listen to what it has to say.

Engage in active dialogue with the chakra, using discrimination about what it says.

Ask it about its relationship with the other chakras, particularly the ones directly above and below it.

Ask it about itself and particularly its *purpose* in this life.

Thank the chakra and ask it to continue to perform effectively for you in this life.

Write about your experience immediately in your diary.

THE CADUCEUS

The Caduceus is a symbol representing the balance of opposing forces throughout both the universe as a whole (macrocosm) and each individual (microcosm). The movement is the dance of life, the joy of separating and joining, of parting and re-merging. As the diagram shows, its relationship to both the system of chakras and the Tree of Life is fairly clear.

GROWTH AND INITIATION

Growth and initiation can take place, in terms of the Tree, in two directions – from the bottom up (the ascent of the individual towards the spiritual) or from the top down (the descent of spiritual energy into the individual). Sometimes the first process from the bottom up is termed 'mysticism' and the process from the top down 'magick'.

Growth from the bottom up

Key words: *Synthesis/Transformation*

For example, an atom synthesizes with other atoms to form a molecule, then a cell, then a tissue, then an organ, then the whole body.

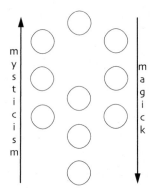

Synthesis respects the individuality of each part and thus each part must be made whole in itself before being integrated.

All so-called conflicts in life can be seen as the growing point for synthesis, the energy of growth. If you have a problem, you can't get rid of it (that would be exclusion) but have to transform it (that is, synthesize it).

The methods of growth from the bottom up may be resumed under the headings of 'love' (that is, loving the Self) and 'will' (that is, choosing to do it).

Growth from the top down

Key words: *Self-identification/Emergence*

The key is to realize yourself as a Self with a personality (rather than a personality with a self). The best methods for growth this way are self-identification exercises – such as the ones you have already done and the 'stop' exercise you will find in the next section.

It is also a matter of *allowing* the Qualities (truth, beauty, joy, and so on – see Chapter 8, section 2) to manifest in the personality, grounding them through asking yourself: how do I express this energy? – then doing it!

the stop exercise

This is a simple exercise to describe and a simple one to do if you remember to do it.

Simply remember to *stop* yourself during the day.

For example, you might be lifting a glass of water to drink, about to step off a pavement, reading this book, eating, watching television, making love – whatever the activity, every now and again recall this exercise and *stop!* Then when you have stopped, look at yourself in terms of the Tree of Life.

Don't make a big thing out of this or try to analyse what you find. Simply look at Malkuth (what are you sensing, what position is your body in, what is your direct physical relationship to the outside world?), then Yesod, Hod, Netzach, the soul and the spirit: what state is each in? What is predominating? With what are you identified? What do you sense, think, feel, believe? How centred are you? How connected to the universe?

This sounds like a lot of questions but do not try to answer them as such. Simply be aware that these are the sort of questions to have in mind when you *stop*. I would recommend that each stop lasts not more than a few moments. It is the attention that counts, not what you do with it.

CREATIVE DISSONANCE

The Chinese ideogram for *crisis* is a combination of two others which mean *danger* and *opportunity*. This is a good way of viewing any crisis, however large or small. In the spiritual realms there is no conflict whatsoever because there is no duality. Below the Abyss, however, all is duality and in all dualities crises occur. A crisis leads to a 'pulling apart' of the components of the crisis, which leads to a tension that is termed 'Creative Dissonance'. Paying attention to both poles or 'parts' involved in the crisis leads to the 'emergence' of the resultant resolution of the crisis.

As an example, a crisis between a mental part of the personality ('I think we should ...') and a feeling part ('I feel we could ...') may be seen as a tension between Hod and Netzach. This tension, as it deepens, in a sense 'separates' the poles of Netzach and Hod until they have no recourse but to come back together again. The separation is the creative dissonance, the coming back together is the emergence of the new. This

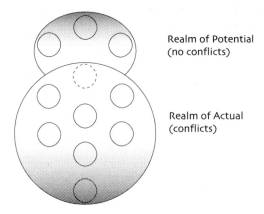

Realm of Potential
(no conflicts)

Realm of Actual
(conflicts)

emergence is achieved through a third factor coming into the conflict, in this case the higher resolving factor of Tiphareth. In other words, the personal identity asserts itself, views the dissonance and finds a resolution that is appropriate to and honours the integrity of both the conflicting parts.

It is also worth remembering that *everything* has a spiritual component. Try always to see what this is, both in yourself and in other people. Remember that whatever conflict you are experiencing, whether internally or with others, everything and everyone is ultimately part of the same one spirit.

Experience and expression may be seen as two poles that have tension or creative dissonance between them (in fact they inevitably will do, as does all duality). Experience is related to Chesed and the right-hand pillar, whilst expression is related to Geburah and the left-hand pillar. The true Middle Way is then the path that goes between these two poles, *but not* in a straight line, rather in a wavy one as it constantly adjusts itself. In most people it is much more wavy than shown in the diagram! No one goes straight up the middle; one minute you are over-balanced to one side, the next you are back in the middle, then you will overbalance the other way. This is a *dynamic* rather than a static description of balance.

Think of how this relates to your own experience, then consider how you would relate this to your experience and knowledge of the society in which you live, then the world as a whole. Try if you can to see how this may relate to the whole universe.

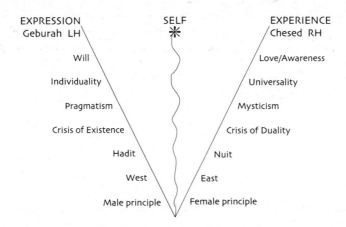

EXPRESSION   SELF   EXPERIENCE
Geburah LH   ✳   Chesed RH

Will   Love/Awareness

Individuality   Universality

Pragmatism   Mysticism

Crisis of Existence   Crisis of Duality

Hadit   Nuit

West   East

Male principle   Female principle

GLAMOUR – THE VEILING OF ENERGY

The 'subjective' is created through identification with the consciousness as the 'ego' or 'I'. The 'objective' is what this awareness perceives as being 'outside' itself. The Self (Kether) creating sparks of individual consciousness (Tiphareth) becomes aware of the duality of 'subject' and 'object'. We all know this duality between what we 'know' and 'feel' to be true inside and what we perceive outside, whether it agrees with our perceptions or not.

This is part of a process of the successive veiling of energy from Kether to Malkuth accompanied by an increasing loss of awareness of 'cosmic consciousness' or 'connectedness to the whole', that is the pure experience of Kether. The 'personal self' at Tiphareth not only lives within the duality of subject and object but also, in clothing itself with a personality, learns to completely attach itself to, or identify itself with, the personality spheres – that is, with the mind, feelings and body. Instead of *having* thoughts, feelings and sensations, it speaks as if it *is* them: 'I see', 'I taste', 'I feel' instead of 'I have seeing, tasting, feelings' and so on. This is the creation of the phenomenal world, the apparently 'real' world we experience as separate from ourselves when we are self-identified, or as part of ourselves when we are identified with it.

This is what is meant by 'glamour' – the identification of the Self with the contents of the personality, the attachment of the subject inside to the object outside. This is described in Buddhism as mistaking the unreal (samsara) for the real (nirvana). Hindu thought describes this as a four-fold process. First there is sushupti, which is 'sleeping' – related to

Malkuth; then svapna, 'dreaming' – related to Yesod; jagrat, 'wakeful-ness' – related to Daath; and finally the only real element, considered to be both behind and inside the other three, called turiya, related to the undifferentiated consciousness of Kether, and in the individual to the pure experience of Self-identity in Tiphareth.

You need not be attached to the 'glamour' of the world. Realize it is a veiling of energy for your use and convenience for experience and expression, but not real in itself.

THE WAYS TO SPIRITUAL REALIZATION

There are seven main Ways to spiritual realization, although these Ways are not sharply divided and in fact frequently overlap. Each of us has one, two, three or more of these Ways manifesting through different aspects of our being. In essence (on the level of the Supernals) we are, each of us, on all seven of the Ways, but in terms of our soul and personality, some of these Ways become the foreground to our particular stage of evolution.

The seven Ways are sometimes numbered as shown in the table below. The usual names are given, but these can vary. The Ways are also sometimes called 'Rays'.

Name of Way (or Ray)	Number	Alternative Name
Will	1	Power
Love	2	Wisdom
Action	3	Action
Beauty	4	Harmony
Science	5	Knowledge
Devotion	6	Idealism
Ritual	7	Organization

The Ways are attributed to the Tree of Life as shown in the diagram.

Most people have two primary influences – one for the soul and one for the personality. Then, within the personality, one Way will be found to particularly influence the mind, another the feelings and a third the body and senses. When looking for the influence of these Ways or Rays within yourself or anyone else, it is important not to be dogmatic. The divisions between the Ways are not clear-cut and it is often difficult to tease out the difference between the influence various Ways have on various parts of the person.

The 'height' of the Way is how it manifests in its pure form; the 'depth' of the Way is, to a greater or lesser degree, how it manifests through the personality. The task, once a Ray's influence has been identified, whether in its 'height' or 'depth', is to *elevate* it. This means to use techniques to create dynamic balance between the various components involved in the manifestation of that Way. This might take the form of personality work, meditation and/or visualization. Always, however, it will involve a deep-rooted connection with Tiphareth.

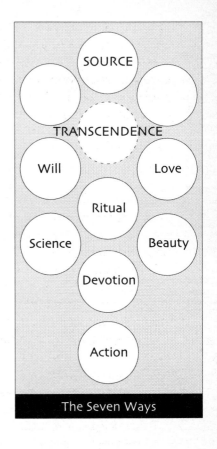

The Seven Ways

The Way of Will (Geburah – Will)

Sometimes called the 'heroic' way, the Way of Will is more rarely manifest than other ways. People strongly associated with this way tend to be leaders, for 'good' or 'bad'. They will be wilful, one-pointed, quick to act, prompt, decisive, competitive and have powers of physical endurance. They tend to judge emotions as negative. If distorted they are self-centred and isolated, assertive in a judgemental way and even violently psychopathic.

Their task is to temper their Will with Love. To become more understanding and co-operative, to build as well as to destroy and to align their personal Will (in Geburah) with their true Purpose (in Chockmah).

The Way of Love (Chesed – Love)

It has been said that the outcome of all the Ways is Love. For this reason, and because love permeates all things, the Way of Love is particularly difficult to separate from the other Ways. Yet it is a specific path. People on this way tend to be 'servers' to humanity, whether through medicine and healing, or in more indirect ways. It is the path of inclusiveness, of seeing the divine in everything. Co-operation, brotherhood, and group-consciousness are all important concepts to these people. Their purpose in life is to love – ultimately to transform individual love into universal Love. The person on the Way of Love will want to include as much as possible and will realize him- or herself through relationships. They tend to be soft – sometimes to the point of inertia. If very distorted, they become like a cushion that accepts all impressions and holds the impression made by the last person to 'sit on them'. They are without boundaries.

Their task is to enlarge and to refine their overall positive attitude and to cultivate love in its pure form. They also need to learn to use their Will more, to be courageous, to have direction, and to be able to say 'no'.

The Way of Action (Malkuth – Sensing)

People of this type tend to have no ultimate goal, the 'going' being sufficient in itself. They can be passionate and dispassionate at the same time. They can act on behalf of others with absolutely no self-interest. They are pragmatic and skilful, and deal with the matter of Malkuth very successfully. On the negative side, they tend to be unconscious of Netzach, so they are often insensitive and/or manipulative and devious. They are very efficient and effective at getting a job done, but can get caught up in their activity and loose touch with its purpose.

Their task is to be still, to slow down, to allow 'being' as well as 'doing'. They need to cultivate Love, connect with their feelings, and develop aesthetic appreciation.

The Way of Beauty (Netzach – Feeling)

It is said that Harmony manifests as Beauty. This could be the watchword of this Way, as people of this type are creative, intuitive and often have a deep understanding of both themselves and others. They see the divine in all forms and they can see true beauty in all manifestations. Ecstasy and agony are both familiar to these artistic types. On the negative side they find it difficult to make choices and are easily spaced out (both in pleasant and unpleasant ways). Often they are adversely affected by other people's negative energies. They can be dreamy and impractical.

Their task is to cultivate persistence and Will, particularly in self-assertion, and to connect with their creative impulses and manifest them in as pure a form as possible.

The Way of Science (Hod – Thinking)

These types are very connected with observing, using the mind in both its abstract and concrete modes – with a strong intuition and imagination, they love exploring and are often filled with waves of curiosity. Bright and clear of mind, they can be tireless in the pursuit of knowledge. They tend, however, to be very out of touch with their emotional life and are often stuck in mental identification. They can be excessively analytical and opinionated, even arrogant about their beliefs. They are also insensitive to others.

Their task is to get in touch with their feelings, develop and appreciate their emotions. They need to balance their head and heart. They can also learn to use the mind to go beyond itself.

The Way of Devotion (Yesod – Sub-conscious)

This is the way of mysticism, of devotion to a god, guru, ideal or cause. The devotion of this type is intense and they are often completely dedicated to their work. They have a great urge for unity and union with their desired transcendent goal. On the negative side they often lack joy in their lives and are overly serious. Often they don't see alternatives and want to convert others to their 'one true' way. They include those who become harsh fanatics and 'fundamentalists'.

Their task is to enlarge themselves both mentally and emotionally and refine their sense of devotion.

The Way of Ritual (Tiphareth – Centre)

This is the way of magick, of organizing matter in such a way as to change consciousness, both on the inner and outer planes. People of this type tend to be organizers, making order out of chaos. They are in touch with Purpose and how to achieve that purpose. They are disciplined at their chosen creative tasks. Although not as inspired as the Beauty type, they will usually get a lot more done. They give tremendous attention to detail and are in touch with the rhythms of life. On the negative side they are often controlled by routines, and their endless organization can be boring both to themselves and others. They can also be rigid and, if given the opportunity, bureaucratic.

Their task is to develop their ritual, to put matter into rhythm, to give order to things that help people appreciate the rhythms and cycles of nature. Also to build a bridge between Tiphareth and Kether.

You will probably recognize some of yourself in all these types but your task is to find which of these ways you particularly connect with (a) on the personality level, and (b) on the soul level.

For (a) it is useful to ask yourself: From which Way do I live my everyday life? and for (b): Which Way do I experience during peak experiences?

When you have elucidated this, then ask yourself the following questions for both the personality and soul level:

What needs to be refined?
What needs to be elevated?

The 'tasks' as described above should help you answer these last two questions.

Once you have found your Way it is a useful exercise then to apply your knowledge of this 'map' to other people; what Ways do your parents, lovers, friends, colleagues, etc. operate from? What do they need to elevate and refine?

In our modern world, there is a 'new' way that has sometimes been called in the past 'The Way of Transcendence'. It is associated with Daath, as opposed to the Way of Devotion, which is associated with Yesod. The link between these two spheres and the movement of energies between them will be developed later. For now just be aware of this 'new' way that is 'transcendent' in that it includes all the other ways yet is more than them. In another sense it could be called the 'Way of Immanence' for by including all the other ways it also manifests them.

It is worth noting that whatever way each of us follows we are all 'pilgrims' with the same goal, notwithstanding the difference of method. Through the diversity of the seven Ways we make an approach to the essential divinity in us all, individually and collectively.

THE QLIPHOTH

Daath is the gate to the reverse side of the Tree of Life. This 'negative', 'dark' or 'evil' Tree that exists behind the usual, outward Tree is the world of the *Qliphoth* (singular Qlipha). These are the demons (literally 'harlots') or shells of the positive energies.

Everything positive has a negative side. The negative of 'goodwill', for example, might be 'unprovoked anger'. The Qliphoth, or 'Qliphotic forces' radiate negative Qualities, the reverse of the positive Qualities of the front side of the Tree. Thus Peace becomes War, Love becomes Hate,

Joy becomes Sorrow, Truth becomes Dishonesty and so on. The traditional Vices of the Sephiroth are, in a sense, these very Qliphotic forces.

Demons inhabit what are often called the 'averse' Sephiroth. The term 'averse' is used for they cannot be considered as independent spheres – rather, the unbalanced, destructive aspect. (Of course the reverse is then true for the positive Qualities, thus asserting the actual existence of both good and evil, for one cannot exist without the other. Whether they are equal or not is a philosophical question.)

There are two kinds of 'evil', which may be termed positive and negative evil. Positive evil moves against the current of evolution; it is destructive to progress and change. Negative evil includes all opposition, blocks, restrictions to free movement. This is relative – thus conservation may be 'evil' to a money-identified farmer but 'good' to many others. Positive evil is not relative.

We can also see that both positive and negative 'evil' manifests in two forms: conscious or unconscious. Conscious evil is that done purposely, for its own sake and with malice. Unconscious evil, on the other hand, is that which occurs from blindness, stupidity, carelessness, but not with any conscious intent or malice.

---

positive and negative qualities

Follow the usual starting procedure.

On a piece of paper make two lists, headed thus:

My Positive Qualities   My Negative Qualities

Continue the lists until you have at least half a dozen on each side.
    When ready go through the list of positive qualities and look for the negative aspects of each positive, and list them.
    Do the same for the negative qualities, finding their positive counterparts.
    Your original list of positive/negative qualities represents what you need to refine. The second list of negative/positive qualities represents what you need to cultivate, that is, develop.

Remember the principle of inclusion – do not cut anything off or try to discard it, however negative it may appear. It is better to transform and absorb it, harmonize with it and create an active, dynamic balance within yourself. Recall the triangles used to illustrate the higher resolving factor. The point of 'neither A nor B' is neutral, inert, there is no growth. The point of 'both A and B' is inclusive – it is a place of equilibrium – there is strain and stress, but this gives the possibility of growth.

If you look in the correspondence tables (Appendix 4) you will find comprehensive lists of demons, Qliphotic entities and the like. It was believed in the past that these creatures prolonged their existence by preying on the 'vital fluids' (for example, semen and vaginal secretions) of the living. This is the origin of the 'vampire' who is a particular kind of demonic entity, typical of the type that exists on vital fluids (in this case, blood). It is true that there are phantom forms created by 'sexual desire' and 'morbid cravings' which exist within the Qliphoth, but these are only a small part of the total demonology. It is also true that contact with these creatures can be beneficial, if directed with clarity and clear purpose. The magickal system of AbraMelin uses this form of contact with good effect. The following section on healing describes another way of using forces for positive ends.

Qliphotic entities, whether demons, vampires, succubi, ghouls or whatever, can 'seep through' in all the Sephiroth from Chesed through Malkuth. They do not cross the Abyss. But they are also always present in a sense, as the 'negative' side of each positive Sephirotic quality, as described above. They are particularly prone to come into consciousness through sexual imagination. Thus Yesod is important as an ingress point for their influence. As Yesod is also associated with the 'denizens' of the lower unconscious, the monsters and demons of dreams and the lower astral, it is particularly important in terms of demonology. All sexual acts, including masturbation, should be performed with some kind of protection ritual beforehand. This could be a pentagram banishing ritual or simply the imagination of a blue egg around the individual/couple.

Intentional contact with the Qliphoth for balance and positive growth can make use of this ingress through Yesod. Alternatively, contact can also be made through Malkuth by using Karezza (a passive form of love-making) or through suppression of orgasm. But primarily contact is made, at least by the initiate, through Daath. This inevitably leads to contact with Choronzon, the 'boss', as it were, of all the demons. Although this is a potentially rewarding form of contact, it is important to realize the dangers involved and this work shouldn't really be undertaken without an experienced guide.

THE HEALING OF DISEASE

In the correspondence tables for each sphere you will find a category of 'Physical Disorders', listing the most commonly occurring disorders as attributed to the various paths of the Tree. They represent, in one sense, the *result* of what happens if the demons or Qliphoth get to you. Diseases of these kinds are the result of these forces on the body. It is as if they are using your physical vehicle to come through into manifestation on the front side of the Tree. This is particularly true of viruses.

The way to deal with these disorders is through contacting the appropriate positive force to counteract the intrusion of the demon. Thus if the disease was associated with Hod, the use of the positive attributes of this sphere will counteract the disease. By using other correspondences you can devise appropriate ways of doing this. As an example, for a Hod-related disease you might wear orange next to the diseased place, or chant the name of/invoke a corresponding divine-force, elohim tzabaoth, or you might fill your room with the corresponding flowers, concentrate on the animals, take appropriate herbal infusions, and so on – using all the correspondences to bring more of the positive aspect of the path into your field of consciousness.

healing stars

You can do this exercise at any time, but it is particularly effective before going to sleep.
Follow the usual starting procedure, then relax as best as you are able.

Above your head visualize a large blue star. Vividly picture this blue star above your head. Then suddenly this star bursts into thousands of little stars, a shower of tiny, bright blue stars pouring down over you. It is as if it is raining little blue stars.
These tiny stars are healing energy. All the little stars move through your body, healing it. They move through your emotions, your feelings, your thoughts, healing all the parts of your personality. You feel good as the stars mingle with you, healing you.
The tiny blue stars will move through your body whilst you sleep and when you wake up you will feel strong and well.

CHAPTER 11

THE SUPERNAL TRIAD

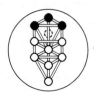

SPIRIT – INDIVIDUAL AND UNIVERSAL

Just as we live in *one* universe composed of an infinite number of parts (galaxies, stars, life-forms, molecules, atoms ...) it is equally true that there is *one spirit* which is totally universal, and in order to know itself (through the process of creation previously described) this one spirit has created from itself an infinite number of parts. The one spirit becomes the individual spirit of Kether. It is still completely connected to the universal spirit but now has a rudimentary consciousness of itself as a single entity. This 'entity', this individual spirit, has will and awareness (Chockmah and Binah) which it uses to create a reflection of itself in each living being (not only human beings!). We call this the soul and represent it on the Tree by the second triad. In order to know itself further, this soul then forms the vehicles of the personality represented by the lower Tree. So we can say that each of us is an individual soul which has a personality. This individual soul is connected to an individual 'spark' of spirit that is connected to the universal spirit.

The three Sephiroth of the Supernal triad – Kether, Chockmah and Binah – are sometimes described as the Trinity (of God), three-in-one and one-in-three. For practical purposes there is a point in separating these three spheres but it is important to remember at all times when studying the Supernal triad that, although we split it into three spheres, it is in essence *one* in its spirituality.

THE THIRD SPHERE, BINAH

Binah, in Hebrew, is spelt:

ה   נ   י   ב

H   N   I   B

It means 'understanding'. Understanding is clearly distinguished from the Knowledge of Daath. There can be, in fact, no true knowledge without understanding. Binah is situated on the second plane, forming a dynamic partnership with Chockmah. On the ascent up the tree it is the *first sphere across the abyss* and it is attributed to *spiritual awareness and love*. On the level of spirit there is no distinction between awareness and love. In other words, love *is* awareness, awareness *is* love.

Binah is sometimes given the title 'Marah', the Great Sea. An image associated with this sphere is of a mature woman. She is equated to *ama*, the 'old' or 'unfertilized' woman (who when Yod [:I] is thrust into her becomes *aima*, the 'fertilized' woman of Malkuth).

The planetary correspondence is Saturn – not so much the heavy, leaden Saturn of the path connecting Yesod to Malkuth, but the Saturn that represents the essence of spiritual awareness.

The vision associated with Binah is the 'Vision of Sorrow', the sorrow of the duality seen below the Abyss. This is the vision often attributed to Buddha, whose 'system' of mystical attainment is based upon the dictate that 'everything is sorrow'. Despite this attribute, Kabbalists tend to believe that the duality below the Abyss is not sorrowful, for the division created is intentional to allow the divided parts the opportunity to know themselves through union or love. This has been described (in the 'Book of the Law') as 'divided for love's sake, for the chance of union'. This attitude is the result of a balanced connection between Binah and Chockmah, Spiritual Love and Will.

The traditional Virtue associated with Binah is silence, whilst the Vice is avarice or greed.

The colour of Binah is black, which absorbs all other colours (representing the lower spheres on the Tree).

In the body Binah corresponds to the right side of the face and the right brain. Along with Chockmah it also corresponds to the 'third eye chakra', the ajna chakra, found midway and a little above the eyebrows.

Symbols associated with Binah are the cup, the yoni and the vesica pisces.

In the Tarot, the four 3s of the minor arcana and the Queens of the court cards are attributed to this sphere.

THE CITY OF THE PYRAMIDS

Associated with Binah is the magickal cup into which, it is said, the Adept who crosses the Abyss must drain every last drop of his blood. This represents symbolically the fact that in order to cross the Abyss, the gulf between the noumenal (potential) world and the phenomenal (actual) world, *everything* has to be given up – everything, that is, which exists within the duality of the creation below the Abyss.

The Adept who achieves this crossing is said to be in the 'City of the Pyramids', each pyramid representing the remains of a successful Adept. There is a 'rebirth' into spirit and the Adept (now called 'The Master of the Temple') is sometimes symbolically represented as a gardener whose sole purpose is the tending of the garden in his or her care. This garden is all the connections with the world the Master of the Temple has 'left behind'; left behind only in order that it may be found again in a *new, transformed light*.

THE SECOND SPHERE, CHOCKMAH

Chockmah, in Hebrew, is spelt:

ה מ כ ח

H   M   K   Ch

It means 'Wisdom'. Wisdom is the result of applying spiritual purpose to understanding. Chockmah is situated with Binah, on the second plane of the Tree. It is attributed to *spiritual will* or *purpose* and sometimes it is simply called the *word*. Yet 'Wisdom is the Word that cannot be communicated with words'.

Chockmah is attributed to the planet Neptune, the controller of the sea of Binah. It is also attributed to the 'sphere of the fixed zodiac'.

The traditional Virtue associated with this sphere is Devotion to the Great Work, that is, devotion to one's true will or purpose. For this sphere (and also for Kether) there is no Vice attributable – once you have reached this level, you cannot consider Virtue and Vice as separate, as nothing is 'dual', the illusion of duality having been totally and finally transcended.

In the body Chockmah corresponds to the left side of the face, the left brain and, along with Binah, the ajna chakra.

The colour of Chockmah is grey, a mixture of the all-resplendent white of Kether and the all-absorbing black of Binah.

The symbols that correspond to this sphere are the phallus and any phallic object. It is also attributed to the wand, the physical representation of the Will.

The image is of a bearded male figure, whilst the vision is of 'seeing

God face to face', which could be described as fully 'knowing oneself'.

In the Tarot the four 2s are attributed to this sphere and also the Knights of the court cards.

THE WORDS OF THE AEONS

This is the sphere of the Magus, the 'perfect magician' who has achieved complete self-knowledge and knows fully his or her True Will or Spiritual Purpose. The Adept, on attaining to this sphere and becoming a Magus, utters a Word which represents his Will. This word compels everything in the world below the Abyss to be seen in the *light* of that word. What the Magus believes he wills, and what he wills is created, exactly as he imagines it to be created.

THE FIRST SPHERE, KETHER

Kether, in Hebrew, is spelt:

ר ת כ

R   Th   K

It means 'the Crown' and it is attributed to the pure 'spirit' of the (transpersonal) Self. Positioned at the top of the Tree of Life, it constitutes the first plane below the negative veils which rest across the top of the diagram. The spiritual experience of Kether is 'Union with God', which in the East is called Samadhi (Sam: together with – adhi: the Lord).

The Virtue traditionally corresponding to Kether is Attainment and Completion of the Great Work.

Kether is *not in the body*. It corresponds to the crown chakra, which is said to 'hover' just above the top of the head.

The colour of Kether is white brilliance. The brilliance of the light is said to obscure what Kether really is; you don't see God but rather the illumination of the brilliant surrounding light. It is the same with a physical light. If you were standing some distance away from a street light for instance, you would not actually be able to see the bulb within it, just a blur of light and the rays that radiate from it. In this example the surface of your eyes (sensory receptor) is equivalent to Malkuth, the radiating light to all the spheres between, and the light bulb itself (which you do not see) is equivalent to Kether.

Another similar analogy can be seen in the projection of films. You

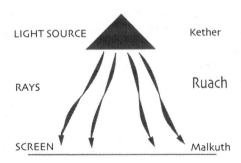

are observing a film; you see the picture on the screen (Malkuth), you can perceive the light that carried the picture to the screen (spheres 2 to 9) but you do not see the light source, the actual bulb of the projector (Kether). It is unfortunate that so many people believe the projected picture to be total reality.

An image traditionally attributed to Kether is of an ancient king seen in profile (there could be no image seen face to face, for no one can 'behold the eyes of god and return to describe that vision'). Sometimes this image is termed the 'Ancient of Ancients'.

Symbols that correspond to this sphere are the crown, the thousand petalled lotus (as the image of the crown chakra) and the swastika (as a symbol of continuous spirit).

Kether is called the 'Vast Countenance' of limitless love, light, liberty and life, not separate in any way from the whole of creation.

In the Tarot, the four 1s, or aces, of the minor arcana are attributed to Kether and are called the 'Root of the Power' of fire, water, air and earth respectively.

CORRESPONDENCES AND THE SUPERNAL TRIAD

All the attributions and correspondences that have just been described for the Supernals are 'false'; false in so far as they are partial. *There is no duality above the Abyss*, so in reality anything you say about the Supernals is *both* true and untrue and *neither* true nor untrue! Another way of saying this is that in the Supernals *all is contradiction* (again because nothing in itself is true of the Supernals unless it contains its opposite).

THE MYSTERY OF SHEKHINAH

The *union* of a god and goddess takes place in the creative World of Atziluth. Briah, Yetzirah and Assiah are the 'fruits' of their union. The God is *Eheieh*, the primary force of Kether. The Goddess is *Shekhinah* who is the indwelling presence, the *essential* form of Malkuth.

All Sephira are 'male' in what they give out and 'female' in what they receive. Therefore, in one sense, Shekhinah is the receptive part of each sphere. Yet there is nothing above Kether so it is totally male – God; and nothing below Malkuth so it is totally 'female' – Goddess (Shekhinah). Recall the maxim 'Kether is in Malkuth and Malkuth is in Kether, but after another manner'. For those familiar with tantra, it will be clear that Shekhinah is equivalent to Shakti. Thus Shekhinah is to Eheieh what Shakti is to Shiva.

The transcendent Self is Kether, the immanent Self is Malkuth. The immanent Self is then the Goddess residing as Shekhinah within the sphere of Malkuth. As it is said, 'When the Self is present, Shekhinah is there.'

We energize our 'desire' in the *Nephesch* (spheres 10 and 9) because of the experience of separation.

We may then experience the 'grace' of the *Ruach* (spheres 4 to 8) in an act of love, an experience of union.

At the climax of this union we know 'reality', contacting the *Neschemah* (spheres 1, 2 and 3), having the experience of being the True Source of all Life, Love, Liberty and Light.

This threefold description of the act of love – energizing desire, experiencing grace and knowing reality, equates with the three 'Grades' of New Age magick – called the Man of Earth, the Lover and the Hermit.

At the moment of orgasm, Shekhinah as the Holy Spirit comes into the participants. The female partner identifies with this spirit and the man takes her within. The Zohar says: '(before the parting) he must allow Shekhinah to rest on him so he remains both male and female'. The woman, who is already Shekhinah, allows herself to be clarified by the experience and may also use the energy for magickal work.

Shekhinah is also called *Asherah*, the 'Queen of Heaven, the consort of God' and is equivalent to Nuit, Isis and her manifestations Asnat, Astarte, Ashtaroth, Ishtar and Esther. The 'Book of Esther' in the Old Testament includes descriptions of the fertility rites and sacred marriages of Asherah, whilst the 'Song of Solomon' was composed in her honour.

Psalms 24:7 says:

lift up your heads, o ye gates; and be ye
lifted up, ye everlasting doors; and the
Kingdom of Glory shall come in.

The 'head' referred to is the penis of Eheieh (located in Yesod of Atziluth) and the 'door' is the vagina of Shekhinah (which leads to Zion, the Holy City). The 'Glory' is the union of Geburah and Gedulah resulting from the love-play of Eheieh and Shekhinah, who, having transcended Yesod and come through the 'door' to Zion, experience the orgasmic reality of 'Soul Union'.

---

soul union

This exercise may be performed with a partner or by an individual using his or her imagination. Both participants follow the instructions at the same time, working together on the same desire or on individual desires.

Follow the usual starting procedure.

Gazing into both eyes of your partner, at the same time pay attention to the midhead area.
  Prolong the gaze and allow yourself to fully relax.
  Visualize your desire (as a sigil or image) on your partner's midhead.
  Visualize its descent to the throat.
  (You may stop here for oracular workings.)
  Physically and/or astrally suck down the desire to the genital area.
  (Oral sexual union may be performed.)
  Unite on earth.
  Conclude by ingesting the resulting bipolar elixir. This androgynized elixir embodies the sigil/desire.
  Do not worry if you do not understand all this. If you return to the exercise after completing this book you will understand it better.

THE NEGATIVE VEILS

Although we have not shown them in this book you will often find in Tree of Life diagrams either one or three Veils above the top of Kether, called the 'Veils of Negative Existence' or simply the 'Negative Veils'. When we studied the creation of the Tree we spoke of Kether as the 'point', the prime source of the rest of creation. This point must in itself, however, come from somewhere. Thus we introduce the Negative Veils – something behind Kether, so ethereal and distant it can only be spoken of in a *veiled* manner. There are usually three Veils described, simply because on the Tree everything happens in a threefold process, so it is appropriate to say there are three Veils. But just as the three Supernals were in reality *one*, this is even more so (if such a thing were possible!) for the 'three' Veils.

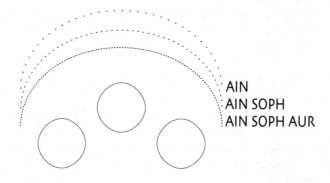

AIN
AIN SOPH
AIN SOPH AUR

These Veils are given the names *Ain, Ain Soph, Ain Soph Aur*, and numbered (if at all) 0, 00 and 000. Perhaps the most useful way to contemplate these Veils is in terms of the creation process. In this sense they can be ascribed thus:

Ain	Nothing
Ain Soph	Nothing Becomes
Ain Soph Aur	Nothing Is

This describes a threefold process where an original 'nothing' which does not exist becomes 'something that does exist' but 'nothing' in so far as it is beyond the comprehension of the normal human consciousness. In a sense they could be correlated with anti-matter.

THE KABBALISTIC SPIRIT

Tiphareth represents the individual soul as a particular 'spark' of the Self or Pure Spirit. The Supernal Triad (and Kether particularly) represents the spirit in both its universal and individualized aspects. It is within you (by being, at least ultimately, the source of you) and without you (by also being 'more than' you). The Negative Veils then represent the spirit that is totally beyond you. This can be termed the 'Universal Spirit'. The three Veils then correspond to the three Supernals, thus:

Ain	Universal Spirit
Ain Soph	Universal Will
Ain Soph Aur	Universal Love

In another sense Ain means 'Absolute and Limitless Void', from which arises Ain Soph, meaning 'Endless and Boundless Infinity', from which arises Ain Soph Aur meaning 'Limitless Light'. Although arising from one another they remain one, totally undivided. The three states together are then true *Negative Existence*, which by being infinite contains within itself the *potential* of all created things. It is the *focusing* of this negative existence which gives rise to the point in Kether, from whence all else springs.

All of these speculations lead nowhere, for by its very nature negative existence is outside of our range of realization. This does not mean, however, that we are outside the range of its influence!

Finally the Veils, by forming a 'background' to manifest existence, allow us to see the latter more clearly.

BEYOND THE VEILS

Metaphysical 'chitter-chatter' about what these Veils are and what they could mean is endless. Thus the Kabbalist's position is that the Veils do exist, and they most definitely veil *something* – but something with which we do not need to concern ourselves for the present. This is not denying the existence of anything; rather, it is asserting the existence of what *is*. It implies that we have our whole work cut out just fathoming the mysteries of the manifest Tree without concerning ourselves with idle speculation about the Veils and what lies beyond them. When we reach Kether perhaps then we will find that the Veils are pulled back and we have more to study, more work to do on ourselves. But for the present, the work of the personality, soul and spirit as represented by the Tree of Life is work enough for anyone. This is not mystification for the sake of it, but a very practical attitude to both individual and group development.

PART IV

THE MAGICKAL AND MYSTICAL KABBALAH

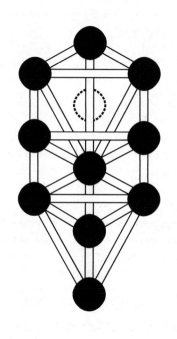

CHAPTER 12

THE MYSTIC
AND THE MAGICIAN

INTRODUCTION

If you have worked through the first three parts of this book, you should
have a thorough grounding in the Kabbalah, particularly in the correspondences to and uses of the Tree of Life. Assuming you have worked
through all the exercises and techniques presented you should also have
a detailed working knowledge of the spheres and paths of the Tree and
the ability to extend your study and practice of the Kabbalah to whatever
ends you need. This chapter and the subsequent ones will present you
with suggestions and techniques aimed at helping you apply your
Kabbalistic knowledge in various areas of psychological work, magickal
and mystical practices and in other applications of the Kabbalah.

Use the Kabbalah as you see fit, doing what you will with your
knowledge so long as you cause no harm to anyone else. Enjoy yourself
along the way, recalling the fact that the Kabbalah is an instrument of
practical research and not a dogmatic system or plan. It is a scheme to
aid your understanding and experience of the 'going', not the goal. 'For
pure will, unassuaged of purpose, delivered from the lust of result, is
every way perfect.'

Your existing knowledge will enable you to relate to other experiences, corresponding ideas and theories in a way that helps you to
understand: (a) the individual parts of your being, analysing yourself and
your 'personality vehicles' in a way that leads to personal growth; and
(b) your being as a single entity, the 'whole you', synthesizing your
understanding into a dynamic picture of the total Self.

The following sections are a series of unfolding suggestions about
ways of looking at Kabbalistic development and understanding aimed at
aiding both your theoretical and practical work with the Kabbalah.

It is an essential task to build up a 'mental image', 'imaginative image' or 'thought-form' of the structural map we call the Tree of Life. You will already have been practising this and by now will probably be quite efficient at holding an image of the Tree in your consciousness. If you already have such an image, use the following suggestions to clearly formulate your Tree in its component parts. If you do not yet have a clear image of the Tree in your consciousness, use these instructions to help you gain one.

Practise being able to form a clear mental picture of the whole Tree in skeletal form. Once this is accomplished, practise filling in the spheres and paths with appropriate sets of correspondences. The colours are a useful set of attributes with which to commence. Once you are holding an image of the Tree in your mind, try 'painting' with your imagination the appropriate colours for the spheres, starting with white for Kether, through to sky blue for Malkuth. Then fill in the paths.

Remember that you do not have to become fully proficient at one set of correspondences before you start practising with others. Allow your work on this to be fluid in nature and try wherever possible to add correspondences to the spheres and paths that you learn from *your own experience*.

Once a clear Tree is held in the mind's eye, so to speak, you can then practise at 'focusing in' on any particular section of the Tree, perhaps one particular plane, pillar, one triad, sphere or path on its own. Study and experience how this is connected to other spheres and its relationship to the whole Tree. Only through practice and by applying your personal experiences to the map, will the image grow within you. As it does grow you will be amazed at the speed with which your understanding of the Kabbalah increases. Also, hand in hand with this, you will find a corresponding increase in your overall knowledge and understanding.

THE MAGICKAL AND MYSTICAL USES OF THE KABBALAH

Magick is causing change to occur, in line with the will or intention of the magician. Mysticism is involved with the attainment of altered states of consciousness, usually through rising above the material planes. In one sense, magick can be described as growth through immanence, and mysticism can be described as growth through transcendence. Both ways can be related to the Tree of Life, which encompasses all possibilities. In a later section we will compare and contrast magick and mysticism, but the basis of both, in terms of the Kabbalah, is to make contact with our own inner world and/or the outer world (which to a magician exists because of his will, whilst to a mystic it exists despite his will).

In the previous section you learned the importance of building up an image of the Tree in your awareness. Techniques were suggested for heightening and improving this image. Once the image is firmly rooted in consciousness, you can then work with the Tree as a whole or focus in on any particular sphere or path as appropriate to your magickal or mystical needs.

In a later section of this chapter we will look at symbols and correspondences as used by the magician (and to a lesser degree by the mystic) but for now it is stressed that the more you live with and integrate the image of the Tree into your consciousness, the more effective your work will be, whatever your purpose in undertaking this training.

THE INNER DIALOGUE

If we stop what we are doing for a few moments and simply listen to what is happening inside, we discover that a lot of the time we are having an inner dialogue with ourselves. 'Should I do what he suggests now, or should I do it later . . . what's for tea anyway . . . look, listen, concentrate on this, it's important . . . I wonder if Mike will phone? . . .' and so on. We create our own reality by keeping a dialogue going with ourselves about our world and what we perceive or imagine is happening. This is not necessarily a bad thing because it helps keep us grounded and able to relate to other people and the world in general. The problem is when we get caught up with this inner dialogue and forget there is anything else. If we learn to turn off the inner dialogue we can reach a place of silence, Tiphareth, in which we contact our *real* inner power and purpose. We reach the real world behind images, thoughts, fantasies, feelings, sensations and so on.

There are many ways of doing this, and it appears as the central theme in many practical teachings. For a shaman, there is no more important goal than turning off the inner dialogue, for when this is achieved everything else becomes possible. In the Western Mystery Tradition, a similar aim is described as one-pointedness. It is claimed that any thought which is held in this state of silence becomes a definite command since there are no other thoughts to compete with it.

In Yoga, there are various practices which also lead to the same goal, all with the single aim of achieving dhyana – which is turning off the inner dialogue, reaching a still, silent place within. Dhyana is the original root of the word zen, and the main aim of zen meditation is the same – to stop the rational mind and reach states beyond the incessant questioning, thinking and reasoning which holds us back from our inner peace and true identity. In Taoism the aim is the same. The Tao is said to resemble the emptiness of space; to employ it we must avoid creating an inner dialogue, which we can do through 'making our sharpness blunt'. Learning to 'turn off your inner dialogue' is an essential requirement for successful magickal practice.

CONTACT WITH 'EXTRA-DIMENSIONAL' BEINGS

All cultures throughout our planet's history have described beings and creatures that exist in other realities or dimensions in parallel with and sometimes interpenetrating our world. In the view of some mainstream psychologists, these 'extra-dimensional' beings are the impersonal forces of nature which we personalize so we can attempt to gain control over them. According to some more farsighted psychologists and those aware of the work of the new physics, however, these beings are representational of real forces. Looked at superficially our world is composed of atoms and molecules which arrange themselves to create the different life-forms we directly perceive. If we examine this basic atomic reality under an electron microscope, we enter the world of sub-atomic particles. This is a level of existence where different laws apply, but it is no less real simply because we cannot see it on a mundane level. The same applies to the 'levels of existence' which we cannot perceive with our usual senses but which are, despite this, no less real.

As our work with the Kabbalah progresses we start to meet 'other beings'. You have already had several such experiences in your visualizations and rituals throughout this course. Your 'guardian angel' is such a being, of course. At first sight, talking of meeting 'extra-dimensional beings' may appear strange, even ridiculous, until we consider their nature. Any being or entity outside of ourselves can be considered this way, including other human beings. Whether these 'beings' actually exist outside or whether they are figments of our imagination, projections, or parts of us that we do not recognize as being part of us, we all have the experience that they exist.

All the beings that inhabit our world, including animals, plants and all living and so-called non-living things, are apparently outside of us and we meet with them primarily in Malkuth. At a deeper level we meet 'astral' entities that inhabit the lower spheres on the Tree of Life. These 'astral beings' include those we meet in dreams, astral projections, fantasies, visualization, and include all symbols and thought-forms. Tiphareth, whilst primarily associated with our own essential selves, is also the sphere for contact with our guardian angels. Whether these angels exist outside of us matters little in practical terms; when we contact Tiphareth we find such beings in attendance. Then on even deeper levels of the Tree of Life we may 'contact' Archangels and, if we reach the Supernal Triad, we may have contact with the Deity or some aspect of it. (And, of course, the 'Deity' is within everything anyway.)

Daath is the unnumbered sphere that resides in the Abyss between the Supernal Triad and the lower spheres of the Tree of Life. It is said to be the access point to the reverse side of the Tree where all the demons that bring 'dis-ease' into our lives exist. Again whether these 'demons' merely represent aspects of our own shadow nature and inhabit the dark recesses of our being, or whether they are actual entities with a life of their own is an irrelevant issue. We can communicate with them and affect our relationship with them as if they are real.

The question arises why would anyone want to make contact with astral entities, Archangels or any other 'being' of this type, particularly demons! If we are to be whole, to include rather than exclude all our energies, one way of achieving this is through making contact with all the forces within our universe. We are usually quite willing to include the 'good guys' – if I suggest you talk to your guardian angel you would probably have little resistance (assuming you believed it possible). On the other hand, once we discuss communicating with demons we are entering the realm of the shadow which includes those parts of ourselves that we would rather not face.

Any aspect of our being and our energy that we exclude from our awareness becomes part of our shadow, which has been usefully described as being like a big bag we drag round behind us. The more shadow we have, the more we are excluding, the heavier our bag becomes and the more it restricts our free movement. Conversely, the more material from this 'shadow bag' we can dredge out, face, deal with, and integrate into our conscious being, the lighter the bag becomes and the more energy we have available to fulfil our life functions, from the loftiest sense of Divine Purpose through to the everyday functions that help us survive in the world.

plant communication

Follow the usual starting procedure.

Choose a plant that you know and love, a plant you look after in normal circumstances (or if outdoors, choose a plant that attracts you and for which you feel an affinity).

Focus your awareness on the plant. Look at the plant, try to be totally aware of the plant as a living being.

Be aware that the plant can communicate with you, that it has a consciousness (although it is very different from yours). Ask the plant if it has anything it would like to tell you or teach you.

Listen carefully and quietly for the answer. The answer can come in a number of forms – as words or pictures inside your mind, as a feeling or a sensation. Really listen to the plant and what it has to communicate.

You can engage in dialogue with the plant if you wish.

When you are ready, thank the plant for what you have learned. Affirm that you will attend to its needs.

Return to normal consciousness.

THE TWO WAYS OF MAGICK AND MYSTICISM

The mystic's intention is to rise up the Tree, to transcend the realm of the actual and merge with the realm of the potential – attaining 'cosmic union', becoming 'one with God', achieving Samadhi. The keywords associated with mysticism are universality and transcendence.

The magician's intention, on the other hand, is to draw down the energies of the realm of the potential into the realm of the actual, changing the latter – transforming it in accordance with Will. The keywords associated with magick are individuality and immanence.

Both the mystic and the magician, in their different ways, have to deal with the realm of the actual, where both personal and interpersonal conflicts exist. In dealing with the actual world the mystic experiences the crisis of duality, realizing his 'stuckness' in the realm of the actual and his separation from the Supernals, the world of potential. He wishes to overcome this duality and realize everything, including himself, as one. The magician in dealing with the actual world experiences the existential crisis, realizing that the world of the actual is not as he desires or wills it to be and realizing the difficulties in manifesting his Will. He wishes to overcome this crisis of existence by overcoming resistance to change, by creating a new world in which his Will is manifest.

It is important to realize the necessity of both ways. The mystic who denies the world of the actual, and thereby magic, is limited. He might transcend this world, but then the question can be asked, what was the point of being here in the first place? The magician who works his Will on the realm of the actual but who does not connect with the higher or deeper realms will not be aligned with the universal and Spiritual Will, and will therefore be working against the currents of evolution. Without connecting to the 'higher' Self, his work is shallow and empty, and ultimately he is doing no more than 'building castles in the air'. The mystic needs to come to terms with the actual world and deal with his personality; the magician needs to connect to the potential world and align himself with the totality of the Self.

freedom in movement

Follow the usual starting procedure.

Stand up straight, put your right arm out in front of you.
   Now move this arm to your side and put your left arm over your head, raising your right foot.
   Lower your foot and stamp on the ground three times.
   Turn around in an anti-clockwise circle twice, then sit down and put your hands on your head.
   Stand up and repeat the whole set of instructions again before continuing.
   Now move around your room in any way you wish – using your arms, legs and whole body to create shapes and patterns that feel good to you and that you wish to make.
   Continue moving freely for several minutes before continuing.
   What is the difference for you in moving to instructions and choosing to move as you wish?
   With which do you feel more comfortable?

In making the choice of how to move you have to own your own personal power; in following instructions (blindly at least) you relinquish your responsibility.

It is important to choose clearly what your Will is, whether you are following the mystical or the magickal path. The problem comes in finding out what you *really* want to do – to be able to choose from your centre rather than from some identified or attached part of your personality. What your feelings want to do and what your thoughts tell you to do might be very different things, and often are. But what you learn from Tiphareth that you 'need' to do is always valid for your growth and development. The more clearly you make *your own* choices from Tiphareth, the more you can manifest energy and change energy (that is, 'do' magick), and/or choose to experience the higher levels of consciousness in unconflicting purity (that is, 'be' a mystic).

the temple of quality

Follow the usual starting procedure.

Be in your meadow, a place which should be familiar to you by now.
Take some time to experience the place, use your senses to be fully there, in a meadow full of scents, sounds, sights, taste and touch.
Feel the ground under your feet as you walk around your meadow.
  Walk towards a nearby hill and, taking your time appreciating the scenes around you, make your way up to the top of the hill.
  At the top of the hill you will find a 'Temple of Quality', alive with soul energies such as Love, Truth, Beauty or Joy.
  Find the Temple and pay attention to its shape, form, size, colour, position and so on. Really get a clear picture of this Temple.
  You may now enter the Temple. As you do so, feel the energies it represents wash over you, fill you, heal you …
  When you feel ready return to the meadow, taking with you the energy of the Temple of Quality.
  How will you manifest this energy in the everyday world?

The mystic is basically involved with 'going up' to the Temple to have the experience; the magician is involved with bringing the energy 'back down' to manifest it in the everyday world. This exercise should show you the necessity for both, and will indicate (by which aspect you are easier with) which type you tend to be, and therefore, by implication, what you need to develop.

THE DEVELOPMENT OF THE MAGICIAN AND THE ATTAINMENT OF THE MYSTIC

Choose which of the following exercises seem most appropriate to you, remembering the basic principle of growth – that you need to refine that which you already have, and elevate that which you lack.

magician and mystic

exercise 1

Visualize a wand and a cup. Get a clear picture of both in your mind's eye, then draw them.

Visualize holding the wand in your right hand, the cup in your left. Let a stream of bright white light come down through your head, through your arms and into each of the Weapons you hold.

How do they change?

exercise 2

Visualize a sword, getting a clear image of all the parts that make it up. Go to your meadow with the sword and take it to the top of the hill. Hold it up to the sky and let a beam of sunlight strike it.

Bring the sword back to the meadow in its new transformed, enlightened state.

What difficulties did you experience? Were your problems associated more with going up or coming back down?

exercise 3

Create a talisman for a chosen purpose (any purpose at all, however large or small).

Visualize this talisman on a hill at the opposite side of a valley. There is a perfectly straight road leading from you to the talisman, through the valley and up the hill. Travel this road, noting any obstructions, diversions and so on, but not stopping or being distracted.

Reach the talisman and, holding it, let its energy fill you up.

Repeat this visualization several times over a period of at least two weeks for any chosen intention.

What effects does this have? Is your Will fulfilled?

exercise 4

This is called doing 'live-a-days'. Live one day as totally as possible with the mystic's way of seeing the world, as if you are a mystic through and through and not at all interested or involved in anything else.

Then on another occasion do the same with the magician's way of seeing the world.

Then with neither.

Then with both.

Try to create settings that fit with your 'live-a-day'. If you are 'being' a magician, do appropriate things, go to likely places, and so on.

How is it? Which do you feel most comfortable with? What do you need to elevate and refine?

Could you live permanently in the world of *both*?

MORE ON THE MAGICKAL LINK

Before continuing, re-read the section in Chapter 9 on the magickal link. The importance of understanding how to create magickal links cannot be overemphasized and you are well advised to ensure you fully understand this, especially on a practical level, if you wish to be a successful Kabbalist.

USE OF MAGICKAL SYMBOLISM AND CORRESPONDENCES

You have already been using the symbolism of correspondences in exercises throughout this book. You have learned that you can assign various animals, plants, Tarot cards, colours, parts of the body, diseases, and so on both to the Sephiroth and to the paths. The Tree is particularly useful as a map to which one can assign symbols because its form lets things be seen in relation to each other, thus causing them to throw light on each other. It may have been thought there was some arbitrary association of various symbols to the Tree of Life but this is not so: they are based upon the direct, practical experience of many magicians, mystics, poets and seers who, by the creative use of their imagination, have penetrated deeply into the secret causes and springs of being, and the identity of all correspondences and associations.

As an example, a plant may correspond with a certain path because of its traditional association with certain gods and goddesses (for example, corn with Ceres), because of the doctrine of signatures whereby plants are assigned to various planets, or because of the research and experimentation of many different investigators through the ages. This is basically true of all correspondences and they should be seen in this light. At the same time, however, it is worth noting again that no correspondence is absolutely certain for any particular individual, so if you find that some other correspondence works better for you then do use that one instead.

You have already been using imagery work in this book and are acquainted with many symbols associated with the Kabbalah.

Images and symbols can be seen as both *transformers* and *accumulators* of psychic energy.

Each individual on the planet has his or her own personal set of symbols. There are also collective symbols, Archetypal symbols and universal symbols (see diagram below). Where would you assign these various kinds of symbols on the Tree?

Imagery is the using of symbols in a form that aids both our reception and understanding of the real, inner meaning of the symbols involved, on whatever level they exist. Imagery can be spontaneous (as in day-dreams, dreams and so on), or guided/structured (as in many of the exercises herein). Imagery can also be long or short, depending upon the nature of the work being done. Some exercises need long, involved

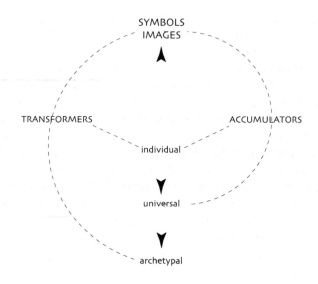

sets whereas others, sometimes called 'short takes', only require momentarily entering the world of imagery.

Imagery is useful:

- to expand awareness, by bringing more information into consciousness and balancing awareness through symbol projection. The general formula is: expand, integrate, expand, integrate, and so on; in other words as you expand your awareness it is important to integrate the new material into the existing body of knowledge and understanding.
- for reliving past experiences (peaks, traumas, and also past lives). Apart from ecstatic reunion or cathartic release, this also gives you the opportunity to replace old patterns with new patterns of experience.
- to 'get to' parts of the body (for example, to cure illness or disease) – see the exercise below.
- for the resolution of conflicts (at least on a symbolic level).
- for transformation and transmutation.

the transformation of disease

Follow the usual starting procedure.

Sitting still, get in touch with the world of sensation in your body. Pay attention to your whole body, becoming aware of disturbed or uncomfortable areas.

Concentrate on the uneasy area and let an image emerge to represent the disturbance. Then transform the image (for example, if it was a house on fire, imagine a fire engine arriving and putting the fire out; then include redecorating the house back to exactly as you want it).

Project the transformed image back to the originally disturbed area.

Alternatively you could imagine yourself becoming very small and visiting the disturbed area to 'do repairs'.

THE ESSENCE OF SYMBOLS

It is essential not to become attached to the form of a symbol, but rather delve into its very essence to find its true inner meaning. Ways of doing this include:

1. Objective consideration of the form and surface of the symbol.

2. Emotional experience of the symbol, including the effects, flavour, sound and so on of the symbol. Try to grasp the quality behind the form.

3. Penetration to the meaning – asking 'what does the symbol teach me?'

4. Grasping the totality of the symbol, its true inner purpose (which may well be abstract and/or formless).

5. Identification with the symbol, again to get its quality and purpose.

You can allow a symbol to emerge in your consciousness or choose to create a specific symbol, but in either case it can then be used to create a new line of force between you and what the symbol represents. It can also unify your knowledge into understanding.

THE POWER OF THE WILL

You have been learning much about the power of the Will and it is timely now to reiterate the principle of all energy work: *as you sow, so shall you reap*. If you use your Will for positive ends and for growth, you will grow; if you use it for negative ends and for repression, you will be repressed. It is as simple as that.

It is worth reviewing where your weaknesses are in this area and using the following techniques to improve your dynamic harmony.

Strengthening the Will

1. Will power/Strong Will:

    (a) realizing the value of the Will. Be aware of how much the Will can do both for yourself and others

(b) evoking feelings towards the Will (perhaps through reading of suitable passages from Will-orientated books)

(c) 'useless' exercises

(d) physical exercise

(e) through daily life (for example, rising earlier)

2. Skilful Will:

(a) general personality work

(b) centring work, contacting Tiphareth

(c) acting as if

3. Goodwill:

(a) never harming another being, always taking others into consideration, helping others when you can without interfering (and doing this because you *want* to, not because you think you should).

4. Spiritual Will:

(a) meditation

(b) all connections you make to your True Will or purpose

the helmsman

Follow the usual starting procedure.

Visualize yourself as being on a ship on the open sea. You are the helmsman at the wheel of this ship. As vividly as possible experience being in control of the ship as you sail on the open seas. The ship is at your command.

Realize this ship is you.

ENERGY EXCHANGE AND THE STORING OF PERSONAL POWER

We sustain our lives through energy, both the energy we derive from our intake of oxygen, foodstuffs and so on, and that derived from more 'ethereal' realms. With an excess or lack of either type, life is altered, either in a depressing or exciting way.

Our left side (corresponding to the right brain) is usually associated with the more feeling-orientated, personally creative manifestations of energy, and our right side with the more deliberate, thought-induced, verbal manifestations. Left is irrational, right is rational. There are extremes of both: the far left is *impulsive*, its Will being to discharge any available energy as quickly as possible; the far right is *compulsive*, its Will being to allow discharge of energy only through rigid patterns of behaviour. What we wish to achieve is a state that is neither compulsive nor impulsive but a balance that includes both.

You create your own environment by how effectively you exchange your energy with the world around you. As you take in energy, any excess can be stored as personal power, but this energy must be discharged when appropriate. It is important that you use your Will and Love energies in an effective way. Hopefully, by following the course of development presented throughout this book, you are now able to do so more effectively.

ORIGINAL RESEARCH AND EXPERIENCE

Whether you 'favour' the mystical or magickal path, as a Kabbalist your task is to use your knowledge and understanding of the Tree of Life to create the right set and setting for your continued growth. Your 'set' is all that makes you up internally; you have to believe in yourself as an Adept and exercise your powers of both Will and Love. Your 'setting' is your environment which you must create as a reflection of your inner world.

Continue with your research and practices with the Kabbalah to help create an experience of life, both in its inner and outer aspect, that fits your purpose for incarnation. Beyond that there is nothing more you can do, for your purpose is ultimately no more nor less than the totality of your existence. Fulfil your purpose and you are fulfilled; ignore or negate your purpose and you are forever lost in a world of illusion and attachment.

CHAPTER 13

THE TAROT AND THE KABBALAH

INTRODUCTION TO DIVINATION

Divination in its widest sense is described as the art of obtaining information about the unknown or the future. In a more restricted sense, divination is using a set of symbols, such as those of the Tarot or the I Ching, to help discover where one is in one's life and where one wants to go. In divination the answers to questions are not usually conveyed directly but through these symbols, which have to be interpreted by the diviner in terms of the problem, whether it be his or her own problem (divination for oneself) or the problem of another (divination for someone else). Divination helps you have an understanding of the past, the present situation and the potential future(s). It helps you find out where you are (here and now), and only by knowing this can you really choose where it is you want to go and how you may get there.

The best-known methods of divination are astrology, geomancy, the Tarot, the Kabbalah itself and the I Ching. There are many other methods. All of them, at least potentially, may be assigned to the Tree of Life, and by so doing one may understand the divination techniques better. For example, the understanding of the Yetziratic attributions to the Tree is an aid to understanding astrological symbols; the correspondences between the trigrams of the I Ching and the spheres on the Tree throw much light on their meaning.

In any system of divination each symbol stands for a specific idea. Combinations of symbols then allow complex interpretations by the diviner, relating the interpretation specifically to the question at hand. Whether there are 'intelligences' or 'spirits' that guide the diviner or whether the intuitive processes used connect to the diviner's unconscious in some way, is not provable. What is certain, however, is that divination works.

THE KABBALAH AND DIVINATION TECHNIQUES

Particles are not isolated grains of matter but
are probability patterns, inter-connections in
an inseparable cosmic web

KAPRA

This quote from a modern physicist, sums up very well the rationale for divination. We are all connected, and it is this interconnectedness that allows divination techniques to be effectively used. The essential components of a successful divination are a knowledge of the symbols being employed and the ability to 'read' intuitive messages. The Kabbalah, based as it is upon pure number, evidently possesses an infinite number of symbols and connections between symbols. It has been said that its scope is as large as the whole of existence itself and it lacks nothing in precision or purity. Thus it is a vital aid to divination. Knowledge of the Kabbalah helps in an understanding of symbols and through Kabbalistic work the Adept builds a stronger and closer connection with the soul (Tiphareth), thus enabling intuition to be more readily accessed. Thus in a twofold manner the Kabbalah and the Tree of Life assist in the divination process.

THE KABBALAH AND THE TAROT

There are 78 cards in a full Tarot pack, four suits of ten cards each: called the minor arcana or 'small cards', 16 court cards in four suits of four cards each and the 22 major cards, the 'Atus' or trumps.

The basis of both the Kabbalah and the Tarot is interwoven, at least theoretically. The 78 cards of the Tarot may be assigned to the spheres and paths on the Tree in a very straightforward and easy to understand manner. If you are not familiar with the Tarot correspondences, look at the appropriate columns in the correspondence tables before going any further. The Kabbalah helps the diviner to develop a living, experiential relationship with all the cards in the Tarot and thus be able to use them more effectively.

The 22 paths admirably support the 22 trumps of the Tarot, and although different authorities do not necessarily agree on the attribution of every card to its path, overall most people find that the experience of the cards does connect with the experience of the particular path in question. Remembering that the paths represent subjective experiences,

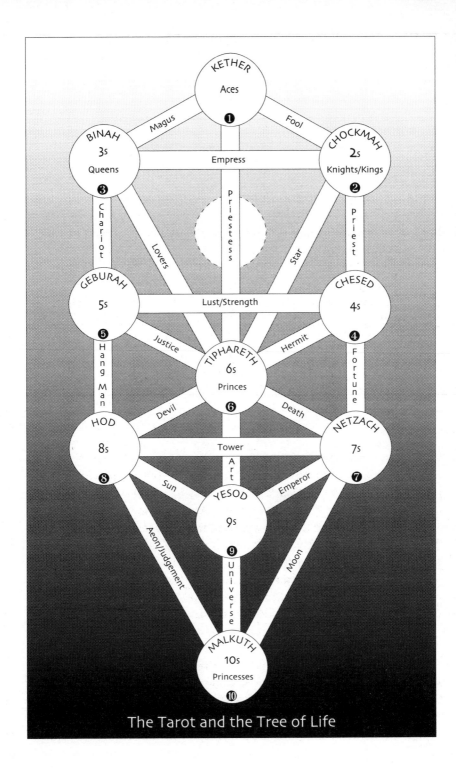

The Tarot and the Tree of Life

it is not surprising there is not total agreement. You will find, however, as you become more familiar with the trumps of the Tarot, that the connections they make between spheres on the Tree will be self-evident.

The ten spheres of the Tree are also ideally suited for the attribution of the 'minor cards' of the Tarot, which, numbered 1 to 10, exactly correspond with the spheres. There are four suits, one for each of the Kabbalistic worlds – so the whole scheme of the Tree is represented.

The court cards of the Tarot do not initially appear to fit on to the Tree so easily, until we consider one Tree divided into the four Worlds. Then we find that they fit admirably: the Knights to Atziluth, Queens to Briah, Princes to Yetzirah and the Princesses to Assiah. The perfection of the attribution is quite staggering.

The four suits of the Tarot, called *Wands, Cups, Swords, Discs* or *Pentacles* correspond to the four elements thus:

wands	fire	creative, 'male' energy; will
cups	water	receptive, 'female' energy; love
swords	air	the mind; intellect; formative energy
discs	earth	material manifestation of energy.

So, for example, the four 4s of the Tarot represent the fiery, watery, airy and earthy part of Chesed (or Love). To put it another way the 4 of wands is the creative aspect of Chesed, the 4 of cups its receptive aspect, the 4 of swords its intellectual or formative aspect and 4 of discs its material aspect.

The ace or 1 of each suit is the pure form of that energy or element, so, for example, the ace of wands is pure creative energy. Each card then represents a progressive degradation of this energy until the 10 which is its most material form. This is a move, in one sense, from the 'ideal' form of energy to its 'actual' form. The 6 then represents its ideal manifestation, the 9 its material foundation and the 10 its complete manifestation which also includes the seed of decay into the next suit.

The court cards also correspond to the four elements: Knights to fire, Queens to water, Princes to air and Princesses to earth. So the court cards of each suit possess a double elemental attribution: for example, the Knight of wands is the fiery part of fire, the Queen of Wands is the watery part of fire, the Prince of Wands is the airy part of fire and the Princess of wands is its earthy form. This holds true for all the court cards. So, for example, the Knight of wands is very creative energy (fire of fire), whilst the Princess of wands is the material manifestation of creativity (earth of fire).

Work out these attributions for all the court cards before continuing.

THE ESSENCE OF THE TAROT

Tarot actually means principle, law or essence. It is equivalent to the word 'tattva' in Sanskrit. Tarot was originally *Ta-Urt*, named thus in Egypt after the goddess Ta-Urt who, sometimes represented by a hippo or 'beast of the waters' (and space), was known as 'The Mother of Revolutions'. Her being incorporated all concepts of the cycles of time, repetition, cyclical return, periodic law and also the 'light in the night' of eternity. She was, as the mother of darkness, the originator of the *living* unconscious.

The Tarot cards, as the essence of the Tarot system, incorporate all these ideas.

So we can say that Taro(t) represents a 'wheeling essence'. If we turn the letters of Taro around we find *Rota*, which is the 'essential wheel', and *Tora* which is the 'essential law'. The *Tarot* of something is its essence, its innermost nature, its principle, the law of its being. In this sense everything has its Tarot within it and the pack of cards of the well-known Tarot are representations of this essence in its various manifestations.

The God allied to the Tarot is Thoth, sometimes seen as the son of Ta-Urt, who as the Lord of Communication, communicates the essence of the Tarot through his *Atus* (that is, the 'major arcana' of the Tarot), which are able, through their connection with the essence of life itself, to take you into and/or out of, and/or beyond the wheel (or life or 'fortune') *at will*.

The court cards are then representations of how different types of people interact with the wheel. These types loosely correspond to the 'types' created by the manifestation of the Seven rays (see Chapter 10). We have all the 'types' within us (thus all the court cards) but some predominate and it is with these predominant 'types' we are usually associated.

The small cards of the Tarot then become representations of the energy of the wheel itself, analysed (into 40 components) so they may be synthesized.

It is useful to imagine the 78 Tarot cards as different people who one wishes to get to know. Imagine you are at a gathering, a party say, of 78 people. You may know some of them very well, a few of them a little bit and most of them hardly, if at all. Really to use the Tarot effectively you have to get to know them all well. Just as at a party you mingle with these guests, meeting them in a fluid, interactive way, so this is the best way to get to know the Tarot cards. As they 'emerge' for you, spend time getting to know them. It has been said, 'the diviner must live with them – and them with him', emphasizing that you should treat them with the same respect (and affection) you would give to someone with whom you share your home.

There are many ways you can get to know the cards and we shall be describing some of these ways throughout this chapter. As you get to know the cards, so you also learn a lot more and experience a lot more, of the corresponding sphere or path on the Tree. Thus the value of such an investigation to the Kabbalist. Perhaps the best way to get to know the cards is through divination, particularly for oneself. Also useful is meditation on each card, and visualization, using the card image as a starting point for the astral investigation involved.

After meditation, visualization or divination, the *grounding* involved in writing up in your diary what has happened is also helpful in getting to know the Tarot cards.

You could also create your own pack, based upon the relationship between each of the spheres, as you understand and experience it. This may sound like a complex, difficult undertaking – which it most certainly is – but the effort would be well rewarded. Even the simplest self-produced Tarot pack is a very effective magickal tool for growth, development and the exploration of consciousness.

getting to know the cards

For this exercise choose any one card from the Tarot trumps (you may want to repeat the exercise at other times for all the 22 trumps).

Follow the usual starting procedure.

Meditate upon your chosen card. Do this through identifying with the character of the card, starting by saying: 'I am the (name of card you have chosen), I …' and let yourself speak *as if* you are that card. Describe yourself in full, in terms of your physical appearance, feelings, thoughts, anything that comes up.

When you feel you have nothing more to say, *keep it up* for a further few minutes.

What Quality does your card represent? Find the answer to this question so that you can express it in one word or a short phrase.

Positively identify with that Quality. Say clearly and distinctly: 'I am … (love, truth, the beauty of light or whatever your Quality is as that card).'

Find ways to express that Quality. Firstly take up the posture of the card as it represents its Quality. What posture is it? Actually take up this posture, then allow yourself to move or dance in a way that expresses the card and its Quality.

What feelings and thoughts do you have as this card?

What is the sound associated with this card? Make that sound.

Try to express as many of these attributes (movement, posture, sound, thoughts, feelings, and so on) as you can in one living expression of the card *here and now*.

Replace the card in the pack. Look at the pack and say: 'Each individual card is whole in itself ... each whole card synthesizes with other cards to create one dynamic wheel of life.'

Find at least one way to express the energy of your chosen card in your daily life.

THE CONSCIOUSNESS AND PREPARATION OF THE DIVINER

The process of divination may be summarized under three headings:

Provision

Preparation

Procedure

Provision is having everything ready before commencing a divination. This includes the cards themselves, incense, a notebook and so on; any preparatory rituals, such as a banishing ritual, and all the study and experience the diviner has previously had with the Tarot.

The *Preparation* is that of the diviner him- or herself. Essential requisites of this preparation are:

| Dis-attachment | — | the diviner must not be attached to any 'sub-personality' or unbalanced part of the personality, but rather needs: |
| Self-identification | — | being in contact with the personal self, dis-attached from, but 'in tune' with the body, feelings and mind, and able to contact the inner wisdom of the self, which is: |

Intuition	—	the ability to 'see' the 'message' or 'plan' presented by the cards in a clear way, through the eyes of the self, in touch with the inner knowledge and connection of intuition; this allows:
Sense of rightness	—	'knowing', 'feeling' or 'sensing' the intuition without bias, which includes :
Making clear all fantasies	—	being aware of the inevitable residue of bias and identification in the diviner and being willing to declare this aspect of the reading in an honest way; this should lead to:
No personal preference	—	whereby the diviner, through clear distinction between what is 'seen' in the cards and what is 'fantasized' to be there, is able to give a reading which is truly 'in tune' with the meaning and message of the symbols involved.

The *Procedure* is the divination itself, which is dealt with later.

All of the above necessities for the diviner may be achieved through the exercises presented throughout this book for the growth of the Adept.

Particularly important is the ability to both dis-identify and self-identify, both procedures being thoroughly presented (see Chapter 7). Please refer to the appropriate section if you are not familiar with these techniques.

Finally it is worth mentioning that the 'wise old person' is a valuable source of guidance to the Adept who is using divination and should be frequently consulted for advice and assistance on this subject.

DIVINATION AND THE TAROT
(PRACTICAL)

After the provision and preparation comes the actual *procedure* for using the Tarot cards for divination. Divination allows an awareness of the past and the present situation, and gives insight into the potential future(s). In other words, it helps you find out where you are *here and now*, and only by knowing this can you really *choose* where you want to go.

divination and the Tarot

Follow the usual starting procedure.

Take the full Tarot pack in your left hand and hold your right hand over the cards.
    Imagine a bright white light over your head, entering you and passing through your hands into the cards.
    The following invocation (or a similar one) may be used, or simply take a few moments silent contemplation.

> *I invoke thee, IAO (pronounced 'ee-ah-oh') that thou wilt send HRU (pronounced 'heru'), the great angel that is set over the operations of this secret wisdom, to lay his hands invisibly upon these consecrated cards of art, that thereby we may obtain true knowledge of hidden things, to the glory of thine ineffable name. Amen.*

If divining for another person: Hand the cards to the querent and have him or her shuffle them whilst either (a) attending to the present position, process or growth (for a general reading); or (b) a particular question. In the case of (b) it is better for you not to know this question unless he or she chooses to tell you, and then preferably at the end of the divination before card 11 is revealed.
    If divining for yourself: follow the process as above but obviously shuffle the cards yourself.
    Instruct the querent to lay the cards out as shown in the diagram overleaf (or do so yourself). This is done as follows:

> Put pack face down in 1st place. Split into three packs (1st, 2nd, 3rd). From 1st pack make 4th and 5th packs. From 2nd pack make 6th and 7th. From 3rd make 8th, 9th, then 10th. Finally from 2nd pack move some up to make the 11th pack.

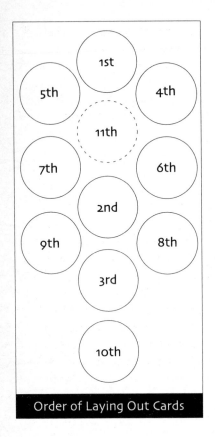

Order of Laying Out Cards

Interpreting the Cards

The diviner next turns over the top card of each pack *except the 11th, which remains face down until the end.*

The divination may now be revealed.

Look at each card in turn, commencing at number 10 and moving up to 1.

Look for relationships and conflicts between cards (particularly 6th and 7th, and 8th and 9th).

Look for any 'bigger pictures' unfolding. Ideally a whole 'picture' or 'story' should emerge from the individual parts.

Use your intuition throughout. If you want to concentrate on any one card more than the rest then do so; if the whole picture is clear then concentrate on that.

Finally, when you (and the querent if there is one) are ready, turn over the 11th card which represents the Next Step. Spend time with this, drawing out from the querent (or investigating in yourself) how this card is understood and, most importantly, how this energy can be earthed or grounded. (If further clarification is required on the next step the cards under the 11th may also be revealed, which then represent aspects of the top card.)

When you are finished conclude the reading by placing the cards back in their container. They should not be used again for a period of time, say around two hours.

The diagram opposite, right, shows you how to interpret each sphere as it is represented by a card in the divination process. As you will see, this follows the usual attributions of the spheres.

Note on Reversals: Some authorities on the Tarot use a method of reversals where upside-down cards are deliberately read in a 'negative' way. This is a poor practice with little to recommend it. All the cards have positive and negative components and it is for the diviner to reveal these through his or her intuition and through knowledge of the card and its relationship with those cards connected to it. Therefore it is recommended that cards should be kept upright and read that way. However, if great care is taken to keep all the cards upright and a reversed card does appear, this can then be taken to mean that that particular force is currently *very* forefront and 'asking' for attention. If more than half of the cards in a layout are reversed, stop the reading and do a banishing ritual over the cards before continuing.

---

card awareness techniques

1. Follow the usual starting procedure.

Choose a card.

Sit holding the card before you. Be as relaxed as possible in your body, feelings and thoughts. Don't try to interpret the card, just look at it.

Notice the lines within the card without thinking about the objects they depict.

Notice the colours. Look at each colour in turn. What is the pattern produced by each colour? How much red is there? How much green? ... and blue? What about black? ... and white?

Look at the outlines of the main features – observe any patterns they form.

Is the card three-dimensional?
Look at the different planes:
  the foreground
  the midground
  the background
Look at the empty spaces – do they form a pattern too?
Consider the light and shadow.
Is there texture in this card?
Now, last of all, look at what is depicted by the card … and realize
this is where we usually start and become fixed.

2. Follow the usual starting procedure.

Choose a card
Look at the card without judging it or trying to interpret it.
Be aware of the foreground and background inside the card.
Be aware of what is 'figure' and 'ground' inside you.
See this card as a unique thing.
Look at the parts; what makes it up?
What is intentional or unintentional about it?
How do you feel looking at it?
What does it make you think about?
What is the card about for you?
Finally, turn the card upside down and look at it that way!

CHAPTER 14

RITUAL AND THE KABBALAH

THE MEANING OF RITUAL

In this chapter we will apply the basic principles of the Kabbalah to the meaning and use of ritual. To do this we need a common ground regarding the meaning of ritual.

Rituals may be classified into two kinds: personal/individual rituals and collective/group rituals. It is easy to see how group ritual contains individual ritual, through the group itself being composed of individual participants. It is perhaps not so easy to see how individual ritual contains group ritual, but this is in fact the case. The individual includes within him- or herself the 'inner group' which is composed of sub-personalities or parts of the personality. Just as a group performing rituals must be in harmony for the ritual to work effectively, so this equally applies to the 'inner group' of sub-personalities.

There is a need for both individual and group ritual, one being dependent upon the existence of the other just as a star (the individual) is dependent upon the galaxy (group) and vice versa.

Individual harmony may be achieved through ritual, of which growth work may be considered an essential part. The inner work necessary to this process of growth is the 'ordering' of the personality round a 'synthesizing centre' or 'I'. This allows and aids the inflow of transpersonal energies (qualities) into the person. This is magically called the 'Uniting of the Microcosm with the Macrocosm'.

Everything said in the previous paragraph may be also applied to group ritual. It must be understood however that the 'synthesizing centre' or 'I' of a group does not need to be any particular group participant or leader. Indeed it is the power of such leadership that so often leads to the corruption inherent in the organizations formed by various Eastern gurus and Western masters. The 'synthesizing centre' of a group should rather be its *common purpose*, centred upon a symbol, object or belief that clearly enshrines and depicts this common purpose. Whilst a person can be such a 'symbol', the dangers of this are all too apparent.

THE UNITING OF MICROCOSM WITH MACROCOSM

The *purpose* of all ritual is the uniting of the microcosm with the macro-cosm. This can be related, in magickal terms, to the invocation and consequent knowledge of and conversation with the Holy Guardian Angel. In mystical terms it is identical to the achievement of Samadhi (meaning 'together with' or 'union with God'). The Holy Guardian Angel is a symbol representing the experience of identity with the centre or 'I' that is part of the whole Self – the clearest part of it. Dhyana is the equiv-alent in mysticism, a kind of 'little samadhi', for in both the mystical and magickal approach to ritual, the union is not eternal. The Adept returns to 'usual' consciousness with the addition, as it were, of a new, inner knowledge.

All ritual, therefore, *essentially* aims to achieve this 'I' or 'centre'. It is said quite correctly that all other rituals are only 'lawful' (that is, in line with the true development of the soul) when their aim is to aid this essential ritual. For example, all the blocks and unbalanced aspects in the personality have to be cleared out and balanced before a true identity with the 'I' can be achieved. They are therefore 'lawful' as adjuncts to the main work. An 'unlawful' or 'invalid' ritual would be one performed for the purpose of gaining certain effects or powers just for the sake of the effect or power itself and not in line with the True Will or purpose of the magician or mystic.

WAYS OF INVOKING 'DEITY'

It is often said that the purpose of most rituals is to invoke (or evoke) deities or 'gods' so that their knowledge and/or power may be conferred upon the individual or group performing the ritual. This is true and coherent with the arguments just presented when it is seen that all deities represent parts or aspects of the individual or group. For example, Jupiter is best understood in terms of open, unconditional love, generos-ity and wealth – all Qualities of the soul which we can find within ourselves. To invoke Jupiter is to get more in touch with these qualities and help manifest them through a balanced personality.

'Deity' thus represents a personification of energy, and a ritualist would identify with the deity to obtain the concurrent energy that the deity represents. In an earlier chapter we looked at the various methods for raising energy and these should be considered again (see Chapter 6). They are useful additions to the process of invoking deity. There are, however, three basic ways of invoking these forces:

1. Devotion — Through devotion to a deity, its force may be felt within the personality. A good example of this kind of ritual is that of the Hare Krishna Temple devotees who dedicate their whole lives to their deity.

2. Ceremonial Invocation — This includes all kinds of prayer, the use of mantra, meditations and 'ceremonial magic'. The aim of this method is to enflame the consciousness of the participant(s) until it is clear and open for the influx of the energies required.

3. Drama — This includes role playing, specifically the psychodrama of deity. This involves assuming the god-form of a particular deity and acting as if one is the deity, until one unites one's consciousness with the energy involved. Some forms of dance are included here, as well as shamanistic ritual.

simple ritual exercise

You will already be frequently using the Kabbalistic Cross if you have been following the course of this book. Perform it now, paying particular attention to the ritual involved.

When you have finished the Kabbalistic Cross consider how effective it is for you as a ritual and how you could improve its ritualistic component *for you*. Consider this in terms of devotion, ceremony and drama, as described above.

psychological ritual work

We all have our daily habitual rituals – such as getting up, dressing, eating and so on in our own particular way; standing to attention when we hear the national anthem(!) or whatever it is we do that is done habitually and repeatedly as a response to a certain cue.

Choose one day to look seriously at your habitual rituals, filling in your journal with everything you do on that day. Underline or highlight in some way those actions you know to be deeply ingrained habitual responses.

When you have completed the above work, construct a second 'rituals of the day' list and fill this one in with what you would really like to do on a typical day of your life. Be honest and 'spare no expense' in putting down all your true desires for a typically 'perfect' day.

Now compare the two. Notice the differences. Be aware that you can *choose* to change your habitual day into your chosen day step by step. The two following procedures can be performed to aid your move from the habitual day to the ideal day. However, do not let either of these techniques become too habitual!

1. Each morning after waking remember the two lists and say to yourself: 'with each new day I move a little nearer to my ideal'.
2. Each evening before going to sleep do a review of the past day, comparing what has actually happened with what you wrote on your second list. Be aware of those points in the day when you have been at least near to your ideal and realize it is possible to live a day in the ideal way. Affirm to yourself before sleep: 'tomorrow will be better than today'.

METHODS OF GROUP INTEGRATION

For a group ritual to be effective there has to be a common, shared group purpose and a common, equally shared group endeavour. A group in the New Age is not held together by a leader but by *common purpose, common intention* and *common plan*.

A group is like a constellation of stars, each individual star making up, and necessary to, the whole constellation. A simpler analogy is the sun and planets, where the planets are the members of the group and the sun is the common purpose. Grouped around the common purpose, the planets follow their course, the common intention, and thereby achieve the common plan, which is the manifestation of an active and growing system. In no way is their individual role in the whole scheme negated.

A group should be viewed as a temporary aid to growth and not as a fixed principle. Just as, say, copper, sulphur and oxygen may come together to form copper sulphate, they will not remain a sulphate (group) together, but through the passage of time and experience will return to the component elements. The copper, for example, will not be changed in itself but will, through the experience of combination, be more aware, expanded in consciousness and further along its path. It is important for the individual members of a group to realize this for it then allows fuller commitment by removing the fear of being swamped or losing identity, except on a temporary basis.

The group working together can be compared to a single 'entity', with the same constituent parts as an individual entity. That is:

Spirit	—	the integrating purpose for the group's existence.
Soul	—	the qualitative aspect of the group, including the soul qualities brought to the group by its individual members.
Personality	—	composed of the group 'mind', 'feelings' and 'emotions' – the blended aspects of its members, working in harmony towards the common purpose but not necessarily in full agreement.
Body	—	the manifestation of the group through its rituals and all its other activities.

If we look at the soul region of the Tree, we can see that Chesed brings to the group the elements of goodwill, caring and so on; Geburah brings the dynamic energy and affirmations necessary to the group; and Tiphareth provides a manifestation and focus for the group's common purpose. A successful ritual needs to include the whole group in all its aspects.

The five main techniques that can be used to help make the work of a group cohesive are: love, meditation, sharing, silence and communication.

Some of the obstacles to these are criticism, personal attachment, the glamour of 'freedom', and all types of communication breakdown. It is up to the individual members of a group to follow their own course of action for dealing with their individual problems and blocks. In the actual preparation for a group ritual, however, individuals may all perform the same procedures, helping themselves individually and also helping the preliminary integration of the group. These methods are:

1. Elimination of the previous 'set' (dis-identification).
2. Elevation of consciousness (self-identification).
3. Contacting the Self through aspiration, prayer and invocation.

After the ritual work the group integration is strengthened through the sharing of experience and the pooling of results. The shared physical manifestation of the intention and plan, where appropriate, may also be useful.

GLAMOURS PREVENTING GROUP EFFECTIVENESS

Glamour may be described as the attribution of false values and/or exaggerated importance to people, objects, situations – and most frequently ourselves.

Obviously glamour is a block to the effective manifestation of the working and plan of a group. Glamour is largely emotional in manifestation (in our present situation anyway), and the main glamours that prevent the group being effective are:

dictatorship – the imposition of authority, personal ambition

dogmatism – certainty of being right

independence (of a pathological degree against the group)

self-interest

narrow vision

fanaticism, and

possessiveness

These glamours need to be watched out for very carefully by all members of the group.

Once identified, a glamour may be dissipated by one or more of the following:

- dis-identification (individual and group)
- awareness of right proportions, keeping a perspective on things
- the cultivation of opposites (elevation of the weak and refinement of the strong)
- the 'as if' techniques, use of our imagination as a clearing energy
- transmutation – the invocation of light being particularly effective

the invocation of light

This is essentially an exercise that groups of people may perform before, during or after a group meeting, as appropriate. It can easily be adapted for individual use.

Having followed all the usual starting procedures, you (and every individual in the group) imagine a light above your head.

You then visualize a light object or symbol (that symbolizes the common purpose) at the centre of the circle.

Visualize the spoke of a wheel coming from you, created from the white light above your head, and attached to the common purpose/symbol in the centre.

Strongly visualize your connection to the centre, and be aware of the spokes (that is, the connections) of the other group members. Be aware that together you make a wheel; individuals at the circumference but united at the centre.

the goodwill ritual

Follow the usual starting procedure.

Imagine a world where the majority of people are concerned with the good of others and not with their own selfish goals.

Realize the part you can play in creating this world.

Visualize the spirit of goodwill (for example, a light) reaching out from your centre of goodwill to all people, problems and situations in your immediate concern.

Now imagine that light spreading from you, and all those areas to which you have already connected, so that it covers the whole planet with a glowing mantle of peace and goodwill. See yourself as part of a network, a web of light, understanding and goodwill.

A particularly useful 'blessing mudra' may be used at any time one wishes to send goodwill to others, either individually or collectively as in the above exercise. Imagine your left hand is aglow with a deep, rich blue light. Once you have visualized this vividly, hold out your left arm, the palm upright and stretched away from you, and see a stream of bright, warm yellow light flow from your hand. Be aware that this is a healing energy that can clear up problems and make people, animals, plants and 'inanimate' objects 'feel' better. It can help create a network of healing energy for the growth of goodwill throughout the whole planet.

THE SCIENCE AND ART OF CEREMONIAL MAGICK

Magick is the science and art of causing willed changes to occur. In other words, it is any intentional act. The method of magick is to 'enflame oneself' through prayer, meditation, dance, ritual, music, incense, barbarous names and so on. All the methods have the common aim of *turning off* the 'inner dialogue' and centring the Adept so that the desired result may happen. An invocation, for example, is completed when the Adept has cleared his or her consciousness, become centred and allowed the new energy to enter, inform and enrich his or her being.

Ceremonial magick is that particular form of magick that uses ritual, in the particular form of ceremony, to obtain the desired change. The result is obtained by using the symbols and techniques that correspond to the particular energy to be dealt with. For instance, if you want goodwill you might invoke Jupiter, using the correspondences to Chesed (the sphere of Jupiter) to focus the work into that particular sphere of energy. Invocation is then the calling down or in of the force and is always performed in a circle. Evocation is the calling up or out of the energies, at least apparently externally, into a triangle which is situated *outside* the magician's circle.

Just as you can picture a laboratory scientist using microscopes, slides, a desk with papers scattered over it, strange formulae, test tubes and so on to study the 'objective nature' or outside world, you can also imagine, inside a specially prepared temple, a magician using the magickal weapons and symbols at his or her disposal, along with strange formulae (the invocations, for example), to study the 'subjective nature' or inside world.

The ritual is mnemonic, as each symbol used in the ceremony must correspond to the desired end, thus focusing the work. For example, if the desired result is 'love' – to concentrate on that force, cedarwood perfume, the wand, a tulip, amethyst and the colour blue might be used appropriately. Correspondences may of course be studied in the tables in Appendix 4.

The ritual leads to:

1. The *exhilaration and purification* of the Will.

2. The *exaltation and clarification* of the Imagination.

Through these processes, the Adept's consciousness is tuned to the appropriate energy or deity and this charges the desired end – thus making its manifestation at least possible if not assured.

A ritual may have a specific goal – for example the celebration of a festival, self-purification, planetary peace, the gaining of money, the acquisition of love, in fact anything – but, ultimately and always, the process involves:

1. The purification of the personality.

2. Contact with the soul energy.

3. Ultimate union with the spirit.

These processes have been described more fully above. Ceremonial magick, despite all its apparent complication and trappings, is no different from any other ritual in its purpose, intention and plan.

THE DEITIES OF THE SPHERES

Gods and goddesses (or 'deities') are natural phenomena which can be interpreted as 'beings', usually akin to a human (in nature and type) but transcending the human in power. These natural phenomena are caused by activities of the same nature as those we can recognize in ourselves (for example, we have all heard of the 'anger of the gods', 'the love of the gods', 'the body of the goddess', and so on), but they take place on a 'higher' or 'deeper' plane which is invisible to our usual perceptions. Ceremonial magic attempts to bring the energies from these other planes into manifestation on our usual earth plane.

There can be various names (within the same culture let alone in different ones) for the same deity or 'energy'; for example an 'angry god' may be called Thor or Mars. The names given to these energies in no way change the nature of the energy. The true formula of a god, as opposed to its common name, may however be more specific. The magickal formula or 'true name' of a god can set his or her energy in motion. Finding the right or true formula is not always easy, however. Generally speaking the Hebrew god names are fairly true and effective (see Tables).

We all know something of each sphere (below the Abyss) of the Tree, therefore by implication we already know something about, and are already connected to, the associated deities. This means the process of invocation through ceremonial magic is not as difficult to achieve as it might otherwise be.

The method of ceremonial magick is no different in essence from the method of any form of ritual, and the gods of the spheres may be contacted through:

1. Invocation: enflaming the being in prayer, turning off the inner dialogue, and holding the god-force/image one-pointedly.

2. Rising on the planes to the required sphere of the Tree, reciting the mantra or name of the required god or goddess, then assuming the form of that deity and acting it out 'as if' the Adept had become the deity.

MAGICKAL INSTRUMENTS

Throughout the chapters on the spheres of the Tree of Life you have learned of instruments and symbols associated with each sphere. These are the 'weapons' used in ceremonial magick, both for correspondence purposes and for the actual enactment of the ritual. The diagram opposite shows correspondences of some of the major magickal instruments and symbols to the Tree of Life.

A magician works in a temple, the external universe as it is found. In this temple a circle is drawn upon the floor to define the limitations of the work, to create a container and to announce the nature of the Great Work (of 'knowing oneself'). The circle is protected by divine names, including the magician's ethics and own oath to Self. Within a magical circle stands an altar, which is described as the solid base or foundation of the work. Upon the altar are a wand for Will, a cup for Love, a sword for Reason and a pantacle which represents the body.

The magician is wearing a robe which conceals, protects and represents the silence and secrecy of the work done. It also corresponds to the aura. The oil, which is usually kept in a phial on the altar, consecrates everything it touches. The oil represents aspiration, and in the Kabbalah all acts performed in accordance with this are said to be holy. A magician

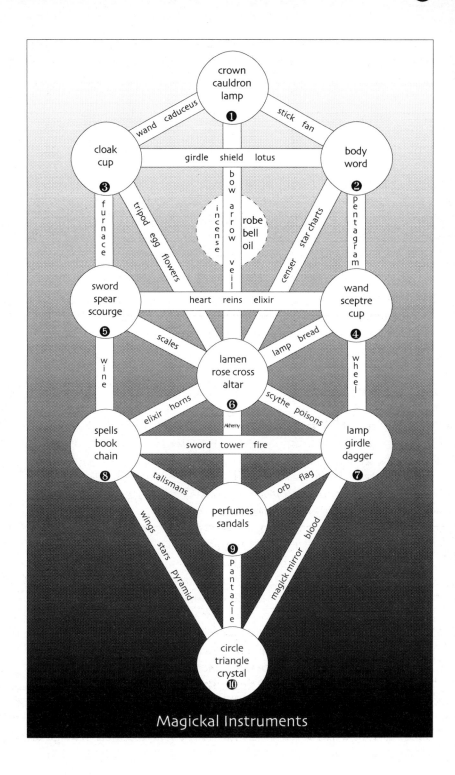

Magickal Instruments

also uses a scourge to excite sluggish nature (challenge), a dagger which calms too great a heat (support), and a chain to bind the wandering thoughts (focused attention). These keep the aspirations pure.

Above the altar hangs a light, representing the light of pure soul. It is a reminder not to be too confident or clever, that something in the Kabbalah is always unknown and beyond (' . . . and I am more than this'). A magician also wears a crown (to affirm his or her divinity), a single robe (to symbolize silence and protection) and over the heart a special seal (to remind the practitioner that the secret keys of power and love are found in the heart). A magician carries a magical record or journal, and a bell (which summons and alarms).

Consider these descriptions of the magickal Weapons in the light of your Kabbalistic knowledge and particularly with respect to their correspondence with the Tree.

BALANCE AND HARMONY IN RITUAL AND CEREMONY

Balance and harmony are *essential* to all ritual work, whether it be of a ceremonial nature, individual or group work. Whilst effects may be achieved through unbalanced ritual work, the consequent lack of harmony will sooner or later lead to problems that will have to be dealt with by the Adept(s) involved. For this reason it is worth emphasizing once again the importance of serious work of a continuous nature being undertaken on the personality of the Adept, and his or her connection with the soul. This is essential to forward the harmony not just of the individual him- or herself, but of the group to which they belong and ultimately of the whole planet.

A COMPARISON OF SEXUAL AND CEREMONIAL MAGICK

As has been stated, the purpose of any ritual, be it ceremonial, sexual or whatever, is to enflame the consciousness and turn off the 'inner dialogue' – success in which enables the required change to occur and the potential 'new' form to manifest.

For enflaming the consciousness, sex has the advantage that:

It works	—	everyone knows this to be true.
It is exciting	—	this goes without saying and is a great aid to enflaming the consciousness.

It is powerful — experience shows this to be the case.

It is simple   — when compared to the long and often
                   cumbersome techniques and methods of
                   ceremonial magick.

Sexual magick may be auto-erotic, or it may involve two people (of any sexual combination) or groups of people, where extra energy is available and where the sexual component may be ritually dramatized rather than actually enacted out. It is the experience of many Adepts working this way that a stable relationship is the best basis for effective magick.

My purpose here is not to describe sexual magick in detail, but rather to draw your attention to its potential benefits as an easy, exciting and effective way of using magick for growth and development. If you look back at Chapter 11 on the Shekhinah you will find a simple sexual magickal ritual.

CONSTRUCTING YOUR OWN RITUALS

There are many books that offer rituals which you can use in your magickal work. Many of the exercises in this book could be seen as rituals or certainly adapted for ritual work. Whilst many of these rituals will be effective, the very best rituals are ones you construct yourself. They are connected to *you* and your energy, so they resonate more with your personal position and potential for growth. Using the knowledge you have acquired in this book, the correspondence tables and your own imagination, you should now be able to construct your own rituals for whatever end you require – whether they be of a ceremonial, sexual, individual or group nature – and feel fairly certain of a good level of success.

As you will realize by now, much of the work you have been performing in the exercises throughout this book, particularly the visualization exercises, has involved the manipulation of what is termed 'astral energy'. Ritual magick, including the construction of a temple, the acquisition of magickal weapons, and even the participation of other beings, can be effectively performed on the astral plane. It is, in fact, often easier and simpler. Also, considering the deep interrelatedness of the astral and material planes, so long as the energy is suitably grounded, there is no reason to suppose the effects of a ritual performed on the astral plane will be any less effective than those performed on the material plane.

healing circles

Follow the usual starting procedure.

Visualize the Tree of Life superimposed on your body ...
Spend some time at this, and each subsequent stage of the exercise.
   Focus on Tiphareth as a yellow sphere in your heart ...
   Be aware of the energy of the whole Tree of Life filling your body,
your feelings and your thoughts with healing energies ...
   Become aware of all the circles with which you are involved:
circles of friends, relatives, work, humanity, life on earth . . .
   Connect to people and places where you wish to send energy,
and in your own time, as appropriate, name out loud these people
or places – as you do so imagine sending energy to that person
or place . . .
   Focus once again on the Tree of Life on your body and feel the
whole Tree now focused in your heart.
   Open your eyes and feel the warmth and healing energy you have
generated. Allow some of this energy to work for your own healing.
   Find some way to show your appreciation of yourself, and the
work you have done in connecting with the spirit of the Tree of
Life.

The Kabbalah, based on pure number, can correspond with an infinite
number of images and symbols – indeed, everything in life and existence
itself. The Kabbalah is a temple for the Holy Spirit, the blueprint for all
life in all its forms. In the light of the Kabbalah the shadows of all transi-
tory things are instantly banished. Use the Tree of Life well and it will
serve you well for the rest of your existence, in this life and, perhaps,
even beyond.

PART V

PRACTICAL APPLICATIONS OF THE KABBALAH

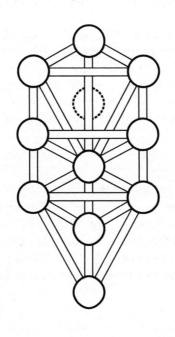

CHAPTER 15

THE PSYCHOSPIRITUAL KABBALAH

LEARNING TO GROW DOWN

Working with the Kabbalah involves more than making connections with the higher realms alone. It's also good to learn how to deal effectively with the mundane and everyday aspects of life. There is an old saying that it is dangerous to put your head in the clouds unless your feet are safely planted on the ground. This perfectly describes the Kabbalistic approach to psychospiritual development. Our task is not to 'trip out' but rather to 'come in', or, as James Hillman so aptly describes it, life is about 'growing down' rather than growing up. Some early depictions of the Tree of Life show the tree growing down into the earth with its roots reaching to heaven. The more we learn how to incarnate fully in our bodies, the more our roots reach up to heaven, the stronger our vessel for journeying into the Mysteries.

The Book of Splendour, an ancient Kabbalistic text, describes how the Creator fashioned all the souls that would incarnate and then told them to go and manifest themselves. Many souls were appalled at this command and said they were happy to stay where they were, in the blissful heaven where they were created. The Creator replied that the whole point in their being created was to go into the world and that they must do so. The souls, unable to disobey their Creator, unwillingly descended into bodies and came to the earth.

We all know how being in life can be very painful in so many different ways. There seems little or no point in bothering to incarnate in the first place, however, if we spend all our time trying to leave. The time to depart will come to us all soon enough. Whilst here, let's enjoy life to the full, appreciate the opportunities it presents to us to learn and grow, and – perhaps most importantly in our modern world – learn to be here with respect for the planet itself and all the life forms it supports. The

Kabbalah, with its grounded, pragmatic approach to spiritual growth, is an excellent guide for such practice. We can work at bringing our spiritual insights, connections and experiences to earth, to illuminate not just ourselves but all sentient beings.

THE FOURFOLD WAY

The American psychologist Angeles Arrien studied the qualities that members of various indigenous tribes brought to group meetings. She distilled these down into four basic conditions, which we can apply not only to group meetings but to all encounters throughout our life journey:

1. The need to show up; this may seem obvious at first sight, but of course to be present physically is not the whole picture. To show up includes to be present emotionally, mentally and spiritually as well, always focused in Malkuth.

2. To speak one's truth without fear of judgement, corresponding to the dialogue between Netzach and Hod within oneself, as well as in relation to others.

3. To listen to what has heart and meaning, corresponding to Tiphareth and its ability to reveal the energy of the higher spheres to us.

4. To be open to outcome rather than attached to it. This corresponds to the best attitude to have towards material from the subconscious aspects of Yesod. This is a good approach to dealing with the life energies and sexual encounters of Yesod.

These four conditions are useful to hold in mind when working on oneself or with others. As well as being good precepts in themselves, they also include all the spheres on the lower Tree of Life, and thus are balancing in effect. It is also important not to make these conditions into super-ego judgements. You cannot 'fail' so long as you are doing your work to the best of your ability. At any moment, of course, you *are* always doing your best, however conscious or not you may be of the process. Soul is not something outside of yourself; it is found in all aspects of your everyday life. The key is in trusting the process and the presence of spirit in the continuing unfoldment of life. That is why the work in this book has stressed that you do not try and memorize techniques or methods. When you *trust* your experience, you open a connection to the 'silent knowledge' that is behind thought and feeling.

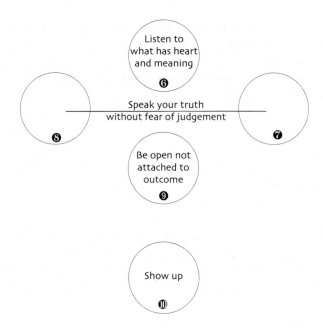

TIKKUN, A PROCESS OF REPARATION

Kabbalists believe that creation takes place through a process of fragmentation. The Source or Creator, originally whole, has the idea – how or why we do not know – that it wants to know itself. To do this it fragments, initially into ten pieces. These fragments are the spheres of the first Tree of Life. The process of fragmentation continues and, as it does, each fragment contains the original wholeness hidden with it. Our task, as living beings and microcosms of the original Creator, is to restore wholeness to the universe. This process is called *tikkun,* which, translated into English, means restoration, restitution or reparation. Reparation is perhaps the most accurate translation as it corresponds to the work of repair that is needed to make us whole again. The aim of tikkun is to restore a sense of wholeness or perfection to the psyche. Perfection in this sense does not mean everything being perfected, but everything *as it is now* being seen and understood as perfect in itself.

As you know, the second triad on the Tree of Life corresponds to the individual soul. Each individual soul is a holographic replica of the original and total Oneness at the Source. Through the process of fragmentation we each have our own individual connection to the original Source. Life becomes a process of refining and elevating the individual

sparks of soul and re-connecting them to the spiritual level. This repara-
tive process will continue whether we co-operate with it or not. As
humans, it is our individual and collective task to find ways of doing so.

Considering your life journey, what acts are you taking or could you
undertake to co-operate with the process of tikkun or reparation?

Child development theories claim that there are various stages we
go through in our development into adulthood, psychologically as well
as physically. This is how we each individually experience the process of
fragmentation. What happens to us at these stages sets the scene for
how we function, neurotically or healthily, on various levels in later life.
If you read the diagram below from the top down, you can see how our
childhood developmental stages correspond to the Tree of Life. The
process of incarnating follows the path of the lightning flash through the
spheres. Each of us is essentially identical to the original creative spark.

Everyone comes into life with issues to work on and, sometimes, to
work *through* – but not inevitably. What happens in our development is a
result of a projection from spirit which
each of us reflects in a slightly different way. We each then have
something to work with that is
suitable for our own soul's particular
growth and development. The repeating patterns at Yesod enable us to stay
connected with our life energy.

We all know how past experiences can affect our flow of energy,
how repeating cycles of behaviour can
sometimes cause us to fail to fulfil our
deepest potential. The Kabbalistic
approach gives us an opportunity to
understand all our experiences as
valuable, rather than looking at these
developmental patterns as negative
and restrictive. Of course, this does
not mean that having been neglected,
abused or mistreated is in itself
valuable; rather, that there is value in
what we can do to learn from and
change in ourselves through having
had our unique life experiences.

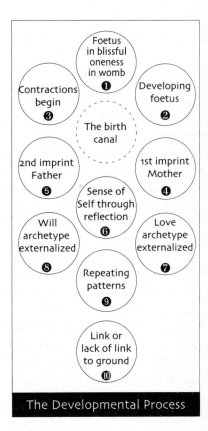

The Developmental Process

THE WORK OF THE SPHERES

Throughout this book you have learned how to work with the spheres and paths of the Tree of Life. This psychospiritual work has offered you a sure way of developing all parts of your being.

The work of Malkuth involves increasing sensory awareness and connection, and realizing the importance of the body and physical manifestation. It is through Malkuth that we have our primary experience of the world. In Malkuth we may discover the mysteries of the physical universe, increase our ability to discriminate, overcome sloth and inertia and increase our ability to heal ourselves and others.

The work of Yesod involves releasing repressed energies, and the subsequent integration of these released energies into their correct spheres, which are consequently strengthened. Releasing the repressed energies surrounding this sphere aids your sexual balance and power. In Yesod we may discover the mysteries of the astral levels and how universal energies operate. Yesod energy enables us, in our human lives, even through our difficulties and suffering, to connect with the divine plan.

Hod and Netzach involve the balancing of thoughts and feelings, which though difficult may be achieved through allowing the experience and expression of both. Hod connects us with the mysteries of information systems, gives us greater ability to speak our truth and communicate with more clarity. Netzach energy brings us into contact with the mysteries of loving sexuality and nature, and can increase our artistic creativity.

The work of Tiphareth involves building a strong centre from where we can direct the personality and our everyday interactions in the world. Tiphareth strengthens our connection to deeper, inner energies which then may manifest in our lives. Strengthening your connection to Tiphareth is vitally important in the Kabbalistic scheme and is equivalent to what is sometimes described as opening the heart. In Tiphareth, through open hearts, we may discover the mysteries of beauty and harmony.

The work of the higher spheres involves the actualization of potential energy. Chesed and Geburah play particular significance in the unfolding of soul energy on earth. Work with the Soul Triad brings purposeful change, awakens love and peace, and stimulates the forces of abundance in our lives.

Working with Daath helps us to discover the mysteries of the shadow side of existence, and brings us knowledge of 'the rainbow bridge.' It also gives us clues to the next step to take in our life journey. The energies of the Supernal Triad always underpin all our work, connecting us to our deepest sense of purpose and our truest values in life. Our spiritual work leads to the amplification of spiritual energies not just in ourselves but also in the world, and the ultimate revelation of divine inspiration.

The many different ways of working with the Tree of Life can enrich our lives through clearing our past conditioning, traumas and controls, dynamically balancing our growth in the present, and through making a link to our innermost purpose and meaning. As the Tree of Life is a holistic model, through working with any part of it we are inevitably linked in ourselves to the whole of creation. Not only is each part, each path and each sphere connected to the whole of creation, but each part in itself, whilst undeniably only a part, nevertheless includes the whole.

the soul cloak

Follow the usual starting procedure.

Imagine you are wearing a dark, heavy, black cloak ... the hood is up and is pulled right over your head, hiding your face ... this dark hooded black cloak is the cloak of all your negativity, your fears and the negative emotions, thoughts and sensations you experience in your life ... really feel the heaviness of this cloak ...

Now become aware that this negative cloak is gradually lifting away from your body, taking with it all your negativity ... really feel this cloak loosening and lifting away from you ...

Imagine the cloak slowly but completely vanishing.

Now it is completely gone, you are free to clothe yourself in a new cloak of your choice, a cloak of love, of joy, protection, or any Qualities you choose ... choose the cloak you wish to wear right now ...

Vividly imagine yourself wearing this new cloak you have chosen, this cloak of light and positive energy ... see its colours and feel its strength and quality all around you ...

Realize this cloak is a symbol for your soul ... realize that as a soul you can wear whatever cloak you choose ... realize you are a soul and choose wisely.

LEVELS OF ATTENTION

To experience how we operate in the world, and to be in a position to make choices about how we want our lives to be, we have to be able to find the inner witness. This is the part of ourselves from where we observe ourselves and all our actions. This is of course the main value in increasing our connection to Tiphareth. To connect with this *witness* inside ourselves is never about escaping from life or disembodying ourselves. The true witness couples awareness with the willingness to feel the totality of oneself, whatever the pain or the joy being experienced. To live the life of a witness is to be passionately involved in life and at the same time centred in the core of your being. This can reduce the fundamental fragmentation that happens when we separate our spiritual nature from our earthly nature. It reduces, in other words, the fragmentation described in the Kabbalistic creation myth, and deeply embedded in our Western cultures.

There are three levels of attention involved in being a witness. The first is when we simply put our attention on something. 'I see – whatever; I touch – whoever; I smell – whatever,' and so on. The second is being aware of the totality of ourselves. 'I am me, everything I do, everything I am is me. I am a centre of pure self-awareness.' The third is becoming aware that there is a source to this attention. Not 'what am I doing or who am I being?', but 'from where does this attention arise?'

Become aware now that at this moment you, yourself, are a totality. There is nothing missing. You are all that you are right now. This awareness is instantaneous. Don't focus on anything in particular: don't focus on your head, your thorax, your pelvis; don't focus on the light above your head, or the earth beneath your feet; don't focus on your breath or anything at all. Just let your attention rest on the undivided presence of yourself.

This is the experience of *the second attention*. You are not doing anything, not being anything, not focused on anything in particular, but simply aware of the undivided presence of yourself. This corresponds to the pure, unadulterated experience of Tiphareth.

At a moment like this you are complete. There is nothing missing (whether you are aware of this or not). You do not have to strive for anything, do any particular exercises; you can just realize, by putting your attention here in this very moment, that you are always here, now, in this moment. You cannot become more or less enlightened or spiritual than this; you are simply you, all you have been, are, and ever will be. For this reason the second attention is sometimes called Self-remembering.

From where does all your awareness arise? Look closely: from where, right now, is your attention coming? Where? Now where? Allow yourself to experience the source of this attention. Be aware of the pure consciousness from which everything arises, including all this witnessing of consciousness. Who or what is this presence, this totality of being that comes alive inside you? Don't look for an answer, but instead look inside your looking.

This is *the third attention* and is equivalent to experiencing the energies of the Supernal triad and even beyond.

To be a witness is not to try and sidestep the everyday world, the limited, the mundane, but to allow your wholeness of being to ensoul the everyday world. This is the work of a Kabbalist: ensouling the world, living the life of a witness with passion and engagement. To put it another way, it is being here now, living life with awareness, including the awareness that sometimes you will not be aware!

THE KABBALISTIC APPROACH TO LIFE

The Kabbalistic approach to life brings both the spiritual into relationship with the everyday ('as above, so below'), and the inner into relationship with the outer ('as within, so without'). The essential aim of Kabbalah is to help us discover our true spiritual nature, then to effectively utilize this discovery in everyday life. The Kabbalah can help both the individual and a group realize creative potential, increase the ability to function harmoniously in the modern world, and improve the quality of relationships. The Kabbalah, from its most ancient roots, has never been just a theory, but is an intensely practical approach to personal and spiritual growth.

Diversity is created from unity in order that all beings can find their own way to realize the source from whence they came and to which they are returning. Divided for the sake of love, we can find ourselves again through love and, in finding ourselves, discover that our separation was an illusion. We have the opportunity from a place of division to form a union, to come together with another being and be at one with him or her, or even to come together with all other beings and realize a total union. Without division no such knowledge would be possible. In the world of duality, working on coming to know oneself, as painful as it can be, is the gateway to soul. This way, we can help bring more beauty and harmony into the world through working at Self-remembering.

A mystical experience which separates individuals from their mundane, earthly existence and, in a state of bliss, leads them to temporarily forget all outer reality is something to be honoured. To become attached to such experiences, however, is to fall into the mystical trap. We can avoid this trap through always paying attention to bringing all spiritual energies back to ground and finding a way of expressing them in the 'ordinary world'.

The mystical experience is not an end in itself but rather a step along the way, from which the individual who is fortunate to have such an experience can draw creative energy and enthusiasm. Indeed, the true mystical experience brings with it the desire to come back into the world to express the energies involved and help one's fellow human beings to also experience this enlightenment. The 'mystic' who remains spaced out has missed the boat, as it were, that carries us all, irrespective of our experiences, towards the final goal of fully realized and consciously shared union.

Another mystical trap is to believe that once one has reached some sort of blissful state, or received some sense of enlightenment, this is all there is to it. It is the experience of all the great mystics that enlightenment is neither an end in itself nor, as such, does it last forever. Nothing remains the same, everything changes, and the enlightened state is no exception to this cosmic rule. Everything that is alive is in a constant state of movement, renewing itself as it moves from moment to moment. Each revelation has to be grounded, expressed and released.

Many people in the modern world suffer from what is sometimes called the 'crisis of meaning'. Particularly in the West but increasingly over the whole planet, many people live in an existential vacuum, where life has lost its meaning (beyond, at best, the purely material). In such a world, with its collective lack of meaning, there is much strife between people. And the ecological state of the planet is poor, due to the greed of some people and the mindlessness of others. There is often an appalling lack of care and understanding and so much imbalance, particularly in the interaction between people. But the Kabbalah offers to help with the healing of this 'illness' through assisting an individual to know her- or himself. To know oneself is to bring meaning back into life, and this then creates a context for living a life in accord with others.

Some of our deepest spiritual connections foster the realization that all life forms, not just human beings, are part of a totally interconnected and inseparable energy field. Whilst most of us may spend a large part of our lives experiencing separation and disconnection, once we start to explore the deeper aspects of our being we discover the underlying truth of our connection. This doesn't make the alienation disappear, but it offers a new perspective from which to experience it. We may not be able to 'be there' all the time – indeed, it may not be right for us to stay in such a state – but once we have an intimation of its existence, once we actually experience it in ourselves, there is no looking back. We can 'set our sights' on the clarity and connection that comes from such realization and, when we remember, try to make each move we take a step in that direction. Working with the Tree of Life helps us remember ourselves a little bit more often.

The realization that we are connected to everyone and everything else brings a different perspective on time and space, allowing us to cultivate within ourselves a sense of 'global consciousness' which we can then start to ground in our everyday lives. When we ground this awareness it helps us to take actions that move the total collective consciousness forward along its positive evolutionary path. It is not an exaggeration to say that one small act made by one individual at one moment in time can make a profound difference. To care for others – not only those immediately within our field of awareness and activity, but also all living and non-living things generally – is the way to ground this consciousness. When we care for our environment, both locally and generally, we are also grounding our deepest, psychospiritual consciousness. Every conscious act that includes such caring furthers the cause of global healing.

CHAPTER 16

THE KABBALAH IN EVERYDAY LIFE

THE DANCE OF LIFE

The best way of understanding and applying the Kabbalah in everyday life is through correspondences. A correspondence exists when there is a similarity about, or a connection between, two or more things. When we make correspondences using the Tree of Life, they become alive in a different and special way. This is particularly exciting when it involves issues that concern us in our lives, for it helps us understand our world in a fuller and richer way. As everything is ultimately interrelated, the scope for growth and understanding through making such connections is truly astonishing.

Take, for example, the Gabrielle Roth Five Rhythms dance programme. Roth describes five rhythms that, when danced successively, bring about increased freedom of movement in not only our bodies but also our emotional, mental and creative lives. These rhythms are called flowing, staccato, chaos, lyrical and stillness. Whilst dancing this series of rhythms might be sufficient in itself, to make a connection between these rhythms and all the dancer's other knowledge and experience puts the work into a wider and more satisfying context. Flowing dance corresponds to Malkuth, staccato to Yesod, chaos to Hod, lyrical to Netzach and stillness to Tiphareth and the spheres above. The five rhythms danced in order open a pathway through the personality spheres to make a connection with the higher realms. This in itself is a gift – but once you start practising this method of dancing you will find there is even more.

Most significantly, you can find out where your particular blocks are and how to work with them. Suppose, for instance, that you found the lyrical movement the most difficult. Through correspondences you would find that, because lyrical connects with Netzach, this difficulty was maybe trying to tell you something about your ability to express your feelings. Through connecting to other appropriate correspondences to Netzach, you can find ways to work with this restriction and free your Netzach energies. For instance, you might create a special dance that invokes lyrical energies. You might pray for the help of the archangel Haniel who corresponds to Netzach. You could wear the colour green, find ways to bring more of the beauty of nature into your life, drink verbena tea and wear patchouli oil, and so on. You might wear a red rose, the flower of Netzach, in your hair! Only through practical work with correspondences will you be able to understand how effective these apparently weird suggestions can be.

Of course in some cases, simply making the connection between different correspondences can be enough in itself. To be able to put any issue into a broader context helps us relate to and find meaning in it. Many of the examples in this chapter offer such a context. You might not agree with my particular correspondences and, if so, all well and good. The point is to create your own correspondences that bring meaning to your life and help you align your journey to the Self with the bigger collective journey we are all undertaking, and, through this alignment, bring yourself into harmony with the unfolding universe.

THE GROUND WE STAND ON

It has been emphasized throughout this book how important it is to start and end all Kabbalistic work in Malkuth, the earth. We wouldn't be here at all if we didn't have the earth to support the biosphere in which we live. In respecting our planet we respect ourselves. Further, we add to the flow of positive energies which counteract the negative energies that bring abuse, famine, war and so on. In respecting our planet, we are co-operating with the unfoldment of life, and passing on to the next generation a place at least as good to live in as the one we knew, and perhaps better. There is another sometimes overlooked benefit, too. When we align ourselves and co-operate with earth energies, our goodwill is returned to us.

Because our ground, the earth, is the best place to begin our Kabbalistic journeying, we will start looking at applications of the Kabbalah by considering the mysteries of the earth itself. The diagram overleaf shows one way of making a correspondence between various aspects of the earth mysteries, particularly sacred sites, and the Tree of Life. The Supernal Triad corresponds to the god and goddess of the earth and emphasizes the need to stay connected with the spiritual depths and

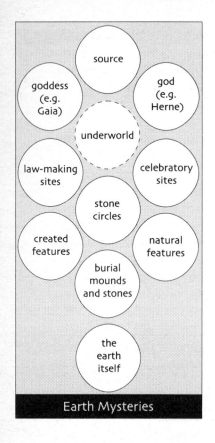

goddess (e.g. Gaia)

source

god (e.g. Herne)

underworld

law-making sites

celebratory sites

stone circles

created features

natural features

burial mounds and stones

the earth itself

Earth Mysteries

connectedness behind our work on the earth. The examples I have given, Herne and Gaia, work for me; it is for each person working with earth mysteries to find the deities (or archetypal principles) that work best for him or her.

It is good practice to create a sacred space in which to do Kabbalistic work, and the following technique is one such way. So long as you focus your attention, acknowledge the presence of 'deity', and intend the space where you work as sacred, you will not go far wrong, and will be aligning yourself with the energies of our beautiful planet.

sacred space

Stand or sit in the centre of the space in which you will be working, either alone or with others. Imagine as strongly and clearly as you can that there is a circle around this place. It will be most effective if you use your hands and body to physically define the boundaries of this circle.

Make three prostrations to the ground. (If you are not able to physically kneel or lie on the floor, then you may simply touch the ground with one or both of your hands. If you cannot do this, then visualize yourself doing it as clearly as possible.)

As you do the first prostration clearly state that you are doing this to connect with the earth energies beneath you. As you do the second, clearly state you are doing this to honour the guardians or spirits of the place in which you are working. With the third prostration, honour the presence of deity in your body.

Stand or sit at the centre of your circle and imagine a strong root coming from the middle of your body and going right down into the centre of the earth, rooting you firmly to your spot. Imagine there is a hook or anchor on the end of the root and feel it attach very firmly to the earth.

Look around your sacred space and imagine, sense and feel the presence of the guardians and angels of this place. Welcome their presence.

Close your eyes, and expand your awareness to the immediate environment and nearby countryside. Silently ask the good spirits of this countryside to be present for you and assist you in your Kabbalistic work.

Return to full awareness of your physical body. Focus on your heart and be aware of the energy there. Breathe into your heart centre now, feeling energy build up. Let your heart centre open as much as is appropriate for you right now.

We can take everything to be a metaphor for something else. Metaphorically, we could see ourselves as gardeners in the 'Garden of Life', rooting out the unwanted weeds, nurturing those things we want to grow, harvesting the fruits of our labours, and so on. But what of 'real' gardening? There is a story about a priest who was passing the house of a keen gardener. Looking over the fence he saw a beautifully tended garden and was impressed. Hailing the gardener, the priest exclaimed, 'What a wonderful garden you and God have created together!'

'Yes, that's true,' said the gardener. 'And you should have seen it when God was doing it on his own.'

The nature of our work with earth is to co-operate with its energies. It is a co-creative process where as we give to the earth so it gives back to us. From the seeds we sow, the plants grow for us to enjoy and harvest. The 'Gardening' diagram shows how the process of gardening can be related to the Tree of Life. Before the gardener arrives there is a wilderness (which corresponds to the negative veils). After the gardener's inspiration, intent and awareness – and the hard work of

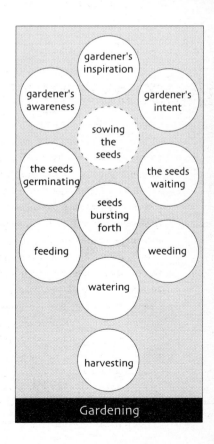

gardener's inspiration

gardener's awareness

gardener's intent

sowing the seeds

the seeds germinating

the seeds waiting

seeds bursting forth

feeding

weeding

watering

harvesting

Gardening

planning, preparing, digging, composting, manuring and so on – it is time to sow the seeds. Each seed, just like an individual soul in the middle triangle of the Tree of Life, waits in full potential, then awakens from its sleep and bursts forth into life. Through the work of the lower spheres (the tending of the little plant), we come to earth and have a harvest. The gardener's original inspiration (at Kether) has been manifested (in Malkuth).

THE POLITICAL WORLD

Living on this earth, we humans have created social and political structures to help us deal with the world itself and with each other. There are, of course, a host of different opinions about how we should govern our societies, what social services should be available to everyone and so on. The rich complex interactions of political difference are both a gift (enabling change and diversity) and a curse (leading to misunderstanding, conflict and war). If we can relate our political world to the Tree of Life, however, we will have a wider and more spiritual context in which to understand our place in the world. It will also enable us to make clearer and more informed choices when we have an opportunity to take action or in some way make a difference in our society.

The diagram here shows one possible attribution of political roles to the Tree of Life. It presents an imaginary people's democracy where the President is informed and guided by a Senate, composed of senior members of the society who have proven their value and goodwill to others, and a House of Representatives who speak, through direct election, for the people. At the soul level we find a Prime Minister, whose work is to direct the government, in particular keeping policy and tactics in line with the party manifesto and the will of the people. In

President

representational Council

senior members of society (Senate)

information (spin)

tactics

policy

Prime Minister

right wing party (govmnt or opposition)

left wing party (govmnt or opposition)

tradition history past

centre party (govmnt or opposition)

Politics

the bottom, personality triangle, we find the different parties, often bickering among themselves and engaging in meaningless dialogue, and at best offering a dialogue that fosters difference and development. The positions that the different parties take are influenced by the traditions of the society as a whole and the history of their particular movement.

Through the left-hand, right-hand and middle pillars of the Tree of Life we find another way to make a correspondence with political parties, enabling a more detailed investigation. What does it mean, for instance, to be 'ultra right wing' in Kabbalistic terms? It suggests an extreme connection to the energies of the left-hand pillar – mentation and willpower particularly. This of course clearly fits. Indeed, extreme rightists would be so far to the right that the energies of the right-hand pillar would control a lot of their actions – that is, they would be ruled by emotional distortions. Similarly 'ultra-leftists' who are far over on the side of love and feelings would be beset with distortions of power from the opposite pillar of the Tree. The 'middle position' in politics usually carries the distortion of being ruled by the lowest common denominator rather than looking for the clearest space available from deeper within.

The ideal political party from a Kabbalistic viewpoint would be one that held a wide perspective on politics. This party would perceive the whole spectrum of political possibilities and place itself appropriately in direct response to each decision. Its position would be based on the enduring and essential principles of fraternity, equality and freedom for all. The left and the right of our political parties describe themselves as holding such principles, yet within their limiting viewpoint and stance they are often not capable of doing this. A Kabbalistic political party would choose what was good from the practices of all other political parties and apply these when effective. It is most unlikely there will ever be Kabbalistic political party because Kabbalists tend to make decisions as individuals, and vote accordingly.

For a Kabbalist, giving is the highest principle in the universe and central to his or her practice. When we remain focused on this central principle, there is no inherent conflict or problem in holding both right- and left-wing viewpoints. The problem arises when such viewpoints hold us, for what has a hold on us also controls us. Conversely, that which we let go of we can direct, making choices appropriate to each situation. Having width of vision that allows the holding of widely divergent viewpoints is the cornerstone of good Kabbalistic practice. It could be the cornerstone for political and social practice, too.

THE LEAVES OF THE TREE

As the diagram on this page shows, social issues, like everything else, are found to correspond to the Tree of Life. Naturally, there are many more social issues than could be shown on such a simple diagram. Maybe some of these would correspond well to various paths. For instance, the relationship between the wealth of society (at Geburah) and its education provision (at Hod) is an area often rife with conflict. How much can we afford to spend on education, or, conversely, can we afford not to spend on education which helps ensure the society's future? This dynamic between Geburah and Hod corresponds with the Tarot card 'The Hanged Man', which graphically depicts how we might feel when debating such an issue.

The Book of Revelations says: 'In the midst of life there is a tree of life which bears all manner of fruits continuously; and the leaves of the tree are for the healing of the nations.' That the Kabbalah flourishes in the modern world depends upon its relevance to political and social issues, as well as for individual development and healing. The central principle of the Kabbalah, the interconnectedness of all things, involves equal respect for ourselves and others. This respect depends upon the acceptance of ourselves and others as we are. We may intend change but we do not require it. From this ground of mutual respect a deep relationship can happen, a relationship of equals, rather than a relationship built upon hierarchy (someone's better than us and someone's worse), or prejudice (this person is the right colour and that person is the wrong one). Deep relationships built on a ground of mutual respect are the basis of healing. When we stop trying to be better (hierarchy) or believing we are better or worse (prejudice), and accept ourselves and others for what we all are – equally humble and equally

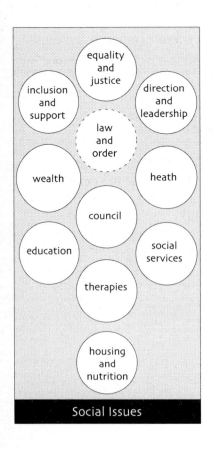
Social Issues

powerful human beings – we free up our ability to interrelate, to understand others for their similarities and differences to us.

When we connect with the Tree of Life it is as if everything becomes brighter, warmer, stiller, because we are no longer confused, we are free. In this state we relate to others in more appropriate ways. This has to be beneficial for any society or nation and all the interactions within them. This doesn't mean we all have to go round radiating love, harmony and light all the time. Sometimes we will feel awful; some days will be filled with conflict, boredom and distrust. There will be differences between us still, but we will celebrate these differences because we will be able to understand them as part of ourselves.

Regardless of what we believe or what religion we belong or don't belong to, we can relate to the Tree of Life and make our own connections. A Buddhist who has connected with the Tree of Life and a South American shaman who has understood the Tree of Life are going to have a much better understanding of one another's ways. A politician who has connected with the Tree of Life will similarly have a better understanding and ability to respond to differing political viewpoints.

Perhaps the Kabbalistic vision seems too radical to apply to politics and society within their current structures. We could arrive at a time, however, when a large enough number of people were working with the Tree of Life for this to be possible. Perhaps it only needs 10 per cent of people, or some such figure, as described in the 'hundredth monkey theory', to cause a relatively large change to the political and social scene. In that context, the shining image of the Tree of Life is really just one facet of a bigger plan, a bigger Tree of Life.

The Tree of Life helps make us whole and gives us the ability to include more of ourselves in our journey through life. We need to be whole in ourselves to be able to combine with other whole beings to create a greater inclusion and synthesis. The more of us who move towards wholeness in this way, the more of us there are to work together for the common goal of societal and eventually planetary harmony. We do not even have to work together: knowing and understanding this togetherness exists may in itself release vast potential. Once we are healing ourselves, the best next step is the healing of others. The Tree of Life is an ideal agent for this change.

THE BUSINESS AND CORPORATE WORLD

Economic factors lie behind many of the changes that happen within societies on a local and international level. Some people put the blame for ecological crises on the actions of individuals; some blame the big multinational corporations that put profits before people. Whatever the truth in these matters – whether it concerns an individual, the owner of a small local business, the manager of a national firm or the director of a global enterprise – of prime importance is effective leadership. Leadership presents a profound challenge both to the leader and those who are led; and leadership isn't just for others, we are all potential leaders. To become a 'leader' is to take on a role or symbol for the insight and power that each of us might be called upon to identify with at various stages of our life within society. Looking at this from a Kabbalistic viewpoint, we can quickly delineate the main challenges to someone working in a leadership role (see diagram below, left).

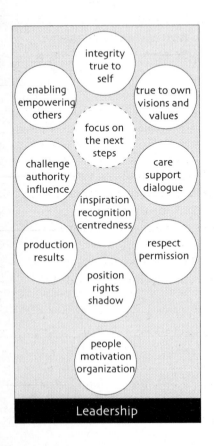

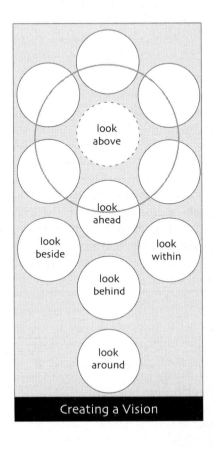

The overriding principles of leadership are the essential components of the Supernal Triad: to be true to oneself and one's own visions and values whilst enabling and empowering others. The true leader does not promote his or her power over others, but endorses and elevates the power of others. Through respect for others (Netzach), the ability to make decisions that get results (Hod), honouring the position or rights of all involved (Yesod), and motivating people and developing the organization (Malkuth), the true leader can remain centred and be an effective channel of power, authority, care and support.

One of the foremost qualities needed for effective leadership is the ability to create and then cast vision. The diagram opposite, right, shows how to understand the process of taking a vision through the spheres of the Tree of Life. In Malkuth the leader needs to look *around* and ask what is happening for the others involved in the organization. In Yesod the task is to look *behind*, offering the opportunity to learn from what has gone before. In Hod the work is to look *beside* oneself at what resources are available; and in Netzach to look *within*, checking out the feelings involved in the issues at hand. Centred in Tiphareth, the leader will look *ahead*, getting a sense of the bigger picture, then, through attending to the next step in Daath, the leader will look *above* to find what is emerging, what is calling the leader and the organization. This way the vision that emerges takes into account the energies of the whole organization. This method for creating a vision can of course be applied in many other spheres of activity.

THE VALUE OF THERAPIES

There are many different kinds of therapies, and different aspects of all of them may be related to the Tree of Life. Whatever the school or therapy, whether a talk-only type or one using hands-on techniques, it involves three basic aspects: the principles behind the work (The Supernal Triad), the relationship between the therapist and patient or client (the soul triangle), and the methods and techniques used (the bottom triangle.)

In psychotherapy for example, through relating psychotherapeutic practice to the Tree of Life we can better understand the processes involved. Of course, there are many different schools of therapy but, generally, psychotherapists do not judge, although they may interpret (Hod); they do not lead, although they may challenge (Yesod); they do not touch, although they do offer support (Malkuth); and they work alongside the unfolding process of their clients, trusting in what manifests as being right for that person at that time (Netzach). Psychotherapists also generally work within the container of the therapeutic space, using the time of the session to be in deep relationship with their client (Tiphareth), involved and witnessing at the same time.

Using the Tree of Life, a therapist can truly work in an integrative way, and not just offer a hotchpotch of borrowed techniques. The Kabbalah is the perfect model or map for this work for, through its simplicity and clarity, it can act as a central synthesizing agent for methods and techniques, other systems, maps and models of consciousness development. Whatever methods are used, however, the principles behind the therapy remain basically the same. There is an attempt to share in an experiential understanding of the relationship between the therapist and client. The use of the Kabbalah as a tool in psychotherapy allows the practitioner to develop his or her own style in accord with universal principles, develop a relationship in line with these principles, and apply techniques where and as appropriate to each relationship.

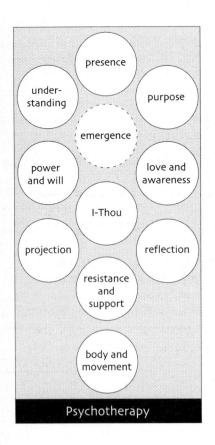

Psychotherapy

Different methods of psychotherapy concentrate on different aspects of the process. For example, Jungian therapists usually work up to Daath, concentrating on the dynamic between Chesed and Geburah (Love and Will archetypes) through the medium of dream analysis (Hod and Yesod). Traditional psychoanalysis works with the lower Tree, attempting to normalize the personality (and, at its worst, denying the deeper or higher aspects of the psyche). This is the opposite pole from the worst forms of transpersonal therapies which work up to Daath or above, but not down into Yesod or Malkuth, potentially leaving clients spiritually connected but totally ungrounded. The differences between approaches become clearer when related to the Tree of Life, which then offers us the possibility of integrating them so the common purpose becomes more apparent.

To use the Kabbalah as a tool in

therapeutic work, whether counselling, psychotherapy or other forms of one-to-one or group healing, it is vital that therapists have someone who can work with them in a supervisory capacity, to help them see what is going on in the work in terms of the model being used. If no such person is available they can supervise themselves, but the work will lack the holding and challenging functions that are possible when working with the help of another.

Of most importance is the awareness of where and how the therapist and client are relating, or not, in terms of the different planes of the Tree, which represent different aspects of the psyche. If therapy is to be successful it is important that the therapist works on creating relationship at all times: establishing 'mindfulness' or focus; making space for the individual experience of the client and the unfolding experience of his or her relationship with the practitioner. The diagram opposite helps show how some of the major issues in such work correspond to the Tree of Life. Through study of the Kabbalah, a therapist could apply the understanding gained to work with groups and individuals.

RELIGIOUS TRADITIONS

In our modern world, therapists often play the role that in early societies was ascribed to the shamans, wise women or healers. Increasingly, however, as people search for meaning in life, whether in terms of existential satisfaction or deeper spiritual quests, different religious traditions once again play an increasingly vital role. When we relate the concepts and practices of different traditions to the Tree of Life, we find there are considerably more similarities than differences. The Tree of Life therefore has the potential to bring harmony where previously there may have been discord and mistrust. Through the Tree of Life, even fundamentalists might be able to arrive at a better understanding of those who hold differing beliefs.

When, for example, we understand the 'gentle' and 'strong' aspects of Jesus' character as corresponding to Chesed and Geburah, we find a correspondence with the compassionate and courageous aspects of Mohammed's life. Further correspondences include the Buddhist meditations on joy and nature; the Hindu deities Indra and Vishnu; the Greek deities Zeus and Ares; the Egyptian Osiris and Isis; and the Scandinavian gods Wotan and Thor. Even ancient cosmologies can be of value, for an understanding of the gods and goddesses of our ancestors not only gives us an understanding of our roots, it can assist in making sense of the mythical aspects of dreams and visions.

If we look within any particular religion, we find different aspects of the religion correspond to different areas of the Tree of Life. In the case of Christianity, we can see how the different components of the Christian faith correspond to the Tree of Life (see diagram below, left).

It is also possible to relate various aspects of the story of Jesus' life to the Tree. The 40 days and nights he spent in the wilderness, for instance, may well relate to the experience of being in the Abyss. The Devil who tempts him is equivalent, in this case, to the demon of Daath. If Jesus had succumbed he would have failed what Kabbalists call 'the ordeal of the Abyss.' This involves giving up everything that has gone before, giving up all sense of power, fellowship, hope and connection. Jesus did not succumb, however, and his experiences in the Abyss strengthened him for his subsequent journey. When he said 'My Father and I are One' he was uniting the Supernal Triad with the middle triangle of the Tree. United, these two triangles form a hexagram, used by both Jewish people and occultists as a symbol of the greatest spiritual truth.

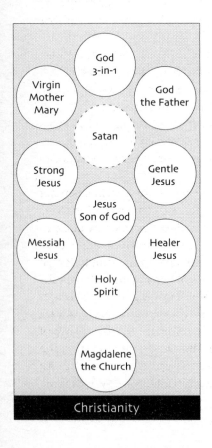

Christianity

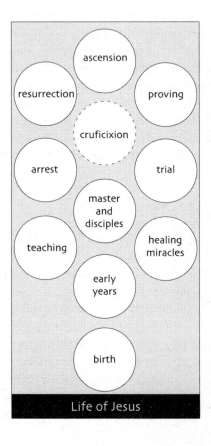

Life of Jesus

The whole life of Jesus can also be seen to correspond to the Tree of Life in different ways. For instance, one way is to place the various stages of his life on the Tree, working from the bottom to the top as the diagram opposite, right, shows. The purpose of relating Jesus' life, or that of any other religious leader, to the Tree of Life, or of relating different religious ideas to the Kabbalah, is primarily that it offers us a greater understanding of our own beliefs and interests. It may also profoundly affect the manifestation of tolerance and understanding between different religious traditions.

GENDER EQUALITY

When people are in grave danger they are often said to call out for their mother. A soldier in a life-threatening battle, for instance, may well do this. Collectively many of us ascribe the properties of mothering to our planet and call her Mother Earth. The mother archetype is the first imprint upon most of us after birth and it stays with us as a primary connection to our source or ultimate origins. After all, *none* of us would be here without a mother!

Many people understand Kabbalah as having its roots in the Judaic tradition. Whether this is ultimately true or not, it is certainly correct that we owe much of our understanding and the development of the Tree of Life to Jewish Kabbalists. Jewish Kabbalists, however, have usually held a different world-view from that held by the Orthodox Jewish faith. In particular, the Kabbalah is neither patriarchal nor matriarchal in its focus, but is people-centred. Women and men are treated as equal in every way.

One example of the suppression of women, not only in Judaism but in many faiths, is through the negativization of menstruation. This aspect of the natural female cycle is considered to be somehow unclean and to be avoided, particularly by men. Apart from anything else, however, the menstrual cycle gives us an excellent opportunity to see how we can use correspondences to the Tree of Life in different, creative ways. Not all correspondences will fit neatly on to the usual pattern of spheres and paths. In the case of the menstrual cycle, as the diagram overleaf shows, we can best understand it through a different way of connecting the spheres. Starting at either the top or the bottom of the diagram, with ovulation or menstruation, through reading round the spheres we can make a connection between the menstrual cycle and the Tree. This way of using the diagram exemplifies a typically 'female' quality that can be found in both men and women: the ability to find new

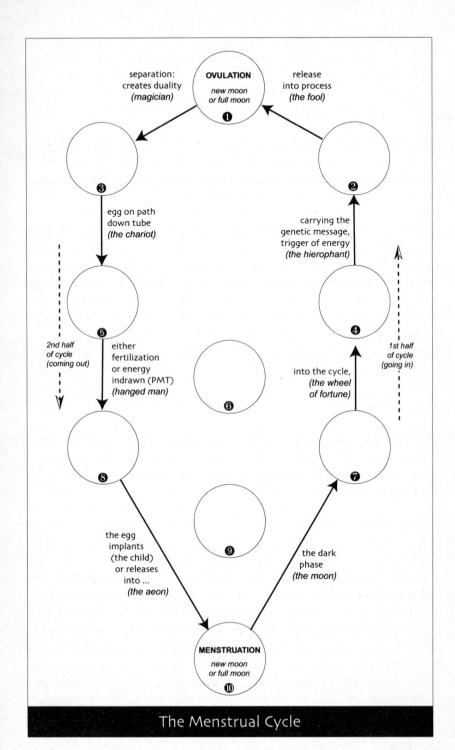

The Menstrual Cycle

and creative ways of using something. It also reminds us that the Tree of Life is infinitely variable and applicable depending upon the ingenuity of the user.

BACK TO EARTH

Whether working with the Tree of Life or any of the many different ways we can work on ourselves, none of this is of any importance if we keep it in isolation, if we keep ourselves separate. You are a fortunate enough person to have the time to read a book like this. At the same time there are many people in your area, in your country, in the world, who are suffering through no fault of their own. Any claim that we are totally responsible for everything that happens to us – that people who are starving in Africa have chosen to be born there, for instance – is absolutely incorrect. There are people on this planet who are suffering through no fault of their own. In our work, therefore, it is important we always make some space to be aware of the energy and the connections we can send out into the world. We can take the time to remember ourselves as part of a wider human, animal, plant and mineral world.

back to earth

Spend a moment to think of or connect with a situation in the world to which you would like to send energy. It can be something very personal – an individual that you know, perhaps – or something on a world scale.

Then do it.

Without denying any of the awful events that occur on our planet, we can also be aware of how far we humans, as a species, have come, and how much has been achieved in terms of consciousness and awareness in the relatively short time we have been on this planet. We are still evolving, and, considering how everything is speeding up in our modern world, should be able to do so much more in this new century. It is hard to imagine anyone only a hundred years ago being able to even vaguely predict all the changes that have occurred during the last century.

Where might we be in a million years from now? And even if we humans were to suffer the same fate as the dinosaurs, the earth would still have another sixteen billion years or so left to evolve without us.

This chapter started through connecting us to the earth and its mysteries. At the end of this chapter, and indeed at the end of this book, we return to earth, the ground from where all Kabbalistic work begins and ends. This last exercise takes you up the Tree of Life and then brings you back to take the next step in your journey. May it have meaning and be fruitful for you personally and for all of life, of which we are each an insignificant and yet essential part.

lighting the Tree of Life

Follow the usual starting procedure.

Then stand up with your eyes closed.

Connect to the ground: imagine you have roots that connect you deeply into the earth.

Visualize the energy of the earth flowing up your legs, into your lower body, your genitals and lower abdomen … As you do this, get a sense of openness and freedom pervading you.

Visualize energy rising up into your belly, your solar plexus and whole trunk … As you do this, feel your centredness in life, how you are rooted in earthly existence.

Visualize energy rising up into your heart, see your heart glowing with energy … As you do this, feel yourself filled with courage and compassion.

Visualize energy flowing from your heart, down your arms and into your hands … Feel how the courage and compassion in your heart gives you the power to link with all other life.

Visualize energy rising up into your throat and mouth, and into your voice … feel this connected energy giving you the power to speak out your truth.

Without opening your eyes, make a sound that expresses your connection with your innermost sense of Self. (Don't force it, but keep making the sound until you feel complete.)

Visualize energy rising to your eyes – open your eyes and see the truth of who you are and where you are … Close your eyes, visualize the energy ascending to the top of your head and feel the presence of the Source of all life.

Imagine yourself as the Tree of Life: feel your roots deep in the earth, your trunk filled with energy, your branches stretching up into the sky, connecting with the light of the sun and stars …

Draw down the energy of the sun and stars into your body ... keep drawing energy through your body and bring this energy right down to earth.

Bring energy right down into your roots, and take up a posture expressing who you are, your own truth when you are connected to your own path through life. Let this energy successfully lead you forward and take the next step into the rest of your life, aware of your inner stillness in the Supernal Triad, your centre in the soul triangle, and your individual integrity in the bottom triangle of the Tree of Life.

The Starting Procedure: how to use the exercises in this book

At the start of most of the exercises throughout this book you meet the phrase 'follow the usual starting procedure'. This 'starting procedure' is aimed at helping you maximize the beneficial effects of the exercises. The basic starting procedure consists of three elements: *banishing, relaxing, centring.*

Before starting an exercise make sure you have enough time to complete it without being disturbed. Even if you can only spend a very short time on a particular exercise do set aside a specific period for it and stick to that.

1. Banishing: as you progress through the work you may find, particularly with more complex exercises and rituals, that you prefer to perform the Kabbalistic Cross or even a Banishing Ritual before commencing. You will find these procedures described in Chapter 2 and Chapter 6 respectively. If you are not using these procedures, your banishing should at the very least consist of visualizing yourself and the space you are using for the exercise as completely enclosed in a sphere of bright blue light.

2/3. Relaxing and centring: take up a comfortable position, either standing, sitting or lying, as appropriate to the exercise, and with an erect spine and closed eyes breathe deeply and slowly a few times. Take a few minutes over this, do not rush. Be aware that you are a unique individual choosing, at this very time, in this very space (that is, 'here and now'), to perform this exercise.

Always take your time with an exercise – it is better to err on the side of 'slowness' rather than rush through it.

Particularly with the longer exercises, it may be necessary to read the exercise through a few times to familiarize yourself with what you have to do. Do not begrudge this time: it will help you to connect with the 'essence' of the exercise and become focused. Some of the exercises could be recorded, if you so wish, thus enabling repeated use of them without interruption. This is particularly useful for long visualizations. Alternatively, of course, working with someone else also assists such work.

If you find a specific exercise(s) especially useful, stick to it for some time, even if you do not notice immediate results. Repetition of an exercise multiples its power.

It is a good idea to keep a journal or magickal diary (see Appendix 2). Get into the habit of recording your experiences immediately after finishing an exercise.

Remember that the fourth power of the Sphinx is *silence*. Do not gossip about your work or prematurely share insights; this can often dissipate the energy.

Keeping a Journal

It is emphasized throughout this book how useful it is to keep a magickal diary or workbook.

You can use your diary to record:

- thoughts, flashes, creative insights
- your practical work, including date, time and any other conditions you think relevant
- a description of pertinent experiences you may have, positive or negative in nature
- drawings, diagrams and other visual items of relevance
- anything else you think of!

Your diary may:

- help you formulate more precisely what you know
- make your knowledge more accessible and increase your understanding
- help you make choices
- call into play your sense of values and keep work in perspective
- attune your mind to your intuitive processes and abstract mind
- be an act of affirmation and commitment, thus strengthening your purpose
- help you see long-term trends in your growth
- aid your memory
- record your successes and difficulties

and be of value in many more ways, depending on how you use it.

Remember, it is *your* magickal diary; it is for your benefit alone, being a record of you as you are and as you progress.

Standard Symbols

The symbols used to represent elements, planets and zodiac signs throughout this book are the standard ones. They are:

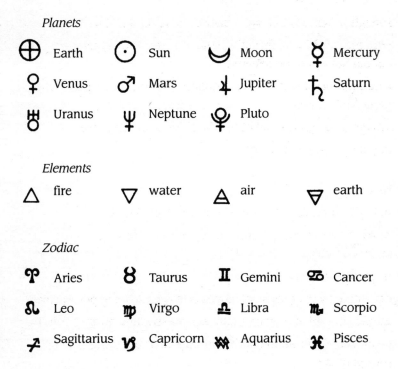

Planets

⊕ Earth   ☉ Sun   ☽ Moon   ☿ Mercury

♀ Venus   ♂ Mars   ♃ Jupiter   ♄ Saturn

♅ Uranus   ♆ Neptune   ♇ Pluto

Elements

△ fire   ▽ water   △ air   ▽ earth

Zodiac

♈ Aries   ♉ Taurus   ♊ Gemini   ♋ Cancer

♌ Leo   ♍ Virgo   ♎ Libra   ♏ Scorpio

♐ Sagittarius   ♑ Capricorn   ♒ Aquarius   ♓ Pisces

The Correspondence Tables

When you look at these correspondence tables, you will see a plethora of images, ideas, concepts and experiences that correspond with the spheres and paths of the Tree of Life. These include the human system, the body, colours, tarot cards, Hebrew letters, trees, flowers and animals. Many items are traditionally attributed to each sphere and path – indeed, one could ultimately ascribe everything in the universe to the Tree of Life. This is part of its value, and is what makes the Tree of Life a wonderful compendium of universal symbols. With all correspondences, however, the most important thing is to make your own connections. So, for instance, if your experience is that a willow tree and goldfish are more appropriate correspondences for Malkuth than the oak and rabbit, then these will be your personal correspondences for working that sphere.

The purpose of these tables is to enable you to understand different symbols, objects, ideas, and so on, in relation to the Tree of Life. This can enable you to find connections between different symbols and categories of symbols, and understand unknown symbols in terms of those with which you are familiar. If you are not sure how to use these tables, refer to the section 'The Meaning of Symbols' in Chapter 4 which explains their use. They are simple to understand: if you read horizontally across any of the rows in the tables you will find matching symbols which are known as correspondences. For instance, if you read across row 14, you will see that this row relates to the path joining spheres 2 and 3, that is, Chockmah and Binah. Reading across, you find this path then corresponds with the letter 'daleth', the nose and mouth, dark grey, Venus, elderflower, a bee, and so on.

The main point of using correspondences is to be able to relate your experience to the Tree, then see the relationship between this and the whole Tree. Any correspondence is appropriate if it works for you. It is useful, however, to stretch ourselves to see why certain correspondences have a more 'universal' application. For example, in Western Europe anyway, most people seem to find the oak tree a good correspondence for Malkuth (the Earth). Why should that be? On the one hand, correspondences can become rather dated. Traditionally the jackal was attributed to Hod, for instance, because in the ancient world it was considered sacred to Mercury, the planet of Hod. In our modern world, however, we may not have much contact with jackals and find that, for instance, a fox is a better correspondence because of its mercurial nature.

The tables in *The Complete Guide to the Kabbalah* are the result of much work at refining and clarifying the system. They are practical in that they include items that you can connect with in our modern world. There is no point, for instance, in telling you that a particular perfume corresponds to a particular sphere if that perfume is completely obscure and virtually unobtainable. Hopefully, many if not all will make sense to you, and can be used appropriately for your Kabbalistic work. Let me stress again, however, that nothing in the Kabbalah is fixed, and as time passes these correspondences may change again, or you may find ones that better suit your psyche. For now I suggest you use these correspondences as a good starting point for your explorations.

Spheres and Paths	Hebrew Letters	Hebrew Names of Letters	English Equivalent	Numerical Value	English Letters
1 Kether			Crown		
2 Chockmah			Wisdom		
3 Binah			Understanding		
D Daath			Knowledge		
4 Chesed			Mercy		
5 Geburah			Judgement		
6 Tiphareth			Beauty		
7 Netzach			Victory		
8 Hod			Splendour		
9 Yesod			Foundation		
10 Malkuth			World		
11 joins 1–2	א	aleph	ox	1	A
12 joins 1–3	ב	beth	house	2	B
13 joins 1–6	ג	gimel	camel	3	C, G
14 joins 2–3	ד	daleth	door	4	D
15 joins 2–6	ה	he	window	5	H
16 joins 2–4	ו	vau	nail	6	U,V
17 joins 3–6	ז	zain	sword	7	Z
18 joins 3–5	ח	cheth	fence	8	Ch
19 joins 4–5	ט	teth	serpent	9	T
20 joins 4–6	י	yod	hand	10	I,Y
21 joins 4–7	כ	kaph	palm of hand	20	K
22 joins 5–6	ל	lamed	ox-goad	30	L
23 joins 5–8	מ	mem	water	40	M
24 joins 6–7	נ	nun	fish	50	N
25 joins 6–9	ס	samekh	support	60	S
26 joins 6–8	ע	ayin	eye	70	O
27 joins 7–8	פ	pe	mouth	80	P
28 joins 7–9	צ	tzaddi	fish-hook	90	X, Tz
29 joins 7–10	ק	qoph	back of head	100	Q
30 joins 8–9	ר	resh	head	200	R
31 joins 8–10	ש	shin	tooth	300	Sh
32 joins 9–10	ת	tau	cross	400	Th

Spheres and Paths	Physical Structure	Inner Body Components
1 Kether	crown	consciousness
2 Chockmah	left side of head	left brain
3 Binah	right side of head	right brain
D Daath	throat	throat, thyroid
4 Chesed	left shoulder	left adrenal
5 Geburah	right shoulder	right adrenal
6 Tiphareth	breast bone	heart, thymus
7 Netzach	left arm and hand	left kidney
8 Hod	right arm and hand	right kidney
9 Yesod	sexual organs	sexual organs
10 Malkuth	base of spine, feet	body as whole
11 joins 1–2	left eye, left ear	left eye, left ear, pituitary
12 joins 1–3	right eye, right ear	right eye, right ear, pineal
13 joins 1–6	backbone	spinal cord
14 joins 2–3	nose, mouth	nose, mouth
15 joins 2–6	left front of neck	arteries, oxygenated blood
16 joins 2–4	left rear neck	posterior pituitary, endocrine overall
17 joins 3–6	right front of neck	veins, de-oxygenated blood
18 joins 3–5	right rear neck	anterior pituitary, endocrine overall
19 joins 4–5	upper chest (breasts)	lymph, spleen
20 joins 4–6	left upper back and sides	left lung
21 joins 4–7	left mid back and sides	large intestine (descending), rectum
22 joins 5–6	right upper back and sides	right lung
23 joins 5–8	right mid back and sides	large intestine (ascending/transverse)
24 joins 6–7	left lower back	stomach
25 joins 6–9	solar plexus	solar plexus
26 joins 6–8	right lower back	liver, gall bladder, pancreas
27 joins 7–8	navel, mid belly	small intestines
28 joins 7–9	left lower abdomen	left inner sexual system
29 joins 7–10	left leg	left skeleton, bones, muscles
30 joins 8–9	right lower abdomen	right inner sexual system
31 joins 8–10	right leg	right skeleton, bones, muscles
32 joins 9–10	perineum, buttocks	bladder, skin

Spheres and Paths	Physical Disorders
1 Kether	lifelessness, soul-less, etc.
2 Chockmah	left brain disorders
3 Binah	right brain disorders
D Daath	thyroid disorders, metabolic rate
4 Chesed	adrenalin-flee (stress, muscular waste)
5 Geburah	adrenalin-fight (stress, virilism)
6 Tiphareth	heart failure and disease, thymus, immunosystem disorders
7 Netzach	kidney disorders
8 Hod	kidney disorders
9 Yesod	sexual disorders
10 Malkuth	death
11 joins 1–2	optical defects, ear disorders, hearing, balance, seeing
12 joins 1–3	optical defects, ear disorders, hearing, balance, seeing
13 joins 1–6	spinal disorders, sensation disturbance
14 joins 2–3	nasal and mouth disorders, vibrational recognition
15 joins 2–6	stroke, coronary thrombosis, arteriosclerosis
16 joins 2–4	inner growth disorders
17 joins 3–6	thrombosis, clotting
18 joins 3–5	outer growth disorders
19 joins 4–5	defence disorders, widespread disorder
20 joins 4–6	numerous disorders (e.g. bronchitis, pneumonia, asthma)
21 joins 4–7	various disorders (including emotional)
22 joins 5–6	numerous disorders (e.g. bronchitis, pneumonia, asthma)
23 joins 5–8	various disorders (including emotional)
24 joins 6–7	various disorders (including ulceration)
25 joins 6–9	nervous disorders
26 joins 6–8	various (liver e.g. jaundice; pancreas e.g. diabetes)
27 joins 7–8	various (including emotional)
28 joins 7–9	reproductive disorders
29 joins 7–10	skeletal disorders (e.g. rheumatism, arthritis, gout)
30 joins 8–9	reproductive disorders
31 joins 8–10	skeletal disorders (e.g. rheumatism, arthritis, gout)
32 joins 9–10	skin diseases, cystitis, etc.

	Spheres and Paths	Colours	Celestial Attributions	Alternative Esoteric Titles
1	Kether	white	Pluto	vast countenance
2	Chockmah	grey	Neptune/zodiac	crown of creation
3	Binah	black	Saturn	the great sea
D	Daath	lilac	Uranus/asteroids	the abyss
4	Chesed	blue	Jupiter	majesty
5	Geburah	red	Mars	justice
6	Tiphareth	yellow	Sun	the child
7	Netzach	green	Venus	the beauty of nature
8	Hod	orange	Mercury	active science
9	Yesod	purple	Luna	the fulcrum
10	Malkuth	sky blue	Earth/elements	the gate
11	joins 1–2	light grey	Air	the holy spirit
12	joins 1–3	mid-grey	Mercury	the messenger
13	joins 1–6	pale yellow	Luna	the virgin
14	joins 2–3	dark grey	Venus	the wife
15	joins 2–6	pale blue	Aquarius	the mother
16	joins 2–4	grey-blue	Taurus	the child priest
17	joins 3–6	pink	Gemini	the twins emerging
18	joins 3–5	crimson	Cancer	the grail
19	joins 4–5	purple	Leo	the magickal union
20	joins 4–6	olive green	Virgo	the secret seed
21	joins 4–7	blue-green	Jupiter	the father of all
22	joins 5–6	orange	Libra	the sexually united
23	joins 5–8	red-orange	Water	the water redeemer
24	joins 6–7	yellow-green	Scorpio	the redeeming belly
25	joins 6–9	mauve	Sagittarius	the pregnant womb
26	joins 6–8	gold ochre	Capricorn	the erect and glad
27	joins 7–8	brown	Mars	the conquering child
28	joins 7–9	bright green	Aries	the ruler
29	joins 7–10	silver	Pisces	the elder witch
30	joins 8–9	bright orange	Sun	the playing gods
31	joins 8–10	pale pink	Fire	the emerging goddess
32	joins 9–10	black	Saturn	pantacle of the whole

Spheres and Paths	Human System	Divine Forces	Archangels
1 Kether	the self	eheieh	Metatron
2 Chockmah	spiritual will/purpose	ihvh	Ratziel
3 Binah	spiritual love/ awareness	ihvh elohim	Tzaphkiel
D Daath	'the next step'	ue	
4 Chesed	love/awareness	el	Tzadkiel
5 Geburah	will/power	elohim gebor	Khamael
6 Tiphareth	personal self/ centre/'I'	ihvh aloah	Raphael
7 Netzach	feeling	ihvh tzabaoth	Haniel
8 Hod	thinking	elohim tzabaoth	Michael
9 Yesod	subconscious/ sexuality	shaddai el chai	Gabriel
10 Malkuth	body (as whole)/ senses	adonai ha-aretz	Sandalphon
11 joins 1–2	[connections between	[Hebrew letters	[various
12 joins 1–3	systems in spheres]	as they	angels
		correspond	correspond
13 joins 1–6	,,	with the paths]	with the
14 joins 2–3	,,		connecting
15 joins 2–6	,,		paths]
16 joins 2–4	,,		
17 joins 3–6	,,		
18 joins 3–5	,,		
19 joins 4–5	,,		
20 joins 4–6	,,		
21 joins 4–7	,,		
22 joins 5–6	,,		
23 joins 5–8	,,		
24 joins 6–7	,,		
25 joins 6–9	,,		
26 joins 6–8	,,		
27 joins 7–8	,,		
28 joins 7–9	,,		
29 joins 7–10	,,		
30 joins 8–9	,,		
31 joins 8–10	,,		
32 joins 9–10	,,		

Spheres and Paths	Pathworking and the Places of Power
1 Kether	the innermost temple
2 Chockmah	the celestial spheres
3 Binah	the great sea
D Daath	the rainbow bridge
4 Chesed	the temple of love
5 Geburah	the temple of power
6 Tiphareth	the mountain of the soul
7 Netzach	the garden of beauty
8 Hod	the house of spells
9 Yesod	the secret valley
10 Malkuth	the meadow of delights
11 joins 1–2	scintillating path, facing the creator
12 joins 1–3	transparent path, seeing visions
13 joins 1–6	uniting path, realizing spiritual truth
14 joins 2–3	illuminating path, fundamental holiness
15 joins 2–6	constituting path, substance of creation
16 joins 2–4	eternal path, pleasure of paradise
17 joins 3–6	disposing path, foundation of faith
18 joins 3–5	influential path, understanding causality
19 joins 4–5	activating path, the experience of blessings
20 joins 4–6	intelligent path, knowledge of existence
21 joins 4–7	conciliatory path, transmitting divine influence
22 joins 5–6	faithful path, increasing spiritual value
23 joins 5–8	stable path, increasing consistency
24 joins 6–7	imaginative path, renewal and change
25 joins 6–9	tentative path, the alchemical processes
26 joins 6–8	renovating path, life force in action
27 joins 7–8	exciting path, the nature of existence
28 joins 7–9	admiral path, understanding the depths
29 joins 7–10	corporeal path, the formation of the body
30 joins 8–9	collecting path, celestial arts and astrology
31 joins 8–10	perpetual path, regulating the creation
32 joins 9–10	administrative path, directing life energies

Spheres and Paths	Aromatic Oils	Herbs
1 Kether	almond	camomile
2 Chockmah	frankincense	rosemary
3 Binah	myrrh	comfrey
D Daath	eucalyptus	balm of gilead
4 Chesed	cedarwood	borage
5 Geburah	cypress	borage
6 Tiphareth	rose	hawthorn berries/bay/heartsease
7 Netzach	patchouli	couchgrass/verbena
8 Hod	rosemary	couchgrass/sage
9 Yesod	lavender	damiana
10 Malkuth	sandalwood	meadowsweet
11 joins 1–2	melissa	hyssop/eyebright
12 joins 1–3	cardamom	hyssop/eyebright
13 joins 1–6	sage	red clover
14 joins 2–3	clove	elderflower
15 joins 2–6	marigold	lime blossom
16 joins 2–4	pine	yellow dock
17 joins 3–6	jasmine/ylang	marigold
18 joins 3–5	thyme	thyme
19 joins 4–5	calamus	echinacea
20 joins 4–6	camphor	coltsfoot
21 joins 4–7	basil	pilewort
22 joins 5–6	clarisage	coltsfoot
23 joins 5–8	camomile	bayberry
24 joins 6–7	peppermint	peppermint
25 joins 6–9	bergamot/hyacinth	passiflora
26 joins 6–8	nutmeg	dandelion
27 joins 7–8	fennel	fennel
28 joins 7–9	geranium	nettle/black cohosh
29 joins 7–10	juniper	bogbean
30 joins 8–9	cinnamon	raspberry leaf/blue cohosh
31 joins 8–10	hyssop	yarrow
32 joins 9–10	marjoram	sarsparilla/rue

Spheres and Paths	Flowers	Trees	Magickal Instruments and Symbols
1 Kether	lotus/almond	almond	crown/cauldron/lamp
2 Chockmah	orchid	beech	penis/body/word
3 Binah	lily	alder	vagina/cloak/cup
D Daath	ivy	magnolia	incense/bell/oil
4 Chesed	tulip	birch	wand/sceptre/crook
5 Geburah	peony	rowan	sword/spear/scourge
6 Tiphareth	yellow rose/gorse	holly	lamen/rosy cross/altar
7 Netzach	red rose/grasses	apple	lamp/girdle/dagger
8 Hod	pansy	hazel	spells/book/chain
9 Yesod	iris/violet	willow	perfumes/sandals
10 Malkuth	clover/ meadowsweet	oak	circle/triangle/crystal
11 joins 1–2	daisy	spruce	dagger/fan/stick
12 joins 1–3	primrose	ash	wand/caduceus
13 joins 1–6	buttercup	maple	bow/arrow/veil
14 joins 2–3	bluebell	sweet chestnut	girdle/shield/lotus
15 joins 2–6	marigold	pine	censer/star-charts
16 joins 2–4	cowslip	cypress	crown/pentagram
17 joins 3–6	honeysuckle	sycamore	tripod/egg/flower
18 joins 3–5	nasturtium	cherry	furnace/grail/chariot
19 joins 4–5	sunflower	fig	heart/reins/elixir
20 joins 4–6	rosebay willow herb	walnut	lamp/wand/bread
21 joins 4–7	anemone	plane	sceptre/wheel
22 joins 5–6	dahlia	palm	equal cross/scales
23 joins 5–8	harebell	lime	christian cross/wine
24 joins 6–7	snowdrop	yew	scythe/poisons
25 joins 6–9	hyacinth	cedar	alchemical items
26 joins 6–8	foxglove	aspen	elixir/lamp/horns
27 joins 7–8	nettle	horse chestnut	sword/tower/fire
28 joins 7–9	geranium	elder	sceptre/orb/flag
29 joins 7–10	poppy	elm	magic mirror/blood
30 joins 8–9	crocus	bay	lamen/talismans
31 joins 8–10	dandelion	balsam poplar	wings/stars/pyramid
32 joins 9–10	daffodil	hawthorn	pantacle/salt/temple

Spheres and Paths	Animals	Legendary Beings	Magickal Visions and Powers
1 Kether	swan	dryad	union with self
2 Chockmah	owl	lemur	vision of self
3 Binah	whale	siren	vision of wonder and sorrow
D Daath	vulture	chimera	dominion over darkness
4 Chesed	dolphin	sphinx	vision of love
5 Geburah	horse	dwarf	vision of power
6 Tiphareth	spider	fairy	vision of harmony
7 Netzach	dove	faun	vision of triumphant beauty
8 Hod	fox	elf	vision of splendour
9 Yesod	cat	vampire	vision of machinery of universe
10 Malkuth	rabbit	gnome	vision of guardian angel
11 joins 1–2	tiger	sylph	fearlessness
12 joins 1–3	monkey	apeman	healing/casting spells
13 joins 1–6	camel	ghost	clairvoyance/dream control
14 joins 2–3	bee	harpy	enchantment/love potions
15 joins 2–6	human	succubus	actualizing true will
16 joins 2–4	cow	banshee	inner voice/physical strength
17 joins 3–6	magpie	incubus	control of double/prophecy
18 joins 3–5	crab	nereid	past life recall
19 joins 4–5	lion	gorgon	dialogue with other beings
20 joins 4–6	crow	apparition	invisibility
21 joins 4–7	blackbird	lemur	divination
22 joins 5–6	elephant	nymph	equilibrium and balance
23 joins 5–8	snake	mermaid/ merman	skrying/body-will
24 joins 6–7	scorpion	lamia	necromancy/mediumistic abilities
25 joins 6–9	peacock	centaur	transmutation/vision of peacock
26 joins 6–8	goat	satyr	fascination/casting evil eye
27 joins 7–8	gnat	dragon	talismanic arts/creating disorder
28 joins 7–9	sheep	minotaur	power of consecration
29 joins 7–10	dog	werewolf	bewitchments/casting illusions
30 joins 8–9	butterfly	will-o'-wisp	power of acquiring wealth
31 joins 8–10	hawk	salamander	evocation/transformation
32 joins 9–10	crocodile	ghoul	astral vision/geomancy

Spheres and Paths	Tarot Attributions	Esoteric Titles of Tarot Cards
1 Kether	four aces	
2 Chockmah	four 2s/knights	
3 Binah	four 3s/queens	
D Daath	-	
4 Chesed	four 4s	
5 Geburah	four 5s	
6 Tiphareth	four 6s/princes	
7 Netzach	four 7s	
8 Hod	four 8s	
9 Yesod	four 9s	
10 Malkuth	four 10s/princesses	
11 joins 1–2	fool	the spirit of the aether
12 joins 1–3	magus	the spirit in the temple
13 joins 1–6	priestess	priestess of the silver star
14 joins 2–3	empress	daughter of the mighty ones
15 joins 2–6	star	daughter of the firmament
16 joins 2–4	hierophant	magus of the eternal
17 joins 3–6	lovers	children of the voice
18 joins 3–5	chariot	magus of the triumph of light
19 joins 4–5	lust/strength	children of the dragon flame
20 joins 4–6	hermit	prophet of the eternal
21 joins 4–7	fortune	ruler of the forces of life
22 joins 5–6	adjustment/justice	spirit of inner truth
23 joins 5–8	hanged man	spirit of the mighty waters
24 joins 6–7	death	lord of the great transformation
25 joins 6–9	art/temperance	the bringer forth of life
26 joins 6–8	devil	lord of the gates of matter
27 joins 7–8	tower	priest of the divine fire
28 joins 7–9	emperor	son of the morning
29 joins 7–10	moon	priestess of the crescent gate
30 joins 8–9	sun	son of the world fire
31 joins 8–10	aeon/judgement	spirit of the primal fire
32 joins 9–10	universe	great one of the night of time

Spheres and Paths	Spiritual keywords fire/wands	Mental keywords air/sword	Emotional keywords water/cups
1 Kether	revelation	illumination	ecstasy
2 Chockmah	dominion	peace	love
3 Binah	virtue	sorrow	abundance
D Daath	recognition	conflict	vitality
4 Chesed	completion	truce	luxury
5 Geburah	strife	defeat	disappointment
6 Tiphareth	victory	science	pleasure
7 Netzach	valour	futility	debauch
8 Hod	swiftness	interference	indolence
9 Yesod	strength	cruelty	happiness
10 Malkuth	oppression	ruin	satiety
11 joins 1–2	wholeness	stimulating	expressive
12 joins 1–3	wilful	quick	unpredictable
13 joins 1–6	intuitive	clear	centred
14 joins 2–3	unconditional	tolerant	forgiving
15 joins 2–6	realization	bright	flowing
16 joins 2–4	channel	establishing	compassionate
17 joins 3–6	integrating	balancing	changeable
18 joins 3–5	questing	focused	secretive
19 joins 4–5	affirming	certain	passionate
20 joins 4–6	introspective	discriminating	sober
21 joins 4–7	change	opportunistic	courageous
22 joins 5–6	idealistic	logical	observing
23 joins 5–8	patience	reflective	stoical
24 joins 6–7	liberation	recognition	fear
25 joins 6–9	harmony	ingenious	optimistic
26 joins 6–8	vitality	original	unrestrained
27 joins 7–8	purifying	motivated	cathartic
28 joins 7–9	discipline	analytical	stable
29 joins 7–10	receptive	reflective	explosive
30 joins 8–9	celebrating	spontaneous	joyous
31 joins 8–10	seeing	perceptive	detached
32 joins 9–10	fulfilling	plenty	exciting

Spheres and Paths	Physical keywords earth/disks	Qualities (virtues)	Distortions (vices)
1 Kether	refinement	unity	confusion
2 Chockmah	change	purpose	illusion
3 Binah	works	silence	greed
D Daath	clearing	expression	dispersion
4 Chesed	power	alignment	bigotry
5 Geburah	worry	courage	restriction
6 Tiphareth	success	devotion	pride
7 Netzach	failure	unselfishness	lust
8 Hod	prudence	truthfulness	dishonesty
9 Yesod	gain	independence	idleness
10 Malkuth	wealth	discrimination	inertia
11 joins 1–2	energetic	original	impractical
12 joins 1–3	graceful	talented	deceptive
13 joins 1–6	pure	contemplative	rigid
14 joins 2–3	embracing	sharing	possessive
15 joins 2–6	sensual	guiding	ungrounded
16 joins 2–4	enduring	traditional	arrogant
17 joins 3–6	synthesizing	choosing	unreliable
18 joins 3–5	moving	explorative	elusive
19 joins 4–5	beautiful	limited	selfish
20 joins 4–6	sufficiency	separated	escapist
21 joins 4–7	extremist	gambling	compulsive
22 joins 5–6	aligned	adjusting	judgemental
23 joins 5–8	stiff	passive	victim
24 joins 6–7	structured	changing	refusing
25 joins 6–9	regenerative	productive	dualistic
26 joins 6–8	expressive	fearless	debauched
27 joins 7–8	releasing	opportunistic	apathetic
28 joins 7–9	solid	materialistic	authoritarian
29 joins 7–10	resting	cyclical	imbalance
30 joins 8–9	radiant	active	insensitive
31 joins 8–10	cautious	planning	critical
32 joins 9–10	integrating	beginning	scattered

The Body and the Tree of Life

To help locate the connections between the Tree of Life and the human body, the following lists introduce the human body systems. Each section shows the system's functions, associated energy centres, related body parts and endocrine system, and a key word or two to connect it to the corresponding ego or soul state. It is intended to further an understanding of Kabbalistic healing, and also to help deepen the connections between your body and the Tree of Life. Use it wisely!

THE CENTRAL NERVOUS SYSTEM

Functions: Experience, response, communication and integration. Expression of life principles, ideals, purpose, revelation.
Associated energy centre: Crown and Mid-head chakras.
Body parts: head and back.
Endocrine: pituitary (left eye), pineal (right eye).
Ego/Soul State: Infinity and Illumination

Tree of Life	Human Body
1: Kether	life force, energy, consciousness
2: Chockmah	left brain
3: Binah	right brain
path joins 1-2	left eyes, ears, pituitary
path joins 1-3	right eyes, ears, pineal
path joins 2-3	nose, mouth
path joins 1-6	spinal cord
path joins 6-9	spinal cord, (solar plexus)

THE ENDOCRINE SYSTEM

Functions: Energy and growth. Survival and expression.
Associated energy centre: Throat chakra.
Body parts: neck, shoulders and arms, endocrine system.
Endocrine: thyroid and whole system.
Ego/Soul State: Inspiration and Intuition.

Tree of Life	Human Body
4: Chesed	left adrenal
5: Geburah	right adrenal
0: Daath	throat, thyroid
path joins 2–4	posterior pituitary and overall system
path joins 3–5	anterior pituitary and overall system

THE CARDIOVASCULAR AND RESPIRATORY SYSTEMS

Functions: Energy exchange, quality of life, defence and transport. Transformation and love.

Associated energy centre: Heart chakra.

Body parts: thorax.

Endocrine: thymus.

Ego/Soul State: Individuation.

Tree of Life	Human Body
6: Tiphareth	heart, thymus
path joins 2-6	arteries, oxygenated blood
path joins 3-6	veins, de-oxygenated blood
path joins 4-5	lymph, spleen
path joins 4-6	left lung
path joins 5-6	right lung

THE DIGESTIVE AND EXCRETORY SYSTEMS

Functions: Ingestion, digestion, absorption, discrimination and elimination. Processing and clearing of desires.

Associated energy centre: Solar Plexus chakra.

Body parts: abdomen.

Endocrine: pancreas.

Ego/Soul State: Imitation.

Tree of Life	Human Body
7: Netzach	left kidney
8: Hod	right kidney
path joins 4-7	large intestine (descending), rectum
path joins 6-7	stomach
path joins 5-8	large intestine (ascending and transverse)

path joins 6-8	liver, gall bladder, pancreas
path joins 7-8	small intestines
path joins 9-10	bladder, skin

THE REPRODUCTIVE SYSTEM

Functions: Connection, propagation, balance. Manifestation of energies.
Associated energy centre: Sacral chakra.
Body parts: inner and outer sexual organs.
Endocrine: gonads.
Ego/Soul State: Impulse.

Tree of Life	Human Body
9: Yesod	sexual organs
path joins 7-9	male: left seminal vesicle, vas deferens
	female: left uterine tube, ovaries
path joins 8-9	male: right seminal vesicle, vas deferens
	female: right uterine tube, ovaries

THE LOCOMOTOR SYSTEM

Functions: Support, movement, expression. Grounding, will to live
   (hereditary, genetic, and cultural).
Associated energy centre: Base chakra.
Body parts: Legs, feet, skeletal and muscular systems.
Endocrine: (adrenals).
Ego/Soul State: Instinct.

Tree of Life	Human Body
10: Malkuth	body as whole
path joins 7-10	left skeleton, bones, muscles
path joins 8-10	right skeleton, bones, muscles

Further Reading

Books may aid our understanding of the Kabbalah and at the same time facilitate our growth if we read in a positive and active way. This means reading slowly, stopping occasionally to reflect and evaluate, copying out or underlining interesting and relevant quotes, reading with attention and interest, and being willing to stop when we find the book uninteresting or depressing. Reading in this way can aid our growth, particularly our will and concentration, and even nourish us spiritually.

This is by no means intended as a complete bibliography. It is a short list of interesting and relevant books that can add to your study of the Tree of Life and related subjects, and act as a jumping-off stage for further study and research.

Publishers are given but many of these books are available in different editions.

ALLI, Antero, *Angel Tech* Falcon 1987

ANDREWS, Ted, *Imagick* Llewellyn 1989

ASSAGIOLI, Roberto, *The Act of Will* Wildwood 1974; *Psychosynthesis* Turnstone 1965

CASTANEDA, Carlos, *The Art of Dreaming* Aquarian 1993

COOPER, David A., *God is a Verb* Penguin 1998

CROWLEY, Aleister, *The Book of Thoth* Weiser 1971; *The Book of Lies* Weiser 1970; *Magick* (Parts I, II, III) Weiser 1974; *777* Weiser 1973; *The Heart of the Master* 93 Publishing Canada 1973

CROWLEY, Vivienne, *A Woman's Kabbalah* HarperCollins 1998

DOUGLAS, Nik and SLINGER, Penny, *Sexual Secrets* Arrow 1982

ELLIS, Normandi, *Awakening Osiris* Phanes 1988

FERRUCCI, Piero, *What We May Be* Turnstone 1982

FORTUNE, Dion, *The Mystical Qabalah* Benn 1970

GRANT, Kenneth, *Nightside of Eden* Muller 1977

HILLMAN, James, *The Soul's Code* Bantam 1997

HOFFMAN, Edward, *The Way of Splendour* Shambhala 1981; *Opening the Inner Gates* Shambhala 1995

JOHANSON and KURTZ, *Grace Unfolding* Bell Tower 1991

KAPLAN, Aryeh, *Sepher Yetzirah* Weiser 1993

KENTON, Warren, *The Work of the Kabbalist* Gateway 1984

KNIGHT, Gareth, *Practical Guide to Qabalistic Symbolism* (I and II) Helios 1970

KRAMER, Sheldon, *Hidden Faces of the Soul* Adams Media 2000

LEVI, Eliphas, *The Key to the Mysteries* Rider n.d.

LOVE, Jeff, *The Quantum Gods* Russell 1976

MASLOW, Abraham, *The Farther Reaches of Human Nature* Penguin 1976

MASTERS, Robert Augustus, *The Way of the Lover* Xanthyros 1988

MATHERS, McGregor, *The Kabbalah Unveiled* Routledge, Kegan Paul 1970

NABY, James, *The Cosmic Serpent* Tarcher 1999

NEEDLEMAN, Jacob, *Lost Christianity* Element 1993

O'REGAN, Vivienne, *The Pillars of Isis* Aquarian 1992

PARFITT, Will, *The Elements of the Qabalah* Element 1991; *The New Living Qabalah* Element 1995

PARSONS, Jack, *Magick* 93 Publishing Canada 1979

PERLS, Fritz, et al., *Gestalt Therapy* Penguin 1973

REGARDIE, Israel, *The Tree of Life* Weiser 1969; *The Golden Dawn* Falcon 1984

SCHACTER, Zalman and HOFFMAN, Edward, *Sparks of Light* Shambhala 1983

SCHOLEM, Gershom, *On the Kabbalah and its Symbolism* Routledge, Kegan Paul 1965

SHAYA, Leo, *Universal Meaning of the Kabbalah* Penguin 1973

SHUTZ, Albert, *Call Adonai* Quantal 1980

STARHAWK, *The Spiral Dance* Harper 1979

WILSON, Robert Anton, *Prometheus Rising* Falcon 1983

WIPPLER-GONZALES, Migane, *A Kabbalah for the Modern World* Llewellyn 1987

Don't forget the Old Testament of the Bible also – it is full of interesting and surprising Kabbalistic information. The scriptures of other religions are worth looking at too for connections you can glean from their 'world view'.

Many works of fiction, particularly those of a fantasy kind, are very illuminative and suggestive regarding Kabbalistic and other symbolism.

Tarot Cards

It is highly recommended, and essential for serious study of the Kabbalah, to have a full pack of Tarot cards. The best cards, became they follow the correspondences to the Tree of Life more closely than any others, are the *Thoth Tarot Cards* by Crowley/Harris. They are also very attractively designed. Other packs of Tarot cards are only recommended if they particularly resonate with the user.

Distance Education and Group Courses

Distance Education. Will Parfitt has been offering distance education courses since 1981. The Practical Kabbalah courses have had hundreds of students from all parts of the world. Currently students come from areas as diverse as Sweden, California, England and Australia. The courses aim to make teachings about the Tree of Life understandable and meaningful to our modern life. Students and graduates include people from all walks of life and a wide variety of religious and ethnic backgrounds; a little over half the students are female.

Using *The Complete Guide to the Kabbalah* and other texts for guidance, students work through the Tree of Life in a practical way with reading, exercises, visualizations, ritual work, meditations and so on. They work at connecting the Kabbalah into their own life experiences, making it of meaningful value to their personal and spiritual development. Students undertake the course work, combined with a personal project of their own choosing, at their own pace. They keep a journal, and send in written material at regular intervals for appraisal and comment. A Diploma in Kabbalistic Practice is awarded upon successful completion of the full programme.

Group Courses. Will Parfitt also occasionally offers weekend, or longer, group courses on Kabbalistic and associated themes.

For full details of distance education and group based courses, or to contact Will Parfitt for any other reason, write to him at:

BCM Synthesis, London WC1N 3XX.

Please enclose a large (C5) stamped, addressed envelope or International Reply Coupons.

Alternatively you can find details of Kabbalah and other courses at:

http://www.willparfitt.dial.pipex.com

1. Index of Diagrams

2. Index of Exercises

3. General Index

This selective index complements the exercises and diagrams indices, and the correspondence tables, and needs to be used in conjunction with them.